# Oracle Application Integration Architecture (AIA) Foundation Pack 11gR1: Essentials

Develop and deploy your Enterprise Integration Solutions using Oracle AIA

Hariharan V. Ganesarethinam

BIRMINGHAM - MUMBAI

# Oracle Application Integration Architecture (AIA) Foundation Pack 11gR1: Essentials

Copyright © 2012 Packt Publishing

All rights reserved. No part of this book may be reproduced, stored in a retrieval system, or transmitted in any form or by any means, without the prior written permission of the publisher, except in the case of brief quotations embedded in critical articles or reviews.

Every effort has been made in the preparation of this book to ensure the accuracy of the information presented. However, the information contained in this book is sold without warranty, either express or implied. Neither the author, nor Packt Publishing, and its dealers and distributors will be held liable for any damages caused or alleged to be caused directly or indirectly by this book.

Packt Publishing has endeavored to provide trademark information about all of the companies and products mentioned in this book by the appropriate use of capitals. However, Packt Publishing cannot guarantee the accuracy of this information.

First published: February 2012

Production Reference: 1170212

Published by Packt Publishing Ltd.
Livery Place
35 Livery Street
Birmingham B3 2PB, UK.

ISBN 978-1-84968-480-4

www.packtpub.com

Cover Image by Tina Negus (tina_manthorpe@sky.com)

# Credits

**Author**
Hariharan V. Ganesarethinam

**Reviewers**
Sandeep Phukan
Senthil Raja
Arun Ramesh

**Acquisition Editor**
Rukshana Khambatta

**Lead Technical Editor**
Dayan Hyames

**Technical Editors**
Mehreen Shaikh
Llewellyn F. Rozario
Azharuddin Sheikh

**Copy Editor**
Neha Shetty

**Project Coordinator**
Jovita Pinto

**Proofreader**
Lynda Sliwoski

**Indexer**
Hemangini Bari

**Graphics**
Manu Joseph

**Production Coordinator**
Alwin Roy

**Cover Work**
Alwin Roy

# About the Author

**Hariharan V. Ganesarethinam** is associated with Aspire Systems Inc, USA as Senior Architect of Enterprise Architecture Solutions. He leads enterprise architecture, integration, and SOA solutions for various customers of Aspire Systems Inc. He has around 15 years of experience in the IT industry with a variety of technologies, strategy, and enterprise solution experiences. He has architected various enterprise-level solutions based on SOA, BPM, and EAI architectures. Prior to Aspire Systems, he was leading various integration and research projects in MGL Americas and Unisys India.

Hariharan is very passionate in researching and learning upcoming technologies, architecture, and industry's best practices. His expertise and knowledge in SOA, EAI, ESB, BPM, and SOA Governance has made him comfortable in providing technical and business solutions to folks across the globe. He has hands-on experience in implementing SOA and EAI projects using Web Services, Oracle SOA Suite, Oracle AIA, iWay Service Manager, and Java CAPS. He is also an Oracle certified Oracle SOA Architect Expert.

Hariharan is well known in the SOA industries through his articles published on IT Toolbox (http://it.toolbox.com/blogs/soa-governance/) and SYS-CON Media (http://vghariharan.sys-con.com/). He has written many articles in the area of SOA and SOA Governance. His articles are related to various decision-making situations in the SOA implementation. He owns a group in www.linkedin.com called "SOA, EA and IT Governance Practitioners Forum" through which he shares and consolidates industries view on SOA and EA practices. He also presented a paper in the IBI Summit 2010 about "Service Reusability and Best Practices".

# Acknowledgement

If everyone is moving forward together, then success takes care of itself. — Henry Ford

As Henry said, the success of this book is made up of many hands. First, I would like to thank Rukshana Khambatta, the Acquisition Editor of Packt Publishing for her confidence in my skills and abilities. Even though I have written many articles online, this is my first book and she guided me very well in the beginning that triggered me to complete it. Jovita Pinto, the Project Coordinator from Packt Publishing would be the next person that I would like to thank since she was very patient in approaching me and gathering my deliveries. I always believe in review because that helps to correct our mistakes and align towards success. Even though I do not have any direct contact with the reviewers of this book, I believe their contribution added a lot of value during the process of writing.

I would also like to thank my wife Shanthi Hariharan who encouraged me whenever I lost my confidence and felt lazy. Many times, she reminded me to complete and deliver my write-ups to the publishing office. Finally, I would like to thank my kids, my dad, and my friends who directly or indirectly have appreciated my efforts.

# About the Reviewers

**Arun Ramesh** started his IT career in 2005 and has since worked on challenging integration assignments. He has been a part of some major IT consulting giants, globally. He has a niche portfolio of skills in integration-related technologies from multiple vendors. He is currently, a Senior Technical Consultant specializing in integrations on Oracle Fusion Middleware based on Service Oriented Architecture. He has been a part of major pioneering implementation milestones using Oracle Fusion Middleware and Oracle AIA. He has also been instrumental in implementations using Oracle stack with the integration layer being Oracle AIA. He is an expert in complex and very large customizations in AIA PIPs and has been a front runner for one such challenging engagement for a telecom major in Europe.

He has been a reviewer for various books on Oracle Fusion Middleware and Oracle BPM. He is distinguishably known in the public domain for his technology blog on Oracle Fusion Middleware and Oracle AIA, which provides numerous technical tips, product reviews, code snippets, and solutions to other blogger queries.

> I would like to take this opportunity to thank my family who supported and encouraged me in spite of all the times that it took me away from them. It was a long and difficult journey for them.
>
> I would also like to thank all those who have helped me in some way to complete the review of this book and whose names I have failed to mention.

**Sandeep Phukan** has more than eight years of experience in integration technologies and Java. He currently works as an Architect in Anatas Consulting, Sydney, a leader in Cloud Computing and next generation Enterprise Architecture Solutions for Asia Pacific region. Earlier, he worked as a Technical Lead for Nokia Siemens Network R&D, Bangalore, assisting on the integration of Next Generation Unified Convergent Billing Systems based on Oracle Fusion Middleware 11g.

Prior to this, Sandeep worked with Oracle SSI, Bangalore as a Senior Consultant, where his key involvement was Oracle AIA for Communications (Telco PIP). During this period he travelled to several countries around the world, aiding customers in developing customizations for Oracle AIA artifacts.

Sandeep is a certified Java Developer and has a keen interest in Low Bandwidth Transports and Distributed Algorithms. During his time at Oracle SSI, he was actively involved with the SSI Innovation Centre, where he created a number of utility extensions to the Oracle SOA Suite. He also maintains an open source repository of several SOA utilities in the Google code repository, `http://code.google.com/p/soalabs/`.

Sandeep is also an avid researcher in the area of SOA Governance. He has published a number of papers in the Oracle Technology Network (OTN) on technology neutral Designtime Dependency analysis of SOA Artifacts. Reference One of his inventions on this subject (Graph Based Designtime Dependency Analysis) has recently been accepted for a Patent in the US Patents and Trademarks Office (USPTO).

> I would like to thank my loving wife, Aparupa, for her patience during those late night researches and my friends and colleagues at Anatas, NSN, and Oracle who were always there whenever I needed them.

**Senthil Raja** is a consultant with Cognizant focusing on SOA technologies with three years of overall experience. He has been involved in development of SOA-based projects throughout his career. Senthil has a Bachelor of Engineering degree in Electronics and Communications engineering from the Anna University.

> I would like thank my colleagues for their help in reviewing this book.

# www.PacktPub.com

## Support files, eBooks, discount offers and more

You might want to visit www.PacktPub.com for support files and downloads related to your book.

Did you know that Packt offers eBook versions of every book published, with PDF and ePub files available? You can upgrade to the eBook version at www.PacktPub.com and as a print book customer, you are entitled to a discount on the eBook copy. Get in touch with us at service@packtpub.com for more details.

At www.PacktPub.com, you can also read a collection of free technical articles, sign up for a range of free newsletters and receive exclusive discounts and offers on Packt books and eBooks.

http://PacktLib.PacktPub.com

Do you need instant solutions to your IT questions? PacktLib is Packt's online digital book library. Here, you can access, read and search across Packt's entire library of books.

## Why Subscribe?

- Fully searchable across every book published by Packt
- Copy and paste, print and bookmark content
- On demand and accessible via web browser

## Free Access for Packt account holders

If you have an account with Packt at www.PacktPub.com, you can use this to access PacktLib today and view nine entirely free books. Simply use your login credentials for immediate access.

## Instant Updates on New Packt Books

Get notified! Find out when new books are published by following @PacktEnterprise on Twitter, or the *Packt Enterprise* Facebook page.

# Table of Contents

**Preface** — 1

**Chapter 1: Overview of Oracle AIA** — 7
- **Various types of integration** — 8
  - Data integration — 8
  - Functional integration — 8
  - Presentation (UI) integration — 8
  - Business process integration — 8
  - Business to business integration — 9
- **Integration architectures** — 9
  - Point-to-point — 9
  - Shared data repository — 10
  - Remote Procedure Call (RPC) — 10
  - Message oriented middleware (MOM) — 11
  - Web service integration — 12
  - Service-oriented Architecture — 13
- **What is Oracle AIA?** — 16
- **What is Oracle AIA Process Integration Pack?** — 16
- **Oracle AIA Foundation Pack concepts** — 17
- **Components of AIA Foundation Pack** — 21
  - Enterprise Business Objects (EBO) — 22
  - Enterprise Business Messages (EBM) — 22
  - Enterprise Business Services (EBS) — 23
  - Enterprise Business Flow (EBF) — 24
  - Application Business Connector Services (ABCS) — 24
  - Oracle Enterprise Repository (OER) — 25
  - Composite Application Validation System (CAVS) — 25
- **Oracle AIA Reference Architecture** — 26
  - AIA Process Reference Model — 27

| | |
|---|---|
| **The role of Oracle Fusion Middleware** | **28** |
| Oracle SOA Suite 11g | 29 |
| **Summary** | **30** |
| **Chapter 2: Enterprise Business Objects** | **31** |
| **Overview of Enterprise Business Objects** | **31** |
| **Exploring EBO** | **33** |
| **Core EBO** | **35** |
| **Core EBO groups** | **35** |
| Common EBO groups | 35 |
| EBO Components group | 38 |
| Business components | 38 |
| Reference components | 39 |
| Common components | 40 |
| **Structure of EBOs** | **40** |
| Custom EBO | 41 |
| **Extending EBOs** | **42** |
| **Industry EBOs** | **44** |
| **Infrastructure components** | **44** |
| Data types | 45 |
| **Summary** | **46** |
| **Chapter 3: Enterprise Business Messages** | **47** |
| **Overview of Enterprise Business Message (EBM)** | **48** |
| EBM characteristics | 49 |
| **Exploring AIA EBMs** | **50** |
| **Structure of EBM** | **51** |
| EBMHeader | 53 |
| EBMHeader components | 55 |
| EBMHeader child components | 56 |
| DataArea | 62 |
| **EBM use cases** | **64** |
| EBM request and response message | 64 |
| **Summary** | **66** |
| **Chapter 4: Enterprise Business Services** | **67** |
| **Overview of Enterprise Service Bus** | **67** |
| Role of EBS in AIA | 69 |
| Characteristics of EBS | 70 |
| **Structure of the EBS definition** | **71** |
| Definitions element | 71 |
| Types element | 72 |
| Message element | 72 |

| | |
|---|---|
| PortType element | 73 |
|    One-way operation pattern in EBS | 73 |
|    Two-way or request and response operation pattern in EBS | 73 |
| **Exploring Enterprise Business Service Library** | **74** |
| **Types of EBS** | **75** |
|   Entity type EBS | 75 |
|   Process type EBS | 77 |
| **Understanding the EBS architecture** | **79** |
|   Architecture for entity services EBS | 80 |
|   Architecture for process services EBS | 81 |
|   EBS Message Exchange Patterns (MEP) | 82 |
|    Synchronous request and response pattern | 83 |
|    Asynchronous fire and forget pattern | 84 |
|    Asynchronous request and delayed response pattern | 85 |
|   Steps to identify the message pattern | 87 |
| **EBS design principles** | **88** |
|   EBS routing principles | 89 |
| **EBS implementation** | **90** |
|   Constructing WSDL for process service EBS | 90 |
|   Developing EBS using Oracle Mediator | 91 |
|   Developing synchronous request and response pattern EBS | 94 |
|   Developing asynchronous one-way pattern EBS | 96 |
|   Developing asynchronous request delayed and response pattern EBS | 96 |
| **Summary** | **97** |
| **Chapter 5: Application Business Connector Services** | **99** |
|   **ABCS in AIA** | **100** |
|   **ABCS Architecture** | **101** |
|    Validate | 102 |
|    Enrich | 103 |
|    Transform | 103 |
|    Operate | 103 |
|    Route | 103 |
|   **Key definitions of ABCS architecture** | **104** |
|   **Design principles of ABCS** | **105** |
|    Designing ABM Schema | 105 |
|   **Developing ABCS** | **106** |
|    Developing ABCS using AIA Service Constructor | 106 |
|    Developing ABCS manually using Oracle JDeveloper | 120 |
|    Briefly about extending ABCS using Custom Code | 124 |
|   **Summary** | **124** |

*Table of Contents*

## Chapter 6: Enterprise Business Flow — 125
### Overview of Enterprise Business Flow — 125
Common characteristics of Enterprise Business Flow — 126
### EBF architecture — 126
### Building Enterprise Business Flow — 128
Identifying service contract for EBF — 128
Identifying the EBF candidate — 128
Creating the service contract for an EBF — 129
Building EBF as BPEL Service — 131
### Business use case for EBF — 138
### Summary — 141

## Chapter 7: AIA Security — 143
### Levels of security implementations — 143
Transport level security — 144
Message level security — 144
Access control level security — 144
### Security in Oracle SOA Suite — 145
### Implementing security in AIA — 146
Securing AIA services — 147
Appling predefined policies to AIA services — 148
### Securing ABCS — 152
### Summary — 153

## Chapter 8: Versioning — 155
### Importance of version management — 155
### Services version management — 156
### AIA versioning — 157
AIA versioning approach — 158
Schema (EBO/EBM) versioning — 159
Services (EBS) versioning — 162
ABCS versioning — 164
### Summary — 164

## Chapter 9: AIA Design Patterns — 165
### AIA message processing patterns — 166
Synchronous request and response pattern — 166
Asynchronous fire and forget pattern — 168
Asynchronous delayed response pattern — 170
Guaranteed delivery pattern — 172
Other message processing patterns — 174
   Service routing pattern — 174
   Competing consumers pattern — 175

| | |
|---|---|
| **Asset centralization pattern** | **175** |
| Data model centralization | 175 |
| Service contract centralization | 176 |
| **Asset extensibility patterns** | **176** |
| Extending EBO/EBM | 176 |
| Extending EBS and ABCS | 177 |
| Extending EBF and transformation | 177 |
| **Summary** | **178** |
| **Chapter 10: Error Handling and Logging** | **179** |
| **Fault handling in BPEL** | **180** |
| Business faults | 180 |
| System faults | 181 |
| **AIA error-handling framework** | **182** |
| **Fault handling in AIA** | **184** |
| Configuring AIA fault policy files | 184 |
| Customize the association between custom fault polices and bindings | 187 |
| **Enabling error notification** | **188** |
| **Disable error notification** | **190** |
| **Updating MDS** | **191** |
| **Error logging** | **193** |
| Enable trace logging | 194 |
| Enabling system/service level tracing | 194 |
| Configuring system log level | 196 |
| View logfiles | 198 |
| **Summary** | **199** |
| **Chapter 11: Service Management Using Oracle Enterprise Repository** | **201** |
| **SOA Governance** | **202** |
| Design-time governance | 202 |
| Implementation-time governance | 202 |
| Run-time governance | 203 |
| **OER as AIA repository** | **203** |
| **Configuring OER as AIA repository** | **204** |
| **Accessing AIA contents in OER** | **208** |
| **Project lifecycle workbench and OER** | **210** |
| Business process modeling phase | 210 |
| Service design and construction phase | 210 |
| Deployment planning phase | 210 |
| Deployment phase | 211 |
| AIA Project Lifecycle Workbench | 211 |
| **Harvesting design-time composites into OER** | **211** |

| | |
|---|---|
| Set up design-time harvesting using AIA Foundation Pack | 212 |
| **Harvesting deployed composites into OER** | **212** |
| **Summary** | **213** |
| **Chapter 12: Composite Application Validation System** | **215** |
| **Composite Application Validation System testing framework** | **216** |
| **AIA architecture and CAVS components** | **216** |
| Test Definition | 218 |
| Simulator Definition | 218 |
| Design prerequisites for CAVS enabling | 219 |
| **Using CAVS user interface** | **220** |
| Gathering test information | 220 |
| Create and execute a test definition using CAVS user interface | 221 |
| Create Simulator Definition using CAVS user interface | 225 |
| **Enabling ABCS to route through CAVS** | **229** |
| **CAVS routing** | **230** |
| Create routing setup ID in CAVS user interface | 232 |
| **Summary** | **233** |
| **Appendix: Case Study** | **235** |
| **Sales and distribution** | **235** |
| **Business / data flow** | **236** |
| **Integration flow** | **237** |
| AIA Integration Reference Architecture | 238 |
| Identifying EBO followed by EBM | 239 |
| Identifying EBS Service Operations from EBS WSDL | 240 |
| **Defining ABCS process for application interfaces** | **241** |
| **Validating the integration interfaces using CAVS** | **242** |
| **Key benefits of using AIA** | **243** |
| **Summary** | **243** |
| **Index** | **245** |

# Preface

Oracle Application Integration Architecture (AIA) Foundation Pack is a commercial integration framework provided by Oracle Corporation. Oracle AIA provides a systematic approach of building business process integrations for an enterprise that helps it to consolidate their IT assets. Oracle AIA foundation pack also provides a set of application independent Enterprise Business Objects, Enterprise Business Messages, Enterprise Business Services, SOA based reference architecture, and test methodologies that help to build uniform integration infrastructure. Using AIA Foundation Pack, an enterprise can achieve quicker SOA adoptability and reusability. Oracle AIA framework requires Oracle SOA Suites in both design time and runtime environments.

The scope of this book is to provide the readers with essential details about various AIA foundation pack components and the role of each component in integration architecture. The book starts with generic integration architecture, approaches, and importance of building application integrations using the SOA approach.

## What this book covers

*Chapter 1*, *Overview of Oracle AIA* revisits the fundamentals of integrations, advancement of integration using Service Oriented Architecture, and the role of Oracle AIA Foundation Pack in the application integration scenarios. At the end of this chapter, the reader will get a good understanding of various integration types and an overview of Oracle AIA FP and its architecture model.

*Chapter 2*, *Enterprise Business Objects* explains the concept of business objects, need of business objects, Enterprise Business Objects (EBOs), various types of EBOs, and physical locations of the EBO files in the Oracle AIA Foundation Pack. This chapter also covers the need of customizing the EBO components.

*Chapter 3, Enterprise Business Messages* covers integration messaging model, business messages, web service messaging, and Enterprise Business Messages. Also, it explains the relationship of an EBO and EBM in the AIA approach. This chapter also covers the physical location of EBM in the AIA FP installation and the need for customizing EBM.

*Chapter 4, Enterprise Business Services* covers the need of business services, web service operations, and role of Enterprise Business Services in the AIA model. Also, this chapter will help to find the appropriate WSDL file in the AIA FP path and screen-by-screen instructions to build the EBS using JDeveloper.

*Chapter 5, Applications Business Connector Services* covers the role of ABCS in the AIA approach, the need of ABCS, and screen-by-screen approach to build ABCS using JDeveloper. At the end of this chapter, the reader will have hands-on experience in building the ABCS component.

*Chapter 6, Enterprise Business Flow* covers the need of business processes in application integration and building business processes using Oracle BPEL. This chapter also covers the systematic instructions to build the business processes by making use of AIA components.

*Chapter 7, AIA Security* covers the various levels of security requirements for application integrations and how Oracle AIA supports security through Oracle SOA Suite. This chapter also explains the steps required to build AIA security by defining security policies and securing ABCS.

*Chapter 8, AIA Versioning* covers the importance of version management in integration and versioning approach followed in AIA. This chapter also covers versioning techniques for various AIA components including EBO, EBM, EBS, and ABCS.

*Chapter 9, AIA Design Patterns* covers the various message exchange patterns with diagrammatic explanations. This chapter also covers the AIA supported message exchange patterns, asset management patterns, and so on. At the end of this chapter, the reader will have a detailed understanding of various AIA integration design patterns and samples.

*Chapter 10, Error Handling and Logging* covers the various type of faults including business faults and system faults. Also, it covers the AIA error handling framework, configuring fault handlers, error notification approach, and various logging mechanisms supported by AIA configurations.

*Chapter 11, Service Management using Oracle Enterprise Repository* covers the SOA governance models, introduction to Oracle Enterprise Repository, and service management using OER. This chapter also guides the reader to import the AIA configurations in the OER and harvesting design time configuration.

*Chapter 12*, *Composite Application Validation System* explains the Oracle AIA CAVS framework, CAVS role in the AIA approach, test definition, simulator definitions, and CAVS user interface. As this chapter guides the reader to create and test definitions and simulators using CAVS, the reader would get a basic understanding of applying CAVS in the AIA project.

*Appendix*, covers a case study with real time scenarios, which explains how AIA components are used to accomplish the integration requirement. The case study explains the approach followed to identify the EBO, EBM, EBS, and ABCS components required to build the integration for the real time use case. At the end of this chapter, the reader should have a good understanding of how to approach AIA integration project from design to implementation

# What you need for this book

You will need the following software to be installed or required to configure Oracle AIA Foundation Pack 11*g* R1 before you go through the chapters:

- Oracle SOA Suite 11*g* (11.1.1.5.0)
- Oracle AIA FP 11*g* (11.1.1.5.0)
- Oracle Express Edition XE (10.2.0.1)
- Repository Creation Utility 11.1.1.5.0
- JDeveloper 11.1.1.5.0
- SOA Extension for JDeveloper 11.1.1.5.0
- Oracle WebLogic Server + Coherence - Package Installer 10.3.5
- Oracle Enterprise Repository 11*g* (11.1.1.5.0)

Please refer to the Oracle installation documents for configuration, and install the these software. Also, please ensure that you have sufficient systems configurations to run these software.

# Who this book is for

If you are a Business Analyst, Integration Architect, or a Developer working in Oracle applications integration, who is looking forward to understanding Oracle AIA fundamentals and development practice, then this is the best guide for you.

This book assumes that you have a fundamental knowledge of Oracle SOA Suite and its components.

# Conventions

In this book, you will find a number of styles of text that distinguish between different kinds of information. Here are some examples of these styles, and an explanation of their meaning.

Code words in text are shown as follows: "We can include other contexts through the use of the `include` directive."

A block of code is set as follows:

```
<xsd:element ref="corecom:CustomerPartyReference" minOccurs="0">
  <xsd:annotation>
  <xsd:documentation>
</xsd:element>
```

When we wish to draw your attention to a particular part of a code block, the relevant lines or items are set in bold:

```
<xsd:annotation>
<xsd:documentation>
  <svcdoc:EBO>
    <svcdoc:Description>BankAccount...</svcdoc:Description>
    <svcdoc:Type>EBM</svcdoc:Type>
    <svcdoc:Industry/>
    <svcdoc:EBOName>BankAccountEBO</svcdoc:EBOName>
  </svcdoc:EBO>
</xsd:documentation>
</xsd:annotation>
```

**New terms** and **important words** are shown in bold. Words that you see on the screen, in menus or dialog boxes for example, appear in the text like this: "On this page, refer to the **Child Components** section where we can find the **ItemLot** EBO as a child component."

> Warnings or important notes appear in a box like this.

> Tips and tricks appear like this.

# Reader feedback

Feedback from our readers is always welcome. Let us know what you think about this book—what you liked or may have disliked. Reader feedback is important for us to develop titles that you really get the most out of.

To send us general feedback, simply send an e-mail to feedback@packtpub.com, and mention the book title through the subject of your message.

If there is a topic that you have expertise in and you are interested in either writing or contributing to a book, see our author guide on www.packtpub.com/authors.

# Customer support

Now that you are the proud owner of a Packt book, we have a number of things to help you to get the most from your purchase.

# Downloading the example code

You can download the example code files for all Packt books you have purchased from your account at http://www.packtpub.com. If you purchased this book elsewhere, you can visit http://www.packtpub.com/support and register to have the files e-mailed directly to you.

# Errata

Although we have taken every care to ensure the accuracy of our content, mistakes do happen. If you find a mistake in one of our books—maybe a mistake in the text or the code—we would be grateful if you would report this to us. By doing so, you can save other readers from frustration and help us improve subsequent versions of this book. If you find any errata, please report them by visiting http://www.packtpub.com/support, selecting your book, clicking on the **errata submission form** link, and entering the details of your errata. Once your errata are verified, your submission will be accepted and the errata will be uploaded to our website, or added to any list of existing errata, under the Errata section of that title.

## Piracy

Piracy of copyright material on the Internet is an ongoing problem across all media. At Packt, we take the protection of our copyright and licenses very seriously. If you come across any illegal copies of our works, in any form, on the Internet, please provide us with the location address or website name immediately so that we can pursue a remedy.

Please contact us at copyright@packtpub.com with a link to the suspected pirated material.

We appreciate your help in protecting our authors, and our ability to bring you valuable content.

## Questions

You can contact us at questions@packtpub.com if you are having a problem with any aspect of the book, and we will do our best to address it.

# Overview of Oracle AIA

Application integration becomes the most common project in every enterprise and corporate. Integration is an important core component in IT systems. **Oracle Application Integration Architecture (AIA)** is a framework based on a **Service Oriented Architecture approach** that provides proven methodologies and best practices for integrating application systems. However, before we jump into AIA, let's understand the need for an application integration and various integration methodologies.

Small and large enterprises invest in building various business systems and applications to facilitate business functions and growth. However, due to various technology advancements, most of the applications and business systems developed over a period are in different ages and capabilities. Many enterprises are quite successful with their business applications, but not very successful in collaborating the data and business functions. In earlier days, data collaboration between applications systems was through manual entry that lead to a lack of data integrity and human errors. In order to avoid the data integrity issue and human errors, most of the investments were made towards integrating business systems. Therefore, integration becomes one of the mandatory agendas in every quarter. Why is such an investment going towards that? It is because of the organization's growth, acquisition, partner relationships, lack of standards, and technology barriers.

In this chapter, we will revisit some of the fundamentals of integration and Oracle AIA components. As part of that, the following topics will be covered:

- Various types of integration
- Integration architectures
- AIA and its flavors
- The Oracle AIA framework approach
- Components of AIA
- The Oracle AIA Reference Architecture
- The role of Oracle Fusion Middleware

# Various types of integration

There are various types of integrations which are followed by enterprises and industries. Integrations can be classified based on the need, scope, and architectural approaches.

## Data integration

Data integration is about transferring or sharing the information between business systems and partners. In this approach, only the data will be shared between systems and partners in the form of binary files, text files, documents, and objects. It does not include sharing business functions and processes. Shared folders, file transfers, FTP transfers, SQL loader, and ETL are the most common data integration mechanisms used by many enterprises. These approaches have some limitations such as data integrity, duplicate transfer, network failure, and delivery guarantee.

## Functional integration

Most of the business application products and custom solutions provide API-based interfaces for certain business functions or logic, which can be executed by external systems. A functional integration has a more flexible approach when compared to the data integration approach. In addition, functional integration encapsulates the business functions and ensures that only certain functions are executed by external systems. It also has a few limitations such as tight integration, increased dependency, and so on.

## Presentation (UI) integration

Presentation integration is about screen scraping and data capturing from the application console and screens. This approach has many limitations and constraints that force a limited success. In addition, it has challenges in maintaining data integrity and security.

## Business process integration

Process integration means collaborating various business functions and partner programs to meet a long-running business process based on data integration and business functional integration approaches. Process integration provides clear separation of the business functions and integration interfaces.

# Business to business integration

As we know, B2B integration is about collaboration between two different enterprises, partners, or vendors through a domain-specific and standard-based integration approach. Such collaboration includes data, business functions, and process integrations. XML-based standards such as EDI, HL7, and RosettaNet are widely-known B2B integration standards.

# Integration architectures

There are various integration mechanisms or architectural approaches followed by industries to achieve integration needs.

## Point-to-point

This approach is also known as one-to-one integration. Point-to-point is basically a decentralized networking approach to directly link two computers or systems. From the integration point of view, it is more about integrating two different systems or interfaces through a common transportation mechanism. A point-to-point integration architecture creates higher dependency between application systems and interfaces as it basically enforces a tight integration model.

This approach initially shows a lower up-front investment, but when more links are created between each application, the complexity of the integration increases. Once the complexity increases, it becomes difficult to customize or enhance the interface. This approach also requires updating each integrated application if any one of the systems require changes in the interface data model. This approach is depicted in the following diagram:

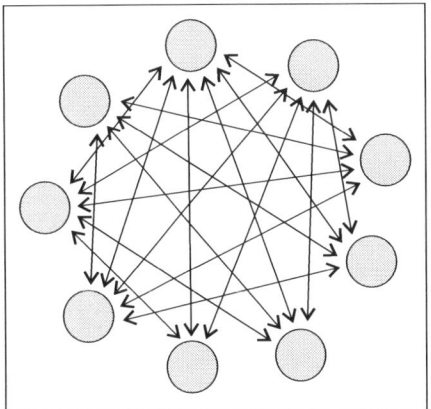

## Shared data repository

Basically, a centralized database repository will be shared across all applications and systems for information distribution. The central database system will act as an integration point. The database schema accepts all applications' input and also provides access to other systems which require that information. This approach increases the complexity in the database systems and a schema should be more generic. This approach also loads more complexity at the application's side as publishing or fetching the data from the repository has to handle all validation and elimination logic. Therefore, this approach increases the maintenance overhead. This approach is depicted in the following diagram:

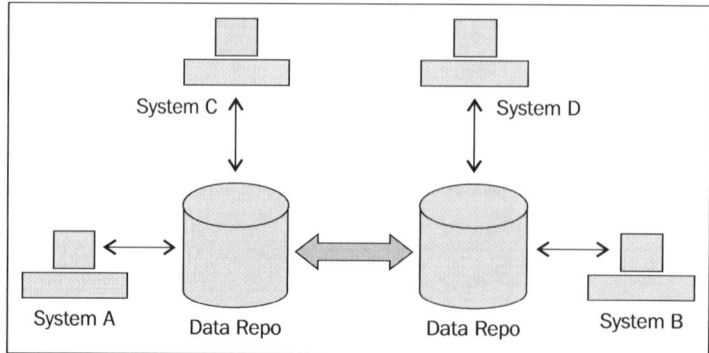

## Remote Procedure Call (RPC)

**Remote Procedure Call (RPC)** is a protocol-based integration approach where one application or system calls the service or the function hosted by another remote application over the network. Basically, RPC uses a client-server model for communication. In addition, RPC works as a request-reply approach, so the requesting systems have to wait for the response from the provider system. Even though the entire communication happens over the TCP/IP network, applications don't need to implement the underlying networking procedures and protocols.

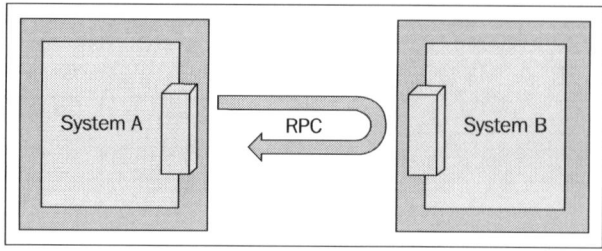

As the end-to-end communication happens over TCP/IP, it is considered an expensive solution. In addition, this approach will affect the performance as compared to other approaches. Java RMI and CORBA are well known technologies that work based on the RPC model, which is a subset of the TCP/IP protocol. Another disadvantage of this approach is that both systems that interact with each other should interpret the language-dependent objects sent over the network.

# Message oriented middleware (MOM)

Message oriented middleware is an infrastructure-based integration approach where distributed systems and applications share data/information as messages over the network. This is the most popular and efficient integration architecture adopted by many enterprises. Comparing to the preceding approaches, the message oriented integration approach facilitates loose coupling, less dependency, and high reliability.

The MOM architecture is, basically, built around the **Message Queue (MQ)** and **JMS** using a messaging broker. A message broker is a server mechanism that persists messages and tracks message deliveries. Typically, a message oriented integration approach follows a publish/subscribe pattern. Most of the messaging brokers are based on **Java Messaging Service (JMS)** standards. IBM WebSphere MQ and TIBCO EMS are based on JMS standards. **AMQP (Advanced Message Queue Protocol)** is another messaging standard which is being followed by brokers, such as Apache Qpid and Rabbit MQ.

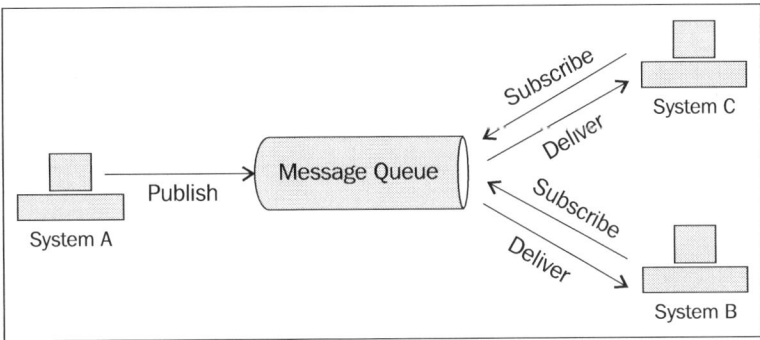

The MOM integration approach is widely adopted in the bulk or large volume of data transfer between multiple systems. As the nature of this architecture supports data exchange between various systems, it also has some limitations. The MOM approach does not support the synchronous request/response message exchange pattern. Moreover, the MOM approach does not enforce any open standardization; so many product vendors have their own implementation approach and standards.

# Web service integration

Web services are open standard-based integration mechanisms which help to establish loosely-coupled integration communication between application systems. Web service provides an interface that can be consumed through an XML-based messaging model over various protocols. There are two types of web service implementations which are SOAP-based web services and REST architecture-based services. As web services are loosely-coupled interfaces, they are being used for the enterprise application integration by exposing legacy application functions. A web service-based integration is basically a point-to-point integration model. However, due to its open standards approach, it is easier to implement and reuse so that it is being adopted widely for the past few years. Web service interfaces are the fundamental for building SOA and BPM solutions.

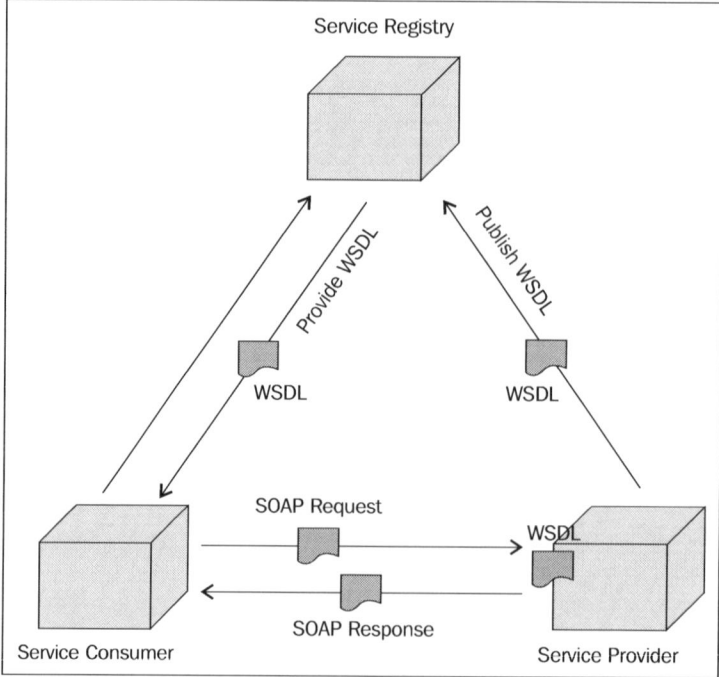

The web service integration approach is based on the following open standards:

- XML: It is a text-based meta language that helps to define a uniform messaging model
- XML schema: It is an XML-based metadata definition based on W3C standards

- **SOAP**: A messaging protocol for exchanging structured information
- **WSDL (Web Service Description Language)**: It is a descriptive artifact which elaborates service operations, input message structure, output message structure, data binding, and service endpoint URI
- **REST (Representational State Transfer)**: It is a style of architecture for service-based integration
- **WADL (Web Application Description Language)**: It is similar to WSDL, but WADL elaborates the RESTful service interfaces and operations in the form of XML

SOAP and REST Web Services are two different styles of service implementation. The SOAP Web Service is basically a standards-based interface whereas REST is an architecture style of interface which provides access to the enterprise resources. The REST-based Web Service architecture best fits for CRUD (GET, PUT, POST, and DELETE) operations only. SOAP-based Web Services are basically meant for implementing complex business functions, which could be consumed by known or third party systems. The SOAP Web Service enforces policy and contract agreements.

# Service-oriented Architecture

**Service Oriented Architecture (SOA)** is a style of architecture which is based on services, open standards, and principles. The SOA approach basically decouples the enterprise system as reusable service components and orchestrates those services to meet various business processes and integration requirements. SOA is predominantly implemented by using web services, enterprise service bus, and process orchestration technologies. As mentioned in earlier sections, each older integration approach has some limitation and complexity, which prevents the adoption of such solutions at the enterprise level. In addition, these approaches tightly integrate the application on a point-to-point basis. Therefore, it takes an enormous amount of effort and cost to enhance and align integration interfaces to meet the dynamic business requirements. However, SOA principles are enforcing to build service components as loosely-coupled, transport independent, reusable, and highly collaborative. The web services-based service architecture provides a better control in building open standard services, business processes, and an integration interface that helps to quickly align when needed. SOAP, BPEL, and WSDL are common open standards which are being used to build services and business processes.

>  Notes:
>
> There is a wrong perception that web services are SOA. Web services basically help to build loosely-coupled interfaces. Even if an enterprise has more than 100 web services, it does not mean that the enterprise has an SOA infrastructure. Service Oriented Architecture means basically, decomposing enterprise business processes and functions as services, and building business processes by orchestrating the services. This can be achieved by using various frameworks and technologies. However, web service is the most commonly adopted approach to implement such architectures. The SOA approach also requires governance and monitoring methodologies to identify the improvement opportunities. Therefore, web services are just integration interfaces and do not mean SOA.

As the Oracle AIA product is based on SOA principles and standards, let's have an overview of the service-oriented architecture, tools, and technologies in more detail:

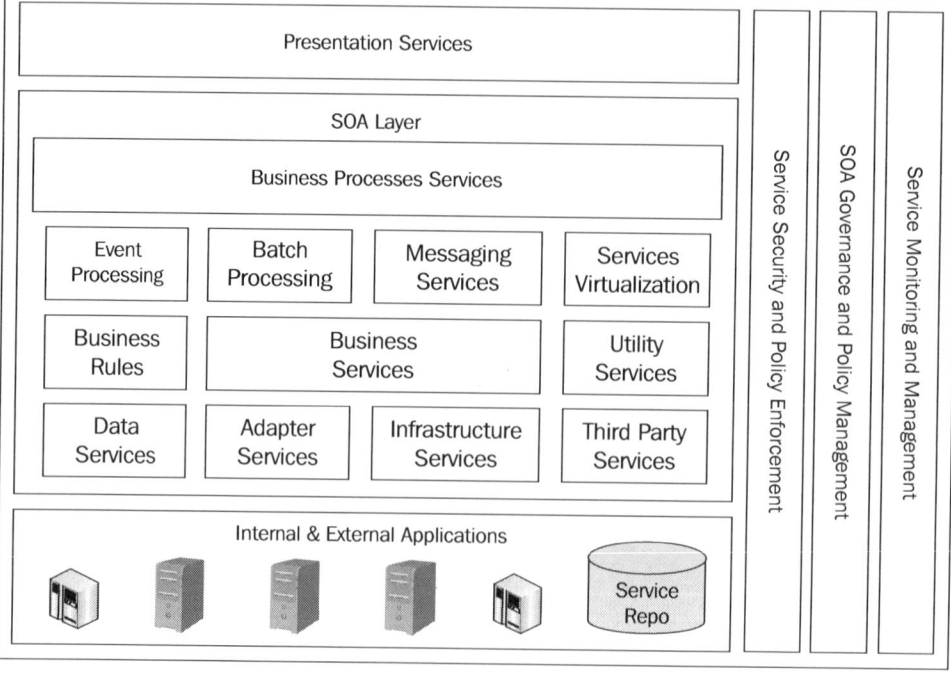

The preceding diagram expresses the typical SOA reference architecture. The SOA reference architecture is used as a blueprint that includes components of solution, guidelines, and development templates for stakeholders, business analysts, architects, and development teams. The reference architecture should outline the layers of service-oriented solution, infrastructure components, architecture layers, building blocks, design guidelines, and policies standards.

The SOA reference architecture should represent various service components involved in the enterprise infrastructure. Typically, the SOA reference architecture should have infrastructure component layers, core business services, adapter service for exposing legacy application functionalities, third party integration services, data/information access services, infrastructure services such as an e-mail services, messaging services, and so on. All such services are consumed by business processes in an orchestrated mode to meet business process requirements. Such business processes are also services which will be triggered by the user interface components or other events.

A service-oriented architecture approach facilitates the creation of most flexible and reusable service components by exposing new and existing IT assets. Basically, this approach enforces to build business functions and resources as services which should be orchestrated to achieve business processes. This also includes integrating business systems with partner services. An SOA approach can be implemented on an application level, a program level, or an enterprise level. However, building mature services and business processes at an enterprise level should boost the return on investment and robotic solution.

Even though the architecture does not enforce it, building a highly-matured enterprise level, service-oriented solution requires a variety of tools and technologies, including web services, Canonical XML, Application Servers, Messaging Services, Enterprise Service Bus (ESB), BPEL, Business Process Management (BPM), Business Rules Engine, Adapters, Complex Event Processer, Business Activity Monitors, Service Registry, and Repository and Security. The Oracle Fusion Middleware platform includes all these tools and technologies in addition to portals, data clustering, and application development frameworks.

Implementing an optimized enterprise service-oriented solution is more complex than the traditional software development approach. It also requires well-defined implementation methodologies and governance to be succeeded. Designing reference architectures is one of the critical phases in the implementation lifecycle.

# What is Oracle AIA?

The Oracle Application Integration Architecture is a complete standards-based integration and processing framework promoted by Oracle Corporation based on the Oracle Fusion Middleware platform. The AIA framework is designed and built based on the various collections of SOA best practices, principles, and standards. Therefore, an AIA approach provides an SOA-based integration framework, reference architecture, implementation methodologies, and best practices for integrating various business applications. This approach helps to build the application integration and enterprise business processes as more generic and align those processes to meet business requirements. The AIA integration approach also helps to build a Plug-and-Play integration solution which lowers IT costs, is faster to build, aligns quickly, and reduces the maintenance overhead. It also addresses the SOA design pain points, such as service decomposition, granularity and standard adoption.

AIA facilitates enterprises to use the existing application assets to build composite business processes and integration solutions. Oracle has a variety of application products which require an integration solution to seamlessly collaborate with each other. Oracle has understood the importance of integrating its application products, so Oracle provides best practices and reference solutions to build such integrations.

Oracle has two flavors of AIA products for its customers. Based on the customer's need and scope, a customer can choose from the following flavors:

- Oracle AIA Foundation Pack
- Oracle AIA Process Integration Pack

# What is Oracle AIA Process Integration Pack?

**Oracle AIA Process Integration Packs (PIPs)** is a prebuilt integration package across Oracle's application solutions such as Siebel CRM, PeopleSoft, Oracle E-Business Suite, Agile PLM, Portal, and SAP. As PIP is a prebuilt package, it facilitates Oracle customers to rapidly deploy it to meet immediate application integration processes for Oracle applications. PIP packs are available not only for Oracle application's integration, but also for various domain-specific processes, such as driver-management for transportation, communication and revenue management for accounting, and so on.

Assume that we have to integrate an Order-to-Cash process flow between the Siebel CRM and Oracle EBS application, and the prebuilt PIP package is already available with Oracle. In a traditional SOA integration approach, we need to validate the application interfaces, messaging schema model, domain-specific standards to make decisions on the interface architecture, standards for messaging structure, data transformation, service interface description, discovery, and many more. All these tasks require enormous effort in analysis, design, development, and testing phases. Oracle AIA PIP implementation eliminates most of these efforts and helps to quickly adopt the AIA approaches. All we have to do is purchase the package, align the data models, and deploy in various environments as per the guidelines. At the time of writing, there are more than 25 prebuilt integrations and business process solutions available and they continue to grow. All these processes and integration solutions are built based on the Oracle AIA Foundation Pack framework. Customers who already have made a lot of investment in Oracle products and want to adopt SOA quickly can benefit from PIPs the most.

The scope of this book is to explore the Oracle AIA Foundation Pack 11gR1 and it does not cover Oracle AIA Process Integration Pack in depth. Let's discuss a little more about Oracle AIA PIP before getting into the AIA Foundation Pack.

# Oracle AIA Foundation Pack concepts

Oracle AIA Foundation Pack is an SOA-based integration framework that includes building blocks of various components. The AIA building block components help to build complex end-to-end integration solutions based on a schema, an abstract or concrete WSDL, and a BPEL or Bus Component and Composite. The Oracle AIA Foundation Pack introduces a standard-based approach to integrate enterprise application systems as process-oriented composite application architecture. A composite application includes building an application solution with a combination of multiple service components, business functions, infrastructure services, business objects, rules, and business processes. Oracle Fusion Middleware helps to build such composite applications, and it can also be used to build the components of composite applications. As Oracle AIA components are running on Oracle SOA Suite, the composite approach could be easily adopted in Oracle AIA.

For better understanding, let's start from a simple point-to-point integration approach. In a point-to-point integration approach, the message/request object should be submitted by the requesting application to the provider application. The communication between the requester and provider could be through a file transfer, an HTTP request/response, a SOAP protocol, or a direct API call. In that case, there is no intermediate compound or layer involved in this approach. It is the requesting application's responsibility to build the message in the format that is accepted by the provider. In addition, the requesting application should transform the response message received from the provider into its own format. Therefore, the requesting and providing applications should communicate directly, as depicted in the following diagram:

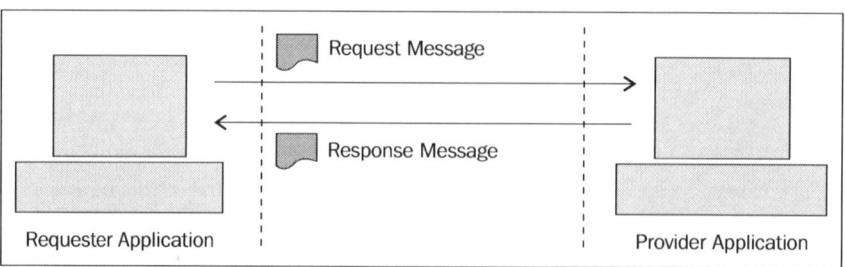

The SOA best practices dictates that there should be an easily extensible canonical model between the two services, so that additional services can be accommodated with minimal changes later. Service virtualization should be used, so that the requesting services and the providing services are de-coupled, and orchestration is done with extensibility points. Therefore, to eliminate the tighter integration, we need to build a common canonical and standard interface middle component to handle all messages. This common intermediate component should handle messages in the standard data format, layout, and business process flows as services. In addition, this component should be deployed in common platforms, so that all applications could consume these services. The common platform should be hosted in a service-oriented infrastructure. As it is a common platform for applications to meet the standard, there should be a transformation component which should transfer the messages that are received from the application to the common standard layout. The transformers are used to map between application-specific messages and a canonical data model. Therefore, communication will navigate through standard layout-based services. There should be a transformer component at the provider application side which should reformat the message from middleware standard format into the provider format. This approach removes the transformation and message formatting responsibilities from the requesting and providing applications.

In addition, the common standard-based middleware can be utilized by other applications which requires message routing and transformation services from the provider. This procedure is depicted in the following diagram:

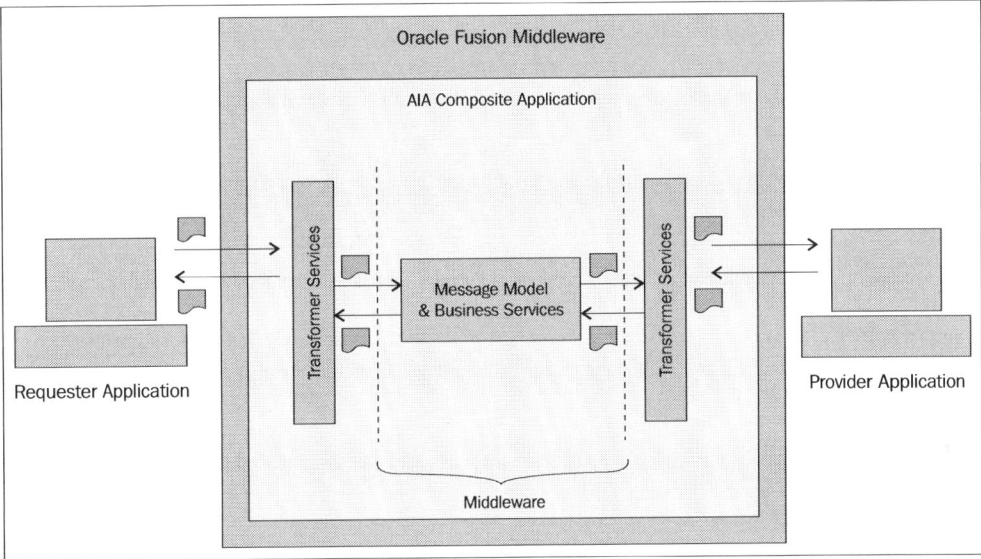

The preceding diagram represents the role of Oracle Fusion Middleware in AIA. The Oracle Fusion Middleware is used as a platform where AIA components are deployed. In the enterprise infrastructure environment, there is a high possibility of having more integration components and business services for all applications. Such environments require a centralized single service reference registry and repository for all schema and WSDL, where the requesting application identifies and chooses appropriate services for specific integration requirements. If there is no similar service available, then enforce to develop new service components and publish those to the service registry for reference.

In addition, such a service integration approach requires an effective error handling mechanism, service and message level security, and integration testing framework to facilitate the integration development. The combination of all these components makes the entire integration a highly mature service-oriented integration platform. This is all about the Oracle Application Integration Architecture framework and approach.

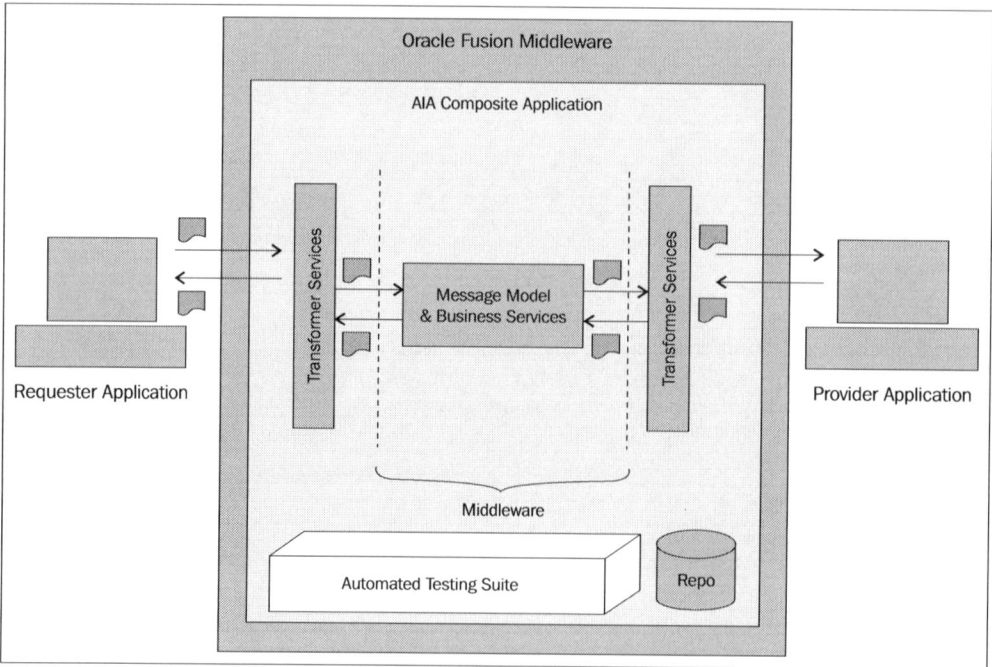

The following are the features of the Oracle AIA Foundation Pack:

- Helps to build a standard-based integration architecture between enterprise applications
- Highly robust integration framework for building service-oriented integration architecture
- Supports a high volume of transactions for enterprise mission-critical applications and infrastructure
- Ability to encapsulate the functionalities provided by Oracle applications and other enterprise application systems
- Supports business process decomposition, analysis, service design, service construction, process definition, and deployment/upgrade plans

- Supports monitoring integration services and process flows at runtime
- Supports design and runtime artifact governance

# Components of AIA Foundation Pack

So far, we have seen the Oracle integration approach and various components (in general) involved in building a service-oriented integration. In essence, the AIA Foundation Pack is a set of artifacts that are used to create, govern, and maintain the SOA-based integration. Now we have to explore the various components of the Oracle AIA Foundation Pack.

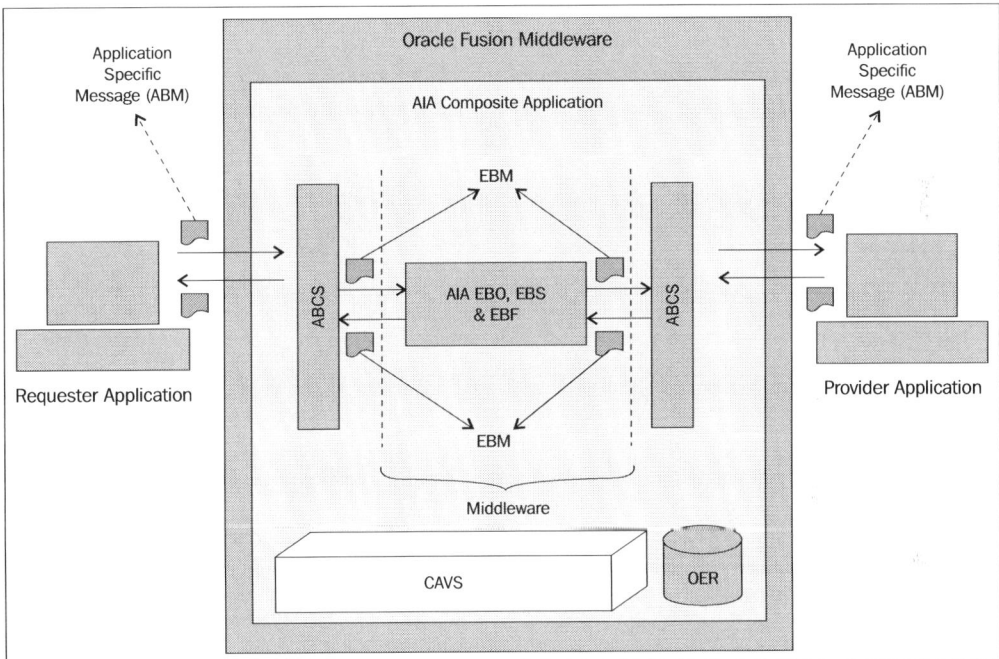

The Oracle AIA Foundation Pack includes several components to meet various standards and best practices to build the enterprise-level application integration architecture. The following is a list of components that AIA includes, and will be explored in this book:

- Enterprise Business Objects (EBO)
- Enterprise Business Messages (EBM)
- Application Business Connector Services (ABCS)
- Enterprise Business Services (EBS)

- Enterprise Business Flow (EBF)
- Enterprise Repository (ER)
- Composite Application Validation System (CAVS)

As this book covers all preceding components in the following chapters, we will have a brief overview of each component in this chapter.

## Enterprise Business Objects (EBO)

An EBO is essentially a design-time view of business entities. In technical terms, it defines the schema of the message types which can be exchanged between different components of AIA. As we have seen in the last section, AIA provides a standard-based integration approach through its centralized component. If we define the standard-based object for all integration communication, it prevents tight integrations and it is easier to manage integration challenges and modifications. EBO is standard-based common business objects that are known to business data models such as sales orders, claims, medical records, customers, and so on. A **business object** is a highly generalized business entity and has been carefully made to be as exhaustive as possible. Therefore, it abstracts the data models at a higher level (application independent canonical model). Therefore, the integration developed based on the AIA approach provides a higher flexibility to manage lower-level changes without changing integration objects and messages. This approach also eliminates the effort required for requesting applications to accommodate the messaging changes. Therefore, EBO helps to design and develop messaging objects at once and reuse as much as possible. Each EBO will be defined in the XML schema (XSD) and refer to each other wherever applicable, minimizing redundancy and promoting reusability.

## Enterprise Business Messages (EBM)

An EBM is an EBO that is used in a particular context. It is the message that is exchanged between services at runtime. While EBOs represent the XSD or the schema for a business entity, an EBM represents the concrete XML in a particular context. For example, a `SalesOrder` EBO used for the creation of a sales order is a `Create SalesOrderEBM`, a `SalesOrder` EBO used for deletion of a `SalesOrder` is a `Delete SalesOrderEBM`, and so on. Therefore, an EBM is one or more EBOs and a verb, or action, used in a particular context. EBSs also exchange XML-based messages between two applications as part of request/response communication. However, EBMs includes business tasks or function-specific enterprise business objects. An EBM could be a generic messaging payload or a content-specific message payload.

In addition, EBM may include one or more EBOs in the same message. As the fundamental messaging architecture does not hold any underlying transportation mechanism, EBM also supports the transport of natural messaging.

> In the messaging architecture, a message includes a header and body. The header helps to carry message-specific metadata information between applications. This header information is used for security, client application ID, and environment-specific information. In the enterprise-service architecture, the header plays a crucial role to keep track of the message information for monitoring and auditing purposes.

## Enterprise Business Services (EBS)

**Enterprise Business Services (EBS)** is a core component in the AIA-based integration approach. EBS is an independent service component based on web service interfaces which helps to execute business tasks and functions. EBS, typically, consists of an abstract WSDL and service routing component. The WSDL defines service operations, messaging patterns, and XML payloads for each operation. Enterprise business services are coarse-grained web services that accept EBM as a message payload from the requesting application, routing the message, and finally, responding back to the requester in the EBM format. EBS makes sure that the interfaces to underlying services are standardized, and helps to specify the granularity of the service. It is an independent service, but can also communicate with other EBSs.

> In an SOA approach, web services can be implemented at different levels or layers. This is called **service granularities**. There are two levels of granularity which are typically practiced. They are **Fine-grained** and **Coarse-grained** web services. Implementing web services at a lower level are Fine-grained web services, such as update the customer address. Coarse-grained web services are at higher/generic level, such as account service.

# Enterprise Business Flow (EBF)

**Enterprise Business Flow** is used for orchestrating flows between two or more services exposed through EBS or other EBFs. EBFs are basically business processes. Business processes are organizational processes being followed to fulfill certain business goals. Such processes are required to interact with various divisions or business group's business activities. Processes kick off by a particular business event, then a process executes various business activities in a step-by-step or orchestrated approach. EBF is nothing but a business process component for Oracle AIA. Oracle AIA supports business processes' orchestration by executing various EBS components defined in the enterprise integration environment. AIA delegates all orchestration flows into the business services and shields such flows clearly from the **Application Layer**. The logic behind this is that the core business logic of an integration changes rarely as compared to the application side or end applications. Therefore, changes at the application end do not necessarily necessitate changes to the Business Flow layer represented by EBFs. In AIA, all processes are also exposed as EBS interface through web services.

# Application Business Connector Services (ABCS)

As we have seen earlier, one of the best approaches is to have a validation and transformation component for each service, which integrates applications through Oracle AIA. **Application Business Connector Service (ABCS)** helps to bridge the gap between AIA EBS and application-specific data models. ABCS is responsible for validating the input request, transforming the message, enforcing security, and handling errors. ABCS can be requester-specific or provider-specific. The requestor is defined by the consuming application and the provider is defined by the service provider application. A requestor accepts the input message in an application specific format (ABM) and sends the response using the same format. A provider accepts the input from EBS or directly from a requester in EBM (common canonical data) and sends the response through the same channel. In addition, the provider ABCS plays a crucial role in exposing application business functions as services, which cannot be directly exposed as AIA's EBO.

# Oracle Enterprise Repository (OER)

In the enterprise SOA infrastructure, application business components, functions, processes, and resources are decomposed as business services. Therefore, in a typical enterprise environment, there is a high possibility of having hundreds of business services. It is highly difficult to manage the lifecycle of enterprise services and processes. There is a need of repository to handle service lifecycle, version management, monitoring, and auditing. **Oracle Enterprise Repository** provides such an enterprise-level service governance support, which is also an integral part of Oracle AIA FP 11g. The earlier version of Oracle AIA (Oracle AIA 2.4 and 2.5) supports **Business Service Repository** (**BSR**). However, the Oracle AIA Foundation Pack 11g release 1 consolidates the BSR functionalities with OER.

If you are using Oracle AIA 2.4 or 2.5 and would like to migrate to Oracle AIA 11g Release 1, you must migrate all your AIA service components from the BSR version to OER. Oracle provides a separate migration guide for its customers.

# Composite Application Validation System (CAVS)

So far, we have seen the various core components of the Oracle AIA Foundation Pack which help to build the AIA approach-based integration solutions. As we know how development components are important in an integration solution, similarly, validating the integration solution is very important to produce a quality product. The Oracle AIA-based integration approach may invoke various business functions of application systems. Therefore, validating such an integration invocation through a simplified testing framework provides more flexibility. **Oracle AIA Composite Application Validation System** is a testing simulation framework which helps to invoke EBS, ABCS, and EBF in real-time scenarios. CAVS also includes a validation framework, service simulator, error handling configuration, and test repository to store the testing definitions and other user interfaces.

# Oracle AIA Reference Architecture

In general, designing and implementing an SOA integration solution is a very complicated process. The SOA implementation requires a strong roadmap and implementation lifecycle to succeed. An iterative development methodology-based implementation lifecycle fits best for the SOA implementation. In addition, the reference architecture plays a crucial role to eliminate the design complexity and redundancy. In a real-time scenario, if we want to construct a corporate office building, we need an architectural blueprint for construction. Similarly, the SOA reference architecture acts as a blueprint for the enterprise SOA implementation. The Oracle AIA reference architecture model is almost similar to the SOA reference architecture, as seen in the following diagram:

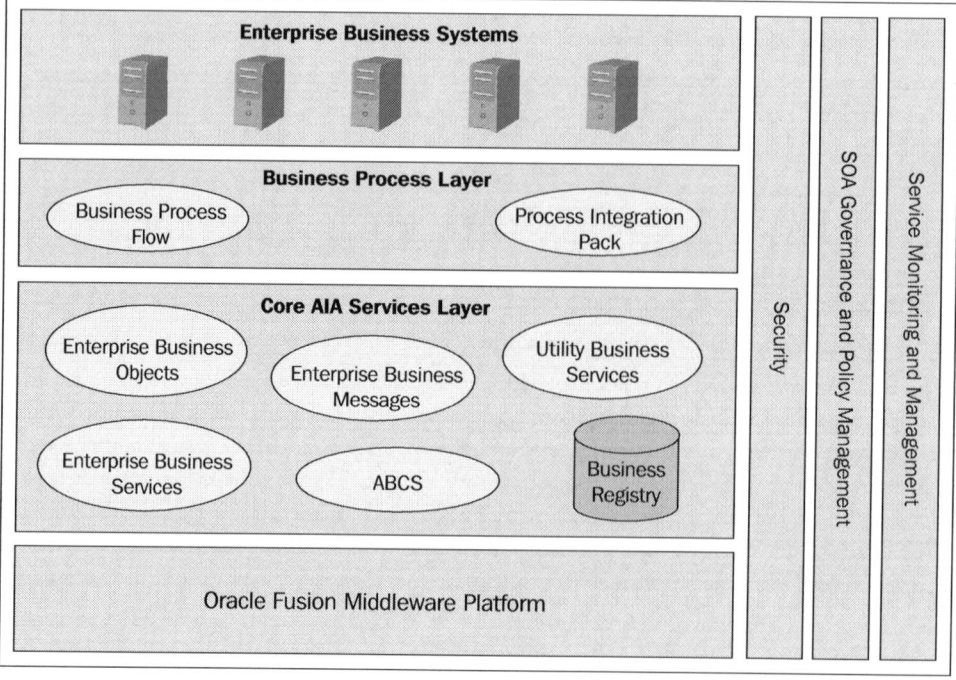

The preceding diagram represents the AIA reference architecture based on the SOA reference architecture approach. As we have seen, the entire AIA application solution should be deployed in the fusion middleware to get service-oriented advantages. If we look at the architecture, we will find that the complete solution is separated as two layers. Basically, this increases the performance of the integration solution. In the architecture world, we should design the solution with simplified layers to increase the performance and reduce latency.

Similarly, the AIA approach requires building an integration solution by the AIA core service layer and business process flow layer. All the AIA service components should be grouped together as part of the core service layer. The AIA components such as EBO, EBM, and EBS are part of the core service layer. All these core services are consumed to build EBF and business processes. The **Oracle Enterprise Repository** could play the role of service repository where all AIA business services can be registered. As the AIA integration solution deployed in the fusion middleware platform, securing services, policy governance, and monitoring can be implemented using fusion components.

Now the question is to identify the processes and business services to define the reference architecture. Oracle has suggested a process reference model in which a collection of best practices is gathered from various Oracle application customers.

## AIA Process Reference Model

The Oracle AIA Process Reference Model is a proven best practice collected from and based on previous application integrations. This approach helps to identify the business processes, business activities, and build repository to keep track of the evaluation of the processes. This model is depicted in the following diagram:

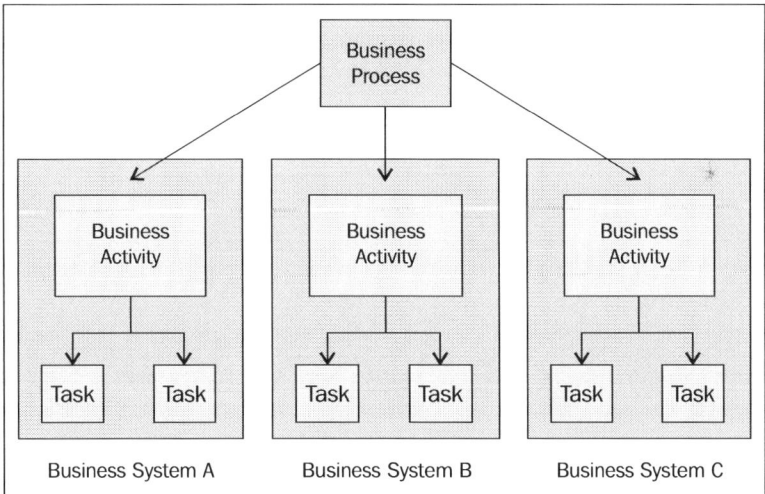

Business processes are a collection of coordinated business tasks and business functions distributed across various business systems, which are executed in order to meet the organized goals. Some of the business processes that we would have come across are Order-to-Cash and Claim processes. Business activities are a set of tasks that execute a business function such as credit payment processing, order fulfillment, and so on. Finally, a task is a small activity which does not have any dependency on other tasks and activities such as create customer, check order status, and so on. In the composite application development, we can follow the top-down drilling approach to identify the business processes and its activities, and expose those functions as business services. Once the business tasks and activities are identified, we then need to build the business process workflow to meet the process requirements.

Apart from regular processes and business components, there are other utilities services that should also be designed as per the AIA reference architectures, which include e-mail notifications, adapter services for legacy integration, validation services, data set processing, and so on. Such services are grouped together as utility services which can be used by AIA integration solutions. This approach also helps to reuse such services for future requirements.

# The role of Oracle Fusion Middleware

The Oracle Fusion Middleware is an enterprise platform that provides solutions for various enterprise needs. Fusion middleware supports a variety of standards for integration, business processes, business intelligence, web development, content management and hosting servers, enterprise governance, and so on. One of the primary integration and process implementation components in the fusion middleware includes **Oracle SOA Suite** and **Oracle Service Bus**. The Oracle SOA Suite is built based on various patterns from enterprise application integration and service-oriented architecture.

# Oracle SOA Suite 11g

The Oracle SOA Suite is a set of components used to build mature, service-oriented architecture at an enterprise level. It is a central component in fusion middleware. The Oracle SOA Suite provides components for enabling services for existing applications and infrastructure assets, securing the service components, orchestrating services to build business processes, and building service composite applications.

The following are the components of the Oracle SOA Suite 11g product:

- Oracle Mediator
- Oracle Technical/Application Adapters
- Oracle BPEL Process Manager
- Human Workflow
- Oracle Service Bus
- Oracle Business Rules
- Oracle Enterprise Manager
- Oracle Complex Event Processing
- Oracle B2B
- Oracle Web Service Manager
- Oracle Business Activity Monitor
- Oracle Metadata Repository
- JDeveloper IDE

The Oracle SOA Suite is the foundation technology for Oracle AIA. The Oracle SOA Suite helps to build the AIA integration application by using various components, such as mediator, Oracle service bus, Adapters, Oracle BPEL process manager, and so on. The mediator is used to build the EBS component, whereas BPEL is used to build integration ABCS, EBF components of AIA. As the AIA approach is based on service-oriented principles, the Oracle SOA Suite best fits for implementing AIA solutions.

## Summary

In this chapter, we have seen the various application integration requirements and architecture methodologies. Oracle AIA provides a standard-based application integration framework to build highly-scalable, processes-oriented integration solutions for enterprise assets. In addition, we have seen a brief overview of AIA concepts and integration approaches using Oracle SOA Suite.

The following chapters in this book cover more details about AIA components and one real-time use case of an AIA implementation.

The next chapter will cover the primary core component of the AIA approach, **Enterprise Business Object (EBO)**, including the following topics:

- An overview of EBO
- Elements of EBO
- Exploring EBO
- The physical structure of EBO
- Various domain-specific EBO components
- Extending EBO

# 2
# Enterprise Business Objects

In this chapter, we are going to learn the core component of AIA called **Enterprise Business Objects**. A business object is a set of business entities combined to meet specific business goals such as a sales order, product, or bank account.

The following topics are covered in this chapter:

- Overview of Enterprise Business Objects
- Exploring EBO
- Core EBO
- Common EBO Groups
- Infrastructure components

## Overview of Enterprise Business Objects

Enterprise Business Objects (EBOs) are a highly grained set of business entity objects, which are used for business information sharing across enterprise business applications. These have been defined using information from several best of breed applications and standards. EBOs define all business information required to accommodate AIA-specific business integration. These are basically used for standard-oriented canonical business data models such as sales order, claims, medical records, customer information, and so on. Understanding EBOs and EBMs is much easier if you are familiar with canonical XML, XSD, and Web Service messages. Even though EBOs have been defined from information available from several applications, they themselves are not attached to any specific application and represent a generic standard based on a canonical model. In a typical integration approach, source and target system data models should be mapped directly from object to object. This type of approach is increasing the risk of frequent modification in the mapping if any one of the system modifies its data model. Oracle AIA EBO components eliminate this risk by providing a data model at abstract level. This approach will also minimize manual coding, data transformation, and validations.

*Enterprise Business Objects*

For example, a sales order arises from two different applications, say A and B, containing two different definitions for sales order. If an application X wants to communicate with both A and B, it is necessary for X to transform messages separately for both A and B. Instead, if a formal definition of a sales order were to be made available, say `SalesOrderFormat`, which abstracts from the definitions underlying both systems A and B, then the application X can simply transform to the `SalesOrderFormat` and communicate with both applications seamlessly. This is the rationale behind EBOs—to create a standards-based abstraction of known business entities that is as exhaustive as possible so as to reduce direct mapping and streamlining data models. AIA extends this concept further to include standard guidelines not only for the content of the EBO, but also for the way in which an EBO is designed, named, versioned, and extended.

The EBOs are in the form of **XML Schema Definition (XSD)**. Also, the EBO structure and design is based on the **UN/CEFACT XML Naming and Design Rules**. It is also based on the **XML Naming and Design Rules** by **OAGIS** and **UN/CEFACT Core Component Technical Specification**. Each and every EBO includes two schema models; one presents the definition of that EBO and another presents the definition of operations (functions) that should be executed by that EBO. EBO does not act independently in the Oracle AIA or Fusion infrastructure; however, it is part of Enterprise Business Messages (EBM) and Enterprise Business Services (EBS).

As EBOs are in the form of XML schema, EBOs follow the best practices in the industry and that includes:

- XML Schema root elements (`xsd:schema`) should be defined using attributes `elementFormDefault="qualified"` or `"unqualified"`.
- The XML `version=" "` attribute should be used to indicate the actual version of the schema.
- All namespaces used in the XML schema must be identified in the `xmlns` attribute at root element level.
- The `targetNamespace` attribute should be used to identify the target namespace in the XML schema.
- XML schema namespace should be used as `xsd`.

Notes:

- Even though Oracle AIA installation and configuration is out of scope for this book, there are a few steps that should be executed properly to install Oracle AIA FP 11g successfully.
- Install Oracle Database or Oracle XE and it should start running.
- Install Oracle Repository Creation Utility (RCU), which should connect to database and create necessary SOA and BPM repositories.
- Install Oracle WebLogic Server 11g and Oracle SOA Suite 11g, and configure the SOA domain prior to installing Oracle AIA FP 11g. Start running the SOA Domain.
- Install Oracle AIA 11g (preferably complete installation).
- Oracle AIA can be installed as complete installation or manually.

# Exploring EBO

Oracle AIA Foundation Pack 11g installation brings a set of predefined EBO schemas packed in the directory structure. The following screenshot will show the physical structure of the EBO groups as directories:

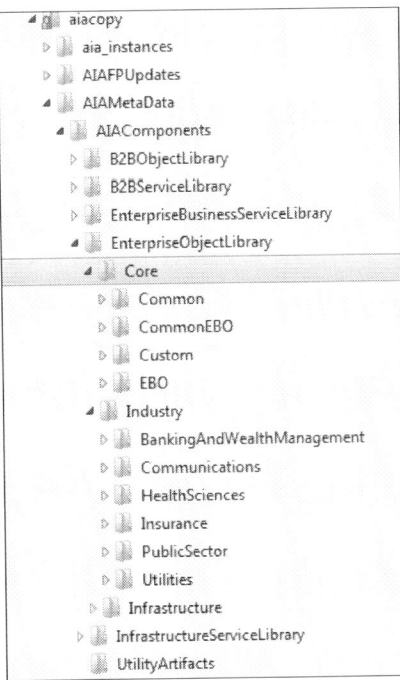

Oracle AIA enterprise objects (EBOs) are grouped as three packages based on the business model of the EBO, which are **Core**, **Industry**, and **Infrastructure** components:

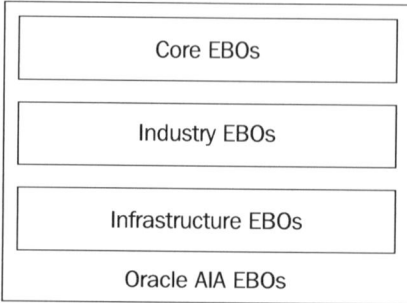

- The Core EBO includes fundamental business objects that are used for various business integrations. The `EnterpriseObjectLibrary/Core/EBO` folder contains EBOs for common business use case such as, sales orders, bill of materials, bank account, project, shipment plan, and so on.
- The Industry EBOs include various specially-designed industry-specific EBO components. The industry business object folder can be found under `EnterpriseObjectLibrary/Industry`:
    - Banking and wealth management
    - Communications
    - Health science
    - Insurance
    - Public Sector
    - Utilities

Infrastructure components can be found under `EnterpriseObjectLibrary/Infrastructure/`. Infrastructure components do not include generic EBO components. They are basically fundamental data types, code lists, and other web services components. Also, infrastructure components include the custom data types and other metadata components designed for specific requirements.

Oracle AIA Foundation Pack 11g includes enterprise objects and other artifacts necessary to build AIA solutions. **Enterprise Object Library** (EOL) comes under AIA Metadata and AIA Component's folder structure. In a typical AIA installation, the Enterprise Object Library is located under the `$AIA_HOME\AIAMetaData\AIAComponents\EnterpriseObjectLibrary` folder.

Enterprise Objects Library folder contains both EBO and EBM components. EBMs are a custom view of EBOs and business entities. EOL includes two varieties of EBO components, which are core EBO components and industry-specific EBO components.

# Core EBO

As the name indicates, Core EBOs are a set of **common business objects**. AIA FP R1 has more than 90 core EBO components, which are used to integrate with various Oracle Apps solutions. In order to identify and browse the list of EBO objects, open the `EBOIndex` html file in the html viewer:

```
$AIA_HOME/AIAMetaData/AIAComponents/EnterpriseObjectLibrary/Core/
EBOIndex.html
```

Oracle AIA Core EBOs includes four different groups of EBOs, which are known as Common, Common EBO, Custom, and EBO. Oracle AIA maintains all the versions of every EBO component to support backward compatibility.

# Core EBO groups

The following packages are parts of Core EBO. All the following groups are separated as folders under Enterprise Object Library.

## Common EBO groups

Common EBOs are also called as reusable EBOs. Reusable business objects represent objects that are commonly used or extended in core EBOs such as item, party, shipment, calendar, person, bill of materials, and so on. Common EBOs are independent business objects but may be part of an another EBO.

*Enterprise Business Objects*

For example, calendar is a Common EBO; however, it has been used as part of the `BusinessCalendar` EBO:

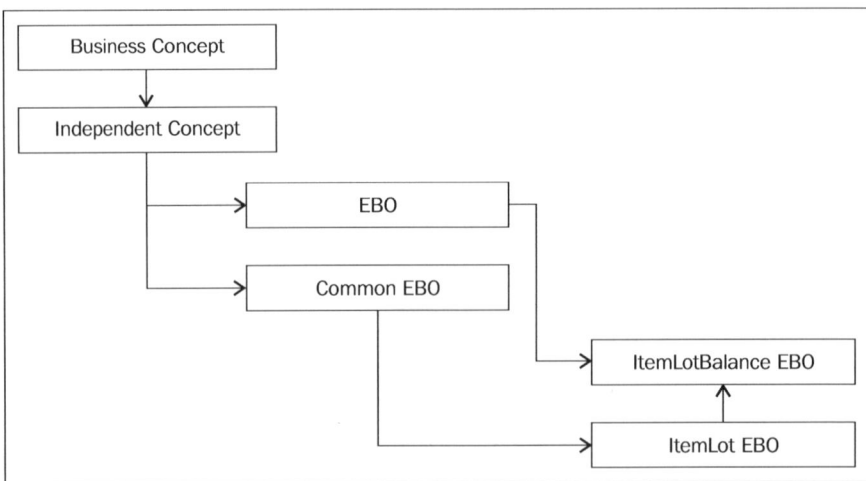

The preceding diagram demonstrates that independent concepts are derived from Business concepts. EBOs and Common EBOs are identified and defined based on the business and independent concepts. The preceding diagram shows that **ItemLotBalance** EBO is part of EBO the package. However, it extends the `ItemLot` EBO from a common EBO. As we read earlier, Common EBOs are a basic level EBO, which are used and extended based on the specific EBO requirements.

Let us cross-check this by physically referring to the AIA Enterprise Object Library. The following steps should be executed one by one for better understanding:

1. Go to `$AIA_HOME/\AIAMetaData\AIAComponents\EnterpriseObjectLibrary\Core\CommonEBO\V1` folder.

2. Open the `ItemLot.html` file in your browser, which will display the following screen:

| ItemLot | |
|---|---|
| EBO Type | Enterprise Business Object |
| CCTS Type | |
| CCTS Dictionary Entry Name | Item Lot. Details |
| Description | This object identifies an item lot, its current state and its specific physical property values. |
| Usage Rule | |
| Extends | |
| Attributes | ExpirationDate<br>Description<br>CountryOfOriginCode<br>GradeCode<br>CreationDateTime<br>LastModificationDateTime<br>Age<br>RetestDateTime<br>MaturityDateTime<br>Volume<br>Length<br>RecycledContentPercent<br>Height<br>Width<br>SourceTypeCode<br>NettableIndicator<br>ExpirationActionCode<br>ExpirationActionDateTime<br>ReservableIndicator<br>BestByDate<br>SellByDate |

3. On that html page, we can verify the ItemLot EBO and its attributes.

4. Now go to the `$AIA_Home/AIAMetaData/AIAComponents/EnterpriseObjectLibrary/Core/EBO/ItemLotBalance/V1/` folder and open `ItemLotBalanceEBO.html` file:

| ItemLotBalance | | | |
|---|---|---|---|
| EBO Type | Enterprise Business Object | | |
| CCTS Type | Aggregate Business Information Entity | | |
| CCTS Dictionary Entry Name | Item Lot Balance. Details | | |
| Description | It contains the Item Lot details including its available balance at a specified inventory location for a specified date. | | |
| Usage Rule | | | |
| Extends | | | |
| Attributes | | | |
| Child Components | Name | CCTS Dictionary Entry Name | |
| | | Description | |
| | LotBalance | Item Lot Balance. Lot Balance. Lot Balance | |
| | | It contains the balance information of an Item Lot at specified inventory on a specified date. | |
| | ItemLot | Item Lot Balance. Item Lot. Item Lot | |
| | | Defines item lot information | |
| | Identification | Item Lot Balance. Identification. Identification | |
| | | Unique identifier for Item Lot Balance. | |
| | PrimaryItemLotIdentification | Item Lot Balance. Primary Item Lot Identification. Primary Item Lot Identification | |
| | | Unique identifier for Primary Item Lot | |

5. On this page, refer to the **Child Components** section where we can find the **ItemLot** EBO as a child component. This shows that the `ItemLotBalance` EBO uses the `ItemLot` EBO as a child component, and that is why `ItemLot` EBO has been packed with common EBOs.

# EBO Components group

Oracle AIA has a list of predefined EBOs as part of EBO package under Enterprise Object Library. Before getting into the package and folder structure, we will dive a little deeper into EBOs for better understanding. Oracle AIA fundamental EBOs are comprised of five major components. They are:

- Business components
- Reference components
- Common components
- Infrastructure components
- Shared components

## Business components

Business Component is a dependant business object, specific to a business, which does not exist independently but only in context of a business goal. In an EBO, Business components are basically business concepts that are specific to an enterprise business object but do not act independently. Business components always depend on the dependent concepts that exist in the context of EBO.

Business components are based on the following characteristics:

1. Business concepts are self-contained components to support a specific business function or operation. For example, a create purchase order function.
2. Business components are independent concepts or dependent concepts. However, an independent concept has its own lifecycle.
3. A dependent business concept does not exist by itself because it is depending on another concept. For example, a purchase order header and purchase order line.

    The following figure depicts this:

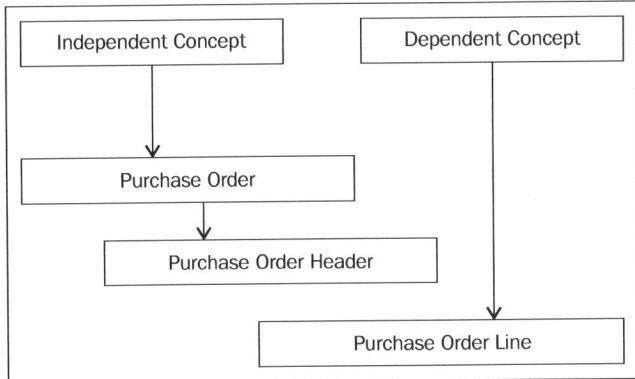

# Reference components

Reference components are actually foreign keys. Also, reference components could be another EBO in the Core EBO package. The most common scenario is that a group of attributes could be a part of reference EBO structure. Also, reference components share namespace with common components.

The advantage of using reference components is that they reduce redundancy, and development and maintenance overhead because they are associated with another EBO.

For example, CustomerPartyReference in the SalesOrder is another EBO itself, which is a `CustomerPartyEBO`:

```
<xsd:element ref="corecom:CustomerPartyReference" minOccurs="0">
<xsd:annotation>
<xsd:documentation>
</xsd:element>
```

*Enterprise Business Objects*

## Common components

Common components include business data types, which are applicable to almost all of the EBOs and EBM components. Common components may also share the same namespace. Some of the common components are `ShipmentType`, `ComponentIndentificationType`, `OperationType`, and so on:

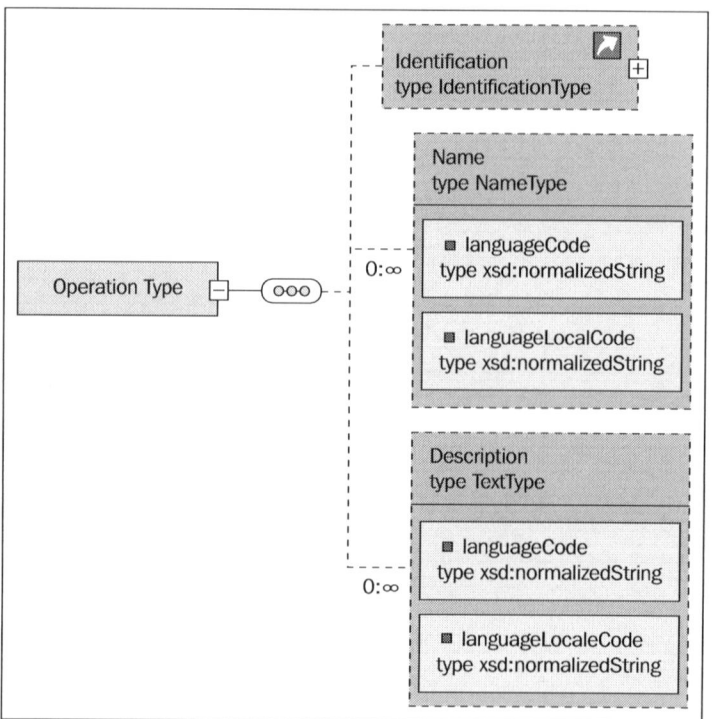

## Structure of EBOs

As we have seen earlier, EBOs are common business objects, which are following standard schema structure in all business objects. The structure of the EBOs are mostly standard structures.

1. The first part of the EBO is `<xsd:schema>` and a list of schema being used in the entire EBO schema.

2. The first part of the EBO should be schema imports `<xsd:import>`. Imports include common components, Metadata, CodeLists, DataTypes, and other EBOs, if any.

3. The third portion of the EBO should be EBO elements `<xsd:element>` for EBO object and followed by `EBOType` objects.

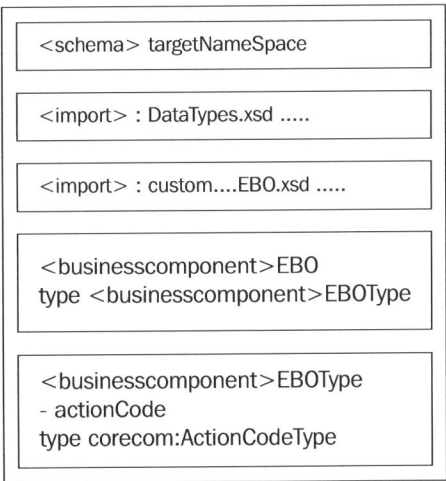

The default set of EBOs are located in the `EnterpriseObjectLibrary/Core/EBO/` folder. Oracle AIA maintains all versions of EBO components. EBO components are continuously updated based on the various inputs received and best practices followed by various customers. So, in order to maintain backward compatibility and support existing AIA implementations, Oracle AIA maintains every version of each EBO.

# Custom EBO

Oracle AIA brings a set of predefined business object used across various industries. As Oracle has a wide variety of business application systems, Oracle collected various business and application objects based on prior implementation and best practices. So, Oracle AIA Enterprise Object Library includes a variety of predefined EBOs. However, Oracle AIA allows its customer to customize the predefined EBOs to meet various individual business integration requirements.

In order to maintain the customizations uniformly (and also to differentiate the customization between various instances of Oracle AIA) Oracle AIA grouped all customizable EBOs as custom EBO packages. So the original EBOs (default version of EBOs) are separated from custom EBOs. Also, in order to facilitate the development to differentiate original EBOs from custom EBOs and also to accommodate custom EBOs as a part of EBM, all custom EBOs are named with a prefix as "Custom". In addition, one of the primary reasons for Custom EBO is that customer does not lose their custom changes during upgrades, as AIA does not update the custom directory in case of upgrades.

Custom EBOs are located in the following location and follow the same package folder structure as Core EBOs: `$AIA_Home\AIAMetaData\AIAComponents\EnterpriseObjectLibrary\Core\Custom`.

For example: `CustomSalesOrderEBO.xsd`, `CustomQuoteEBO.xsd`, and `CustomPriceListEBO.xsd`.

# Extending EBOs

In real-time AIA implementation, we may have to customize the existing EBOs and EBMs to meet the business requirements. Oracle AIA supports customizing EBOs and EBMs to meet potential demands. In the previous sections, we have explored the physical structure of EBOs in the AIA installation. Now, we are going to extend one of the EBOs.

We assume that purchase orders should be shared across business systems through AIA integration pattern. However, the existing PO EBO requires additional parameter as priority. The following steps should be executed to customize the PO EBO in the out-of-the-box AIA:

1. First, we need to identify the EBO schema, which should be customized (in this case, add addition element). Go to the `$AIA_Home\AIAMetaData\AIAComponents\EnterpriseObjectLibrary\Core\Custom\EBO\PurchaseOrder\V1/` folder and open `CustomPurchaseOrderEBO` schema file in JDeveloper.

2. Now, select the `customPurchaseOrderEBOType` and right-click to display the list of options. Now, select **Insert Inside ComplexType** and select **sequence** from the menu items.

3. This should insert a sequence object in the `customPurchaseOrderEBOType`. Now, select the **Sequence** and right-click to display the list of menu items. Again, select the **Insert Inside Sequence** and select **Element**.

4. Rename the element (usually it should be created as element1) as **Priority**. Now, we have to set the type of the element.

5. Now, right-click the priority element and select the **Set type** from the menu item. Now, it should prompt to enter the type of the element. Here, we can select the element type from the list or enter **corecom:identificationType**.

6. Now save the file. We have completed the customization by adding additional elements in the custom PO EBO. The customization should as look as follows:

*Chapter 2*

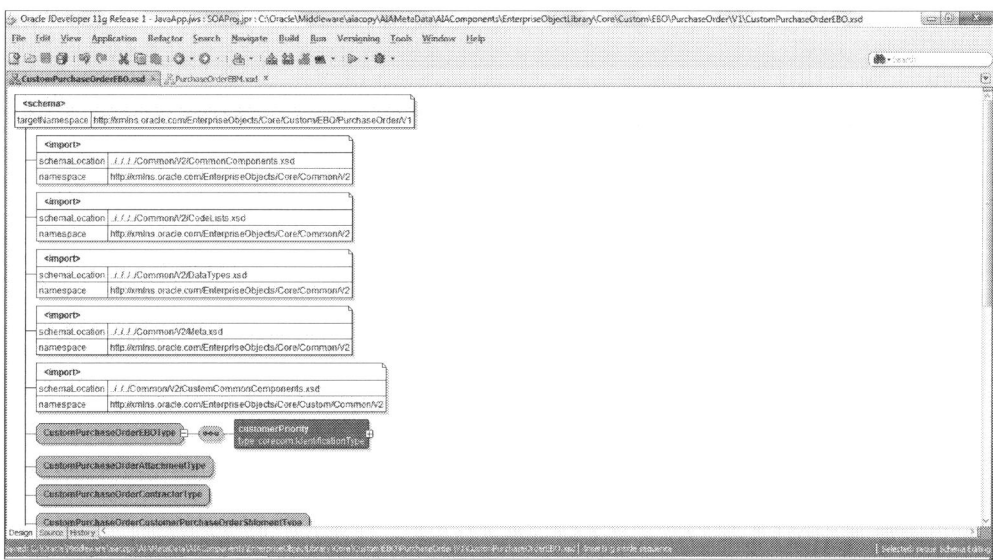

Now, we have to verify that how this EBO customization reflects in the PO EBM (we are going to explore in detail about EBM in next chapter). The following steps should be executed to validate the customization in EBM.

1. In order to verify the EBM, we have to open the EBM object in JDeveloper IDE to verify it.

2. Go to the `$AIA_HomeAIA\MetaData\AIAComponents\EnterpriseObjectLibrary\Core\EBO\PurchaseOrder\V1` folder and open the `PurchaseOrderEBM` schema in JDeveloper.

3. Extend the **PurchaseOrderEBMType** and scroll down to till the end of it where we can view the custom element and its value as **Priority**. The customization should show what is seen in the following screenshot:

Similar to the preceding steps, we can extend any EBO schema according to our customization needs. However, we have to ensure that we are following these steps properly for it to work correctly.

[ 43 ]

*Enterprise Business Objects*

# Industry EBOs

Industry EBO package contains a list of industry-specific EBOs. We can physically view the list of industry EBOs supported by AIA by going to the folder `$AIA_HOME/AIAMetaData\AIAComponents\EnterpriseObjectLibrary\Industry`. The following figure will list down the industries supported by Oracle AIA EBOs:

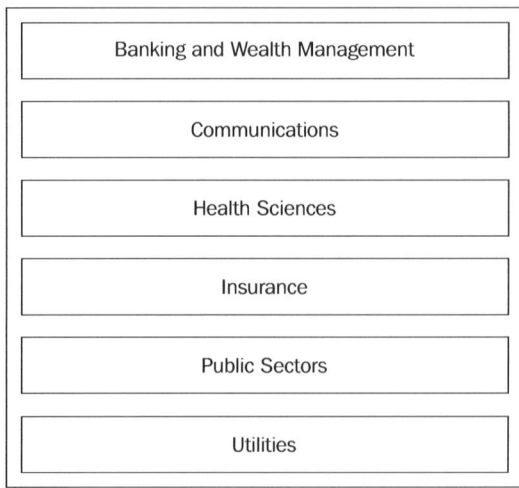

Let us take one of the industry packages and explore it further into those EBOs. Industry-specific EBO packages are also structured like a Core EBO package. Go to Insurance industry EBO folder `$AIA_HOME/AIAMetaData\AIAComponents\EnterpriseObjectLibrary\Industry\Insurance`. In this folder we can see the folder structure as Common, CommonEBO, Custom, and EBO. If we refer to the list of EBOs in the EBO folder, the entire EBOs list in this folder is related to the insurance sector. Similarly, each industry package's EBO folder has its own EBOs. AIA enterprise object library facilitates us to maintain and customize the EBOs, and common data types, metadata, and code lists specific to the industry. This approach allows the development team to maintain a clean EBO repository specific to industries.

# Infrastructure components

Infrastructure components are a collection of various data types, metadata and code lists that are being used to build core EBOs. There are two types of data types being used such as **Simple** data types and **Complex** data types.

Examples for Field Level or Simple data types are `DataType`, `NumericType`, `StringType`, and so on.

Examples for Complex types are `AmountType`, `QuantityType`, and so on.

EBOs are designed by reusing the infrastructure objects that are inherited by different components. Metadata's elements are used in EBM header and body, and code lists are normally values such as `language query` and `debug`.

## Data types

Data types are used to define the data type of each EBO attribute and hence, data types are defined at the infrastructure level. AIA differentiates the data types as **Core** date types and **Business** data types. Core data types are used across all EBOs to define the attribute type. Business data types are restrictive data types applicable only to certain business attribute representations.

The following screenshot shows the list of core and business data types supported as parts of infrastructure components.

| CCTS Core Data Types | | | |
|---|---|---|---|
| AmountType | BinaryObjectType | CodeType | DateTimeType |
| DateType | DurationType | IdentifierType | IndicatorType |
| IntegerType | MeasureType | NameType | NumericType |
| PercentType | QuantityType | RateType | TextType |
| TimeType | StringType | URIType | YearType |
| | | | |
| CCTS Business Data Types | | | |
| PositiveIntegerType | | | |

In order to view the list of infrastructure data types supported by AIA, open the html file from `$AIA_HOME/AIAMetaData/AIAComponents/EnterpriseObjectLibrary/Infrastructure/V1/DataTypes.html`.

## Summary

Enterprise Business Objects are not independent components of the AIA infrastructure. They are used along with Enterprise Business Messages (EBM) in Enterprise Business Services. Application Business Connector Services (ABCS), Enterprise Business Flow (EBF), and EBMs are providing a runtime-specific view for EBOs in the business service integration.

In order to revisit what we learned about EBOs in this chapter, let us go through the following points:

- We learned about the Business objects and EBO in AIA
- Explored the physical folder structure of an EBO
- Various components of EBO and its structure
- Needs of custom EBO folders, and custom EBOs

EBOs cannot be used as is in the AIA implementation; EBOs are basically a design time schema model. We need to bind the specific view of EBO along with EBM. In the next chapter, we are going to explore more about EBM.

# Enterprise Business Messages

Before we jump into the AIA Enterprise Business Message (EBM) standards, let us understand a little more about Business Messages. In general, Business Message is information shared between people, organizations, systems, or processes. Any information communicated to any object in a standard understandable format are called messages.

In the application integration world, there are various information-sharing approaches that are followed. We already explored some of those in the *Chapter 1, Overview of Oracle AIA*. Therefore, we need not go through it again, but in a service-oriented environment, message-sharing between systems is the fundamental characteristic. There should be a standard approach followed across an enterprise, so that every existing or new business system could understand and follow the uniform method. XML technology is a widely-accepted message format by all the technologies and tools.

Oracle AIA framework provides a standard messaging format to share the information between AIA components. In this chapter, we are going cover the following topics:

- Overview of Enterprise Business Messages (EBM)
- Structure of EBM
- EBM Use Cases

# Overview of Enterprise Business Message (EBM)

Enterprise Business Messages (EBMs) are business information exchanged between enterprise business systems as messages. EBMs define the elements that are used to form the messages in service-oriented operations. EBM payloads represent specific content of an EBO that is required to perform a specific service. In an AIA infrastructure, EBMs are messages exchanged between all components in the **Canonical Layer**. Enterprise Business Services (EBS) accepts EBM as a request message and responds back to EBM as an output payload. However, in Application Business Connector Service (ABCS), the provider ABCS accepts messages in the EBM format and translates them into the application provider's **Application Business Message (ABM)** format. Alternatively, the requester ABCS receives ABM as a request message, transforms it into an EBS, and calls the EBS to submit the EBM message. Therefore, EBM has been a widely-accepted message standard within AIA components.

The context-oriented EBMs are built using a set of common components and EBO business components. Some EBMs may require more than one EBO to fulfill the business integration needs. The following diagram describes the role of an EBM in the AIA architecture:

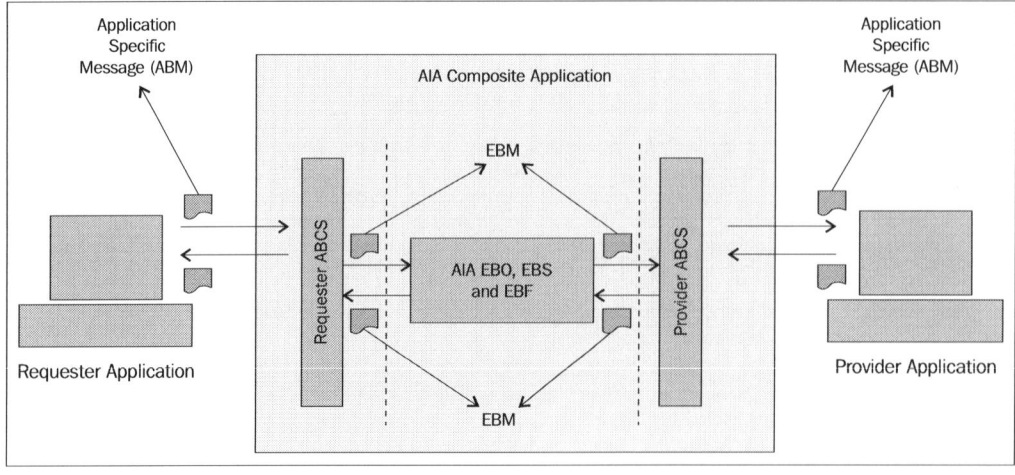

# EBM characteristics

The fundamentals of EBM and its characteristics are as follows:

- Each business service request and response should be represented in an EBM format using a unique combination of an action and an EBO instance.
- One EBM can support only one action or verb.
- EBM component should import the common component to make use of metadata and data types across the EBM structure.
- EBMs are application interdependencies. Any requester application that invokes Enterprise Business Services (EBS) through ABCS should follow the EBM format standards to pass as payload in integration.
- The action that is embedded in the EBM is the only action that sender or requester application can execute to perform integration.
- The action in the EBM may also carry additional data that has to be done as part of service execution. For example, the **update** action may carry information about whether the system should notify after successful execution of update.
- The information that exists in the EBM header is common to all EBMs. However, information existing in the data area and corresponding actions are specific to only one EBM.
- EBM headers may carry tracking information, auditing information, source and target system information, and error-handling information.
- EBM components do not rely on the underlying transport protocol. Any service protocols such as HTTP, HTTPs, SMTP, SOAP, and JMS should carry EBM payload documents.

# Exploring AIA EBMs

We explored the physical structure of the Oracle AIA EBO in the previous chapter; EBMs do not have a separate structure. EBMs are also part of the EBO's physical package structure. Every EBO is bound with an EBM. The following screenshot will show the physical structure of the EBM groups as directories:

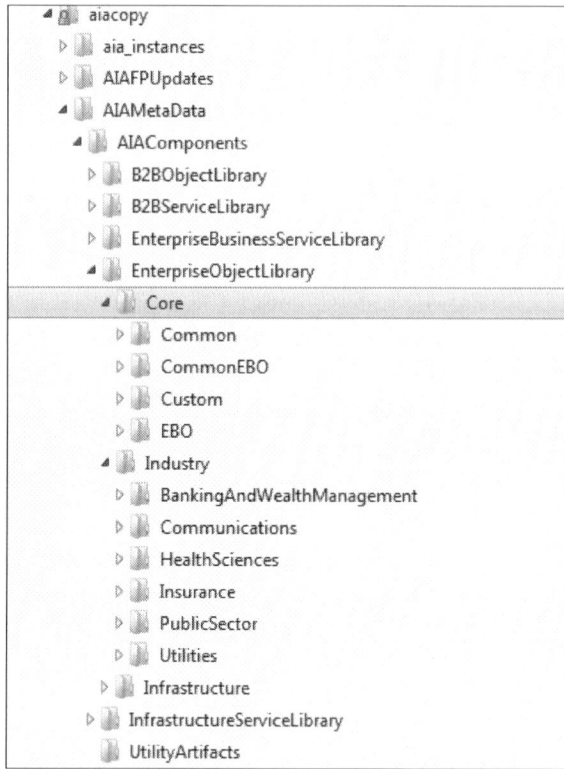

As EBOs are grouped as packages based on the business model, EBMs are also a part of that structure and can be located along with the EBO schema under the Core EBO package.

# Structure of EBM

In Oracle AIA, EBOs and EBMs follow standard structures to meet best practice in business integration. EBMs follow a messaging architecture for all business integration requirements. The following screenshot will show the structure of an EBM (for example, a Bank Account EBM):

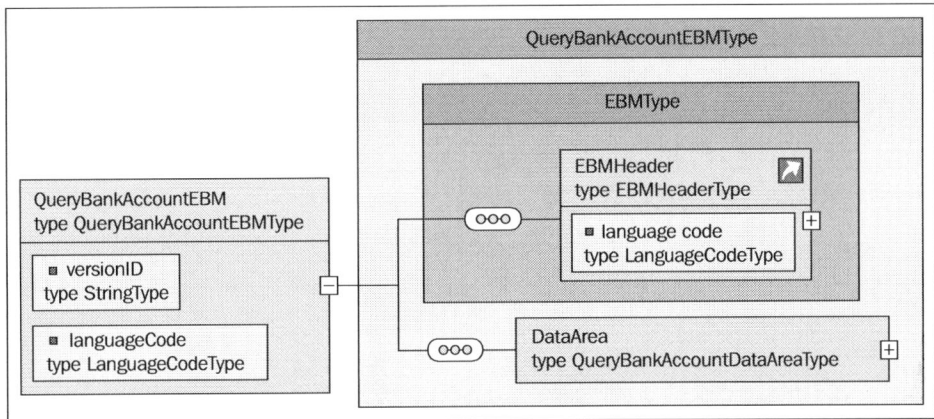

Basically EBMs are divided into two parts, (EBM) **Header** and **Data Area**. The primary structure of EBM includes EBM Header, action to be executed using the given data (Data Area), and global attributes. Every service request and response is presented in the EBM by a combination of operation and instance. EBM cannot process more than one type of operation. For example, both query and update operations cannot be executed in the same message or a single request. In AIA, EBM carries the message payload in both service requests and responses. Each EBM is associated with a specific EBO and thus an EBO package structure includes the EBM schema as well. Let us explore EBM and EBO physical structure and references further.

For our case, we will explore Bank Account EBO and EBM in its physical package location. Go to `$AIA_Home/AIAMetaData\AIAComponents\EnterpriseObjectLibrary\Core\EBO\BankAccount\V1` folder. In this folder we can find both `BankAccountEBO` and `BankAccountEBM` schema definitions. Open the `BankAccountEBM` in the JDeveloper.

# Enterprise Business Messages

The first part of the EBM includes the reference schema elements of `include` and `import` parts where we can see the schema location reference of `BankAccountEBO.xsd` in the `xsd:include` element shown as follows:

```
<xsd:include schemaLocation="BankAccountEBO.xsd"/>
..........
..........
  <xsd:import namespace="http://xmlns.oracle.com/EnterpriseObjects/
Core/Custom/EBO/BankAccount/V1" schemaLocation="../../../Custom/EBO/
BankAccount/V1/CustomBankAccountEBO.xsd"/>
..........
..........
    <xsd:annotation>
    <xsd:documentation>
      <svcdoc:EBO>
        <svcdoc:Description>BankAccount...</svcdoc:Description>
        <svcdoc:Type>EBM</svcdoc:Type>
        <svcdoc:Industry/>
        <svcdoc:EBOName>BankAccountEBO</svcdoc:EBOName>
      </svcdoc:EBO>
    </xsd:documentation>
  </xsd:annotation>
```

The preceding script shows how the common and custom EBOs are included in the EBM.

# EBM global attributes

Each and every EBM has two global attributes apart from EBM Header and Data Area elements. They are used to maintain information about that EBM. These two attributes are shown in the following diagram:

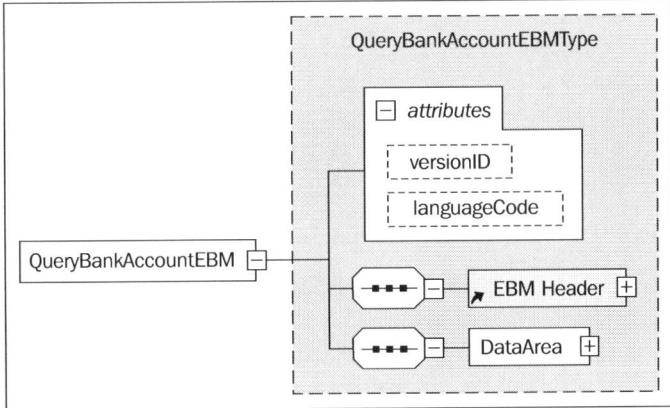

- **versionID**: This attribute is used to maintain the version number of the EBM. Since Oracle AIA, EBM, and EBO supports many versions of business objects and messages, it is necessary to maintain the version number as a global attribute.
- **languageCode**: This attribute is used to hold the EBM message language information from the `Meta.xsd` schema definition. Oracle AIA supports carrying a variety of language-specific information through EBM and EBOs. The default language code is `en-US`.

# EBMHeader

In Oracle AIA, every EBM should have a header in addition to a data area. An EBM header basically provides information to identify the source and target of the message, to log and trace the messages, and additional information to help in the routing and processing of the message. Understanding EBM and EBM header is very important in order to handle different integration scenarios. The goal of the EBM header is to hold the information that can be used for:

- Audit information
- Header errors and traces
- Source and target system information

*Enterprise Business Messages*

The following image will show the EBM header from one of the Oracle AIA EBMs:

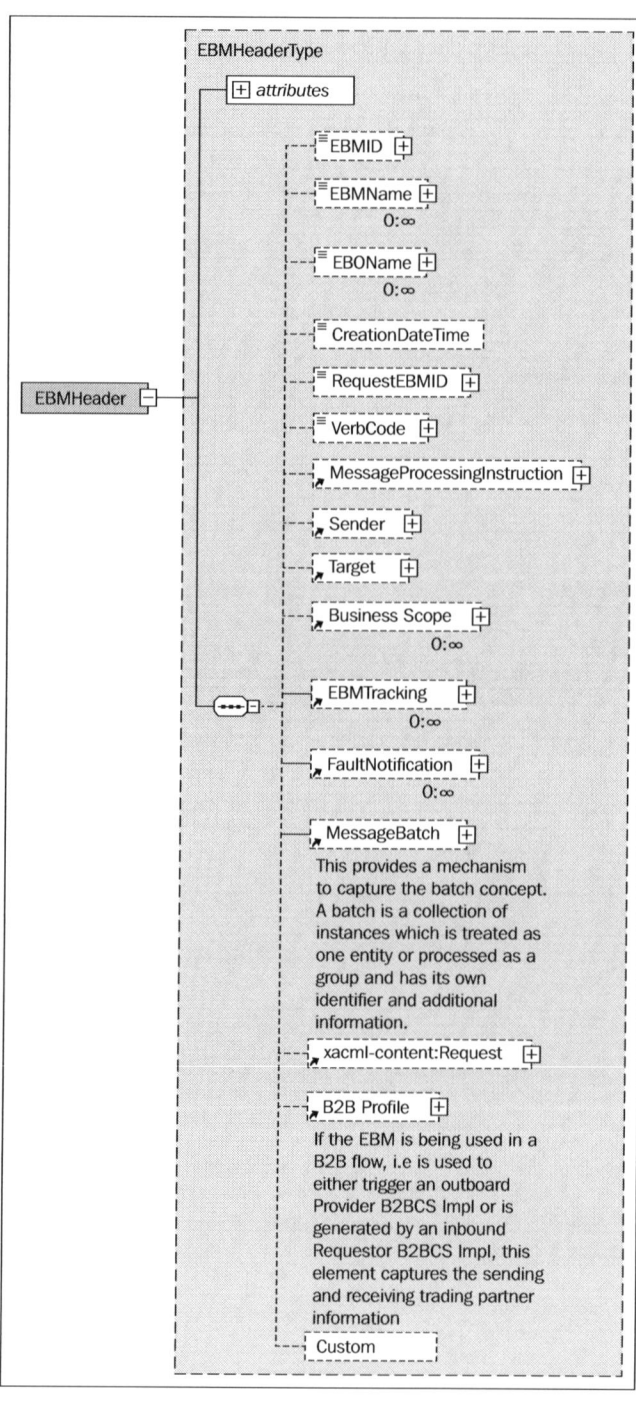

# EBMHeader components

EBM header components are grouped as two sets of components. They are **primary** header components and **secondary** header components. The primary header components hold raw information about the EBM payload. However, the secondary components of the EBM header holds information about the messages, systems, and processes involved in the EBM payload.

## EBMID

This element contains identity information about the EBM. This element's data type should be `IdentifierType`. An ID can be generated by using the `XPath` function, shown as follows:

```
orcl:generate-guid().
<EBMHeader>
<EBMID>888383838383838383883838383838</EBMID>
...
</EBMHeader>
```

## EBMName

This element contains the name of the EBM. This element's data type should be `NameType`:

```
<EBMHeader>
<EBMName>...</EBMName>
......
</EBMHeader>
```

## EBOName

This element contains the fully-qualified EBO name in the following notation. The datatype of this element is `NameType`:

```
{namespaceURI}localpart
<EBMHeader>
  <EBOName>{http://xmlns.oracle.com/EnterpriseObjects/Core/EBO/
    BankAccount/V1}CreateAccount</EBOName>
..
</EBMHeader>
```

## CreationDateTime

As the name expresses the meaning, this element contains a timestamp about the EBM when created. This element supports the `DateTimeType` data type. This timestamp should be UTC, which is also used to present the current timestamp and GMT offsets. The current timestamp can be generated by using the `XPath` expression function `current-datetime()`.

## RequestEBMID

This element contains the GUID that identifies the service requester identity and the unique request ID. The data type for the request ID should be `IdentifierType`. The enterprise business service responds back this request ID as part of the response:

```
<EBMHeader>
  <CreationDateTime>2011-08-02T10:19:23.45-04:00</CreationDateTime>
  <RequestEBMID>...</RequestEBMID>
  . . .
</EBMHeader>
```

## VerbCode

The element contains the verb code of the EBM. The data type supported by this element is `CodeType`. Some of the common verb codes used in EBM are `Query`, `Create`, `Delete`, and so on:

```
<EBMHeader>
  <VerbCode >Query</VerbCode>
  . . .
</EBMHeader>

The overall EBM Header structure should be looks like below.
<EBMHeader>
  <EBMID>88838383838383883838383838</EBMID>
  <EBMName>ProcessFulfillmentOrderUpdateEBM</EBMName>
  <EBOName>{http://xmlns.oracle.com/EnterpriseObjects/Core/EBO/
FulfillmentOrder/V1}FulfillmentOrderEBO</EBOName>
  <CreationDateTime>2011-08-02T10:19:23.45-04:00</CreationDateTime>
  <RequestEBMID>61e315eb-a1e0-4d14-89aa-fa4ff282c4b6<RequestEBMID>
  <VerbCode >process</VerbCode>
.
</EBMHeader>
```

## EBMHeader child components

In this section, we are going to explore some of the common header and child componets that are used in the EBM.

# MessageProcessingInstruction

This element contains information or instructions about the message processing method. This element is used to identify whether this instance of message should be considered as a production message, and if it should go through standard process or is it a test level message and should just pass the test case. Message processing instruction element has the following three attributes:

- EnvironmentCode
- DefinitionID
- InstanceID

EnvironmentCode: This attribute could be set as **Composite Application Validation System (CAVS)** or PRODUCTION. The default value of this attribute should be PRODUCTION. If value of this attribute is set as PRODUCTION then it means the request must be sent to the concrete service endpoint. If it is a CAVS then service request should be sent to the CAVS simulator.

> Note that the Composite Application Validation Systems (CAVS) are testing simulator utility tools provided by Oracle AIA to validate the business integration created by using Oracle AIA FP. We will explore them in detail in *Chapter 12, Composite Application Validation System*, and look at aspects such as approach that should be followed in CAVS and its test case configurations, and so on.

DefinitionID: This property is used to define the test definition ID created in the CAVS. This attribute property should be populated with the value of property from AIAConfigurationProperties.xml.

> Note that the AIAConfigurationProperties.xml can be located after deploying AIA in the SOA Domain environment. However, the template version of the configuration properties file can be located under the $AIA_Home\AIAMetaData\config folder.

InstanceID: This attribute should contain information about the instance of the message processing instruction. This attribute may be populated automatically (may be through Xpath) by the AIA infrastructure. Please make sure that the corecom namespace is declared properly in the schema.

This is explained in the following example:

```
<BusinessScope>
  <ID> Banking-Account-Creation </ID>
  <InstanceID> BANKACCT/10002121 </InstanceID>
  <BusinessScopeTypeCode>BusinessScope</BusinessScopeTypeCode>
  <EnterpriseServiceName>BankAccountEBS</EnterpriseServiceName>
    <EnterpriseServiceOperationName>
       CreateBankAccount</EnterpriseServiceOperationName>
</BusinessScope>
```

## Sender element

This element is used to contain information about the service requester application. The Sender element has a separate set of sub elements to capture and carry forward elaborate information about the requesting application:

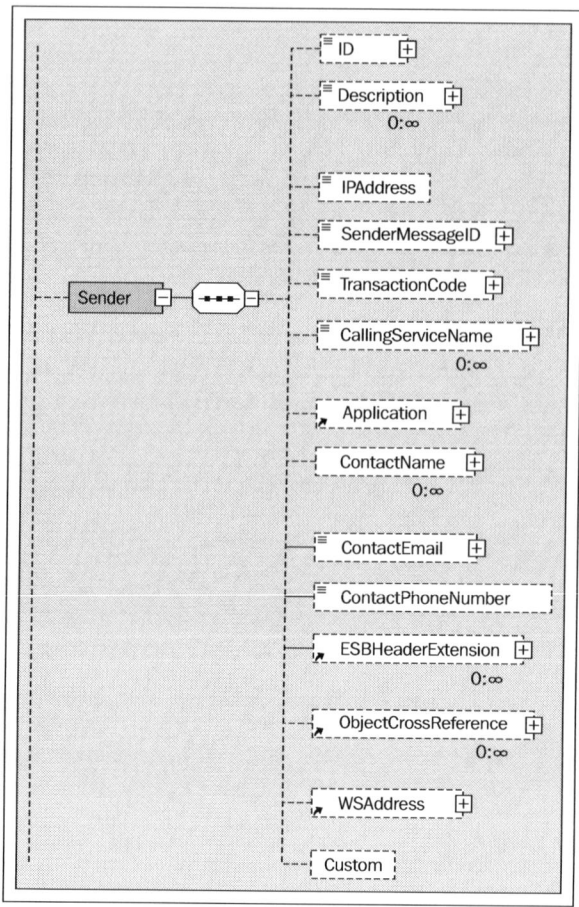

*Chapter 3*

The following table shows details about each sub element of the `Sender` element:

| Attribute Name | Purpose |
| --- | --- |
| **ID** | It contains sender system's unique identification code. It is a mandatory field. |
| **Description** | Description about the sender system. |
| **IPAddress** | This element contains the IP address of the sender system. |
| **SenderMessageID** | This ID can be used to identify the unique message sent by the sender system. |
| **TransactionCode** | This is a task identification code. This element should be used to generate the message by the sender system. |
| **CallingServiceName** | Name of the application business component service. |
| **Application** | This element should have information about the originating application. |
| **ContactName** | Sender application's contact name. |
| **ContactEmail** | Sender application's contact e-mail ID. |
| **ContactPhoneNumber** | Sender application's contact phone number. |
| **ESBHeader** | This element contains more detail about the EBM header. It acts as an extension of the EBM header. This element has attributes such as `Name`, `DataTypeCode` and `Value`. |
| **ObjectCrossReference** | This element contains an identifier of the sender object and corresponding cross-reference identifier. This element can be used for bulk processing messaging. |
| **Custom** | This element is a complex type which can be extended to use custom elements. |

The following sample format shows the header elements of the EBM structure:

```
<corecom:Sender>
  <corecom:ID>PPLS_101</corecom:ID>
  <corecom:Description/>
  <corecom:IPAddress/>
  <corecom:SenderMessageID>898989898989898989898889</corecom:SenderMessageID>
  <corecom:CallingServiceName>{http://xmlns.oracle.com/SamplePeopleApp}
  CreateCustomerSiebelInputFileReader</corecom:CallingServiceName>
  <corecom:Application>
    <corecom:ID/>
    <corecom:Version>1.0</corecom:Version>
  </corecom:Application>
  <corecom:ContactName/>
  <corecom:ContactEmail/>
```

*Enterprise Business Messages*

```
      <corecom:ContactPhoneNumber/>
</corecom:Sender>
```

## Target Element

The **Target** element will be used to send the target system information while sending the EBM. Usually, the Oracle Mediator will be used to define routing rules in the composite application. So, all the messages received from the source system should follow the same routing rule. But for the bulk processing scenario, there may be a use case where the routing rules should be overridden with exception. Such exceptional routing rule could be handled by this target element:

```
<corecom:Target>
   <corecom:ID>PORTAL_101</corecom:ID>
   <corecom:OverrideRoutingIndicator>...</corecom:OverrideRoutingIndic
ator>
   <corecom:ServiceName>Service1</corecom:ServiceName>
   <corecom:ApplicationTypeCode>PORTAL_101</
corecom:ApplicationTypeCode>
</corecom:Target>
```

## BusinessScope

The **BusinessScope** section of the EBM header captures information related to the scope of the business specification. As per Oracle the AIA standard, every EBM must have at least two `BusinessScope` elements. One of the `BusinessScope` elements must be described at the end to end business process that the EBM engaged. The second one should describe as the message associated in the process flow:

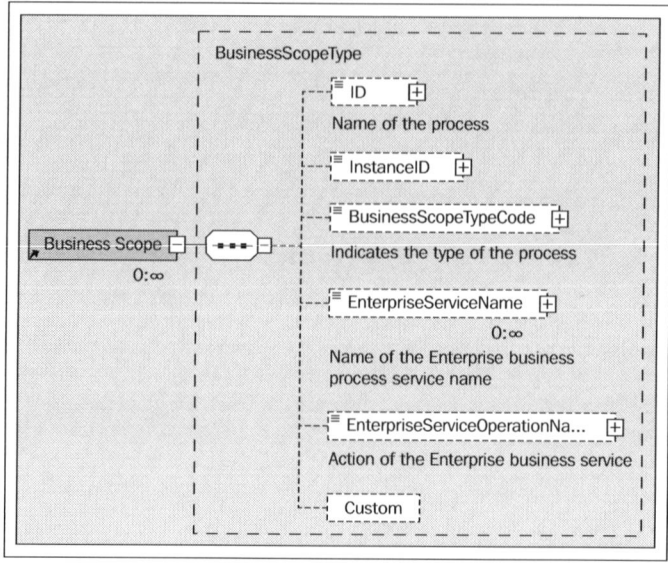

The following elements are used in the business scope as part of EBM header.

- **ID**: This element is an optional identifier for the execution service contract.
- **InstanceID**: This element is used to carry unique identification for a particular scope instance. This could be an alpha numeric code provided by application.
- **BusinessScopeTypeCode**: This element should hold the information about the business scope of the particular message instance. This value should be `BusinessScope` or `BusinessService` or `Message`.
- **EnterpriseServiceName**: This is basically the message creator name. It could be either ABCS or EBS name.
- **EnterpriseServiceOperationName**: This element should store the name of the EBS operation that triggered this message.
- **Custom**: This is a custom element, which can be extended to carry any other information along with scope details.

## EBMTracking

As the element name expresses the purpose, the **EBMTracking** elements are used to track the message passing through the various nodes of integration. So the tracking element may populate multiple times in the EBM in order to record all the execution units that the message passes through. The following are the elements of `EBMTracking`.

- **SequenceNumber**: This element contains the sequence number of the execution node.
- **ExecutionUnitID**: This element contains the ID of the execution node or process.
- **ExecutionUnitName**: This element contains the execution unit name that the EBM passes through.
- **ImplementationCode**: This element references the type of the execution such as BPEL, Mediator, or Java Service.
- **ActivityDateTime**: This element records the execution date and time.

    The below sample schema model shows the structure of the `EBMTracking`:

    ```
    <EBMTracking>
       <SequenceNumber>1</SequenceNumber>
       <ExecutionUnitID>110</ExecutionUnitID>
       <ExecutionUnitName>{http://xmlns.oracle.com/ABCSImpl/Portal/
    BankAccount/v1}Query
       BankPortalABCSImpl</ExecutionUnitName>
    ```

```
            <CategoryCode>Mediator</CategoryCode>
            <ActivityDateTime>...</ActivityDateTime>
    </EBMTracking>
```

## FaultNotification

In a Web Service-based integration approach, the `fault` element is used to populate exception that occurs during message transfer. Integration is more vulnerable due to the independence of each system. In order to build more robotic integration, exception and error should be properly captured, and necessary action should be taken to handle it. In Oracle AIA EBM, the `FaultNotification` element can be used to populate the fault messages while transferring EBM between ABCS and EBS.

## MessageBatch

This element contains information about the batch processes. This element helps to capture collection of instances, which is treated as one entity or processed as a group.

## B2BProfile

This element contains the sending and receiving trading partner information for the B2B integration document flows. This element introduced an Oracle AIA FP 11g along with the B2B integration feature. This element has child elements, which are as follows:

- `SendingTradingPartner`: This element contains information about sending a trading partner.
- `ReceiverTradingPartner`: This element contains information about EBM receiver trading partner.

## Custom

This element is used to extend the EBM header by adding an extra custom element, which it may require. However, we have to ensure that the data type used by custom elements should be in compliance with common data types defined by Oracle AIA FP.

## DataArea

So far we have seen a very elaborative view of the EBM header and its elements. **DataArea** is also an important part of EBM. In EBM, `DataArea` contains information about the message to be processed along with necessary action identifications. Also the `DataArea` will contain the business objects and references. In AIA, the business objects are instances of EBO. The following image will show a high level view of `DataArea` in EBM:

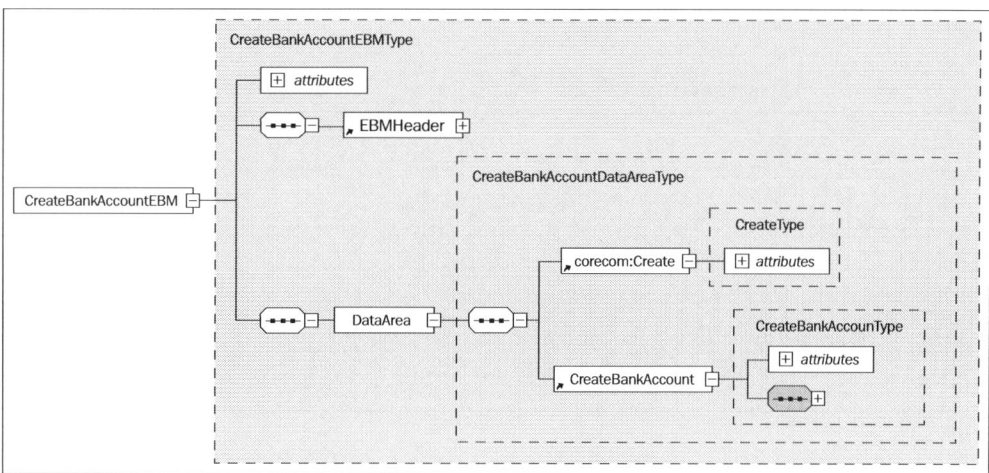

One of the fundamental rules of EBM is that each message request and response should be represented in an EBM by a unique action and an EBO type instance. According to that rule, each `DataArea` (`DataArea` element is sequential) should have one element that represents the action to be taken and another element should represent the context-specific object required to execute that action. So for each service, there should be a request EBM object and response EBM object.

Let us take the example of the create bank account service and its EBMs. In create bank account service request message, `DataArea` of `CreateBankAccountResponseEBMType` has two elements in a sequence. One is `corecom:CreateRequestResponse` and another one is the `CreateBankAccount` object and its attribute. In this, `CreateBankAccount` is an object of `CreateBankAccountType` EBO.

Similarly, in the response EBM of create bank account, there should be an action element that should represent `corecom:CreateResponse` and a response object of the `CreateBankAccountType` element.

# Enterprise Business Messages

The following diagram shows the typical EBM message structure:

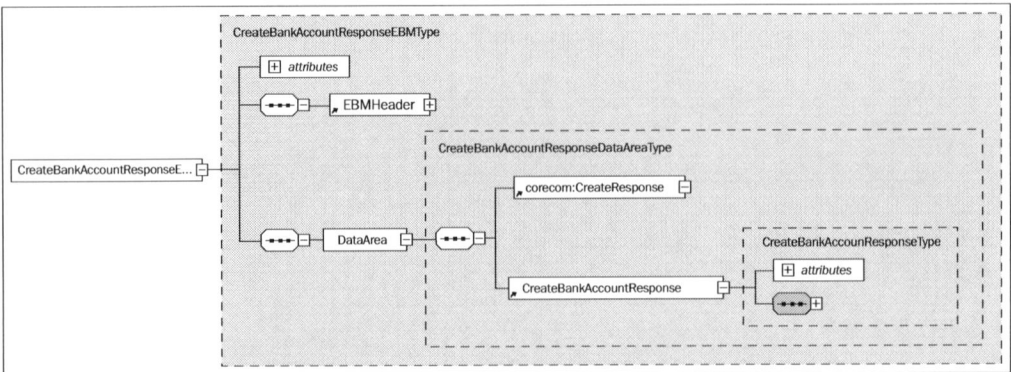

# EBM use cases

In this section, we are going to explore one of the message exchange types and how EBM supports these scenarios.

## EBM request and response message

The most common message exchange model that every integration project might have is request-response type. The requester requests information from another system and the responder system responds with the information based on the request parameters. This model is typically used in the web systems.

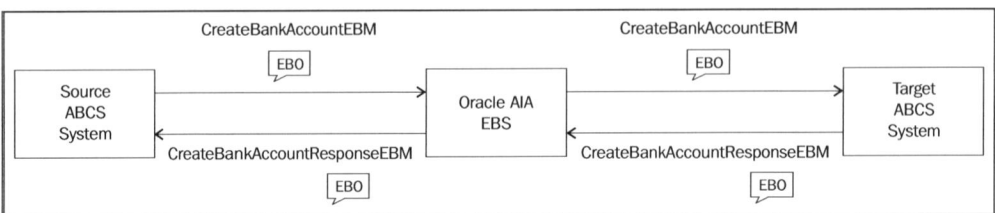

From the preceding diagram, we can see that source ABCS system sends CreateBankAccountEBM to the Bank Account EBS service using BankAccountEBO. The request has been sent to the target system by EBS in the request EBM format. The target ABCS system generates the output in the BankAccountResponseEBM with BankAccountEBO. The same response message forwards back to the source ABCS service through bank account service. The diagram shows the simple version of EBM use case in the AIA model. Basically, it forces to use the standard format within AIA implementation except the area where application requires ABM format.

The following code shows the request EBM format:

```
<BusinessScope>
  <ID>Source System Bank Account</ID>
  <InstanceID>CREATEBankAccount/10081</InstanceID>
  <BusinessScopeTypeCode>BusinessScope</BusinessScopeTypeCode>
  <EnterpriseServiceName>BankAccountEBS</EnterpriseServiceName>
  <EnterpriseServiceOperationName>CreateBankAccount</
     EnterpriseServiceOperationName>
  <BusinessScope>
  <BusinessScope>
  <ID>CreateBankAccountReqMessage</ID>
  <InstanceID> ACCTMSG/10101</InstanceID>
  <BusinessScopeTypeCode>Message</BusinessScopeTypeCode>
  <EnterpriseServiceName>BankAccountEBS</EnterpriseServiceName>
  <EnterpriseServiceOperationName>CreateBankAccount
  </EnterpriseServiceOperationName>
</BusinessScope>
```

The following code shows the response EBM format:

```
<BusinessScope>
  <ID>Source System Bank Account</ID>
  <InstanceID>CREATEBANKACCT/10081</InstanceID>
  <BusinessScopeTypeCode>BusinessScope</BusinessScopeTypeCode>
  <EnterpriseServiceName>BankAccountEBS</EnterpriseServiceName>
  <EnterpriseServiceOperationName>CreateBankAccount</
     EnterpriseServiceOperationName>
  <BusinessScope>
  <BusinessScope>
  <ID>] CreateBankAccountResMessage</ID>
  <InstanceID> ACCTMSG/10110</InstanceID>
  <BusinessScopeTypeCode>Message</BusinessScopeTypeCode>
  <EnterpriseServiceName>BankAccountEBS</EnterpriseServiceName>
  <EnterpriseServiceOperationName>CreateBankAccount</
  EnterpriseServiceOperationName>
</BusinessScope>
```

In our use case, if we notice the request EBM and response EBM, then the primary difference is the message ID. The message ID is considered as a key change in the EBM header, which will help to keep track of the difference between request and response EBMs. We are going to explore EBM and EBO further in the next chapter, along with EBS.

# Summary

So far we have seen fundamental details about the Oracle AIA EBO and EBM structures and their purpose. EBO and EBM are fundamentals of the Oracle AIA data integration. In the following chapter we are going to see more details about Enterprise Business Services (EBS) and Application Business Connector Services (ABCS), which are used to create service interfaces. EBO and EBM are populated as payload in the EBS and ABCS. Before we proceed to further chapters, it is good to refresh our knowledge in the fundamentals of Web Services and Interfaces since EBS and ABCS are based on service interface and contracts.

# 4
# Enterprise Business Services

In this chapter, we are going to learn about the AIA **Enterprise Business Service**. In general, business services are service components that expose a specific business function/task. A business service accepts various parameters as part of a request message to execute the business services and responds back with a message generated by that business function/task. In enterprise infrastructure, exposing application business functions as services is important to leverage application capabilities across the organization. Technically, service can be enabled through various approaches as we have seen in *Chapter 1, Overview of Oracle AIA*.

The following topics are covered in this chapter:

- Overview of Enterprise Service Bus
- Structure of the EBS definition
- Types of EBS
- EBS design principles
- EBS implementation

## Overview of Enterprise Service Bus

In Oracle Application Integration Architecture, Enterprise Business Services (EBS) is a core foundation block. When you read the word "services", immediately it reminds you of web services and its concepts. As Oracle AIA is deployed and runs on top of Oracle SOA Suite, Enterprise Business Services are based on web services architecture. Therefore, EBS represents application or service independent web service definitions for business integration tasks.

EBSs are defined as web services, distributed with service contract as abstract **Web Service Definition Language** (**WSDL**) along with service operations, message exchange patterns, and schema definition for message requests and responses. In addition, EBS can be used as independent service or it can interact with another EBS. EBSs are mostly coarse-grained business services, which perform a specific business activity such as creating a bank account in the banking system or fetching bank account balance information from the same banking system. These coarse-grained EBSs support such synchronous and asynchronous message exchange patterns.

> Note that in a Service Oriented Architecture, services are defined as on two levels, which are coarse-grained and fine-grained services. Coarse-grained services are abstract level business functions, which should include many business task definitions. However, fine-grained business services are absolute business services. They are just at the bottom level only to execute a particular business task.

EBS components belong to the canonical layer of AIA. Basically, EBS's request and response payload uses standards-based enterprise message format, which is nothing but EBM. As we have seen earlier, EBM typically contains one or more instances of EBOs that is defined from business message formats, metadata, and message header formats.

For example, let us consider the Bank Account EBS meta model from Oracle AIA FP. The bank account management-related services are encompassed in the BankAccountEBS.wsdl definition. The BankAccountEBS.wsdl definition includes various operations to handle accounts management business activities. One such business operation is to create a bank account, which includes payload as CreateBankAccount and CreateBankAccountResponse service operation. Both payload message structures are defined as parts of CreateBankAccountEBM. If we refer to the CreateBankAccountEBM, the DataArea is basically referring to the instance of CreateBankAccountEBO (we already have seen this type of EBO/EBM models in detail in *Chapter 2, Enterprise Business Objects* and *Chapter 3, Enterprise Business Messages*). So, the CreateBankAccount operation of BankAccountEBS.wsdl definition should look like the following screenshot:

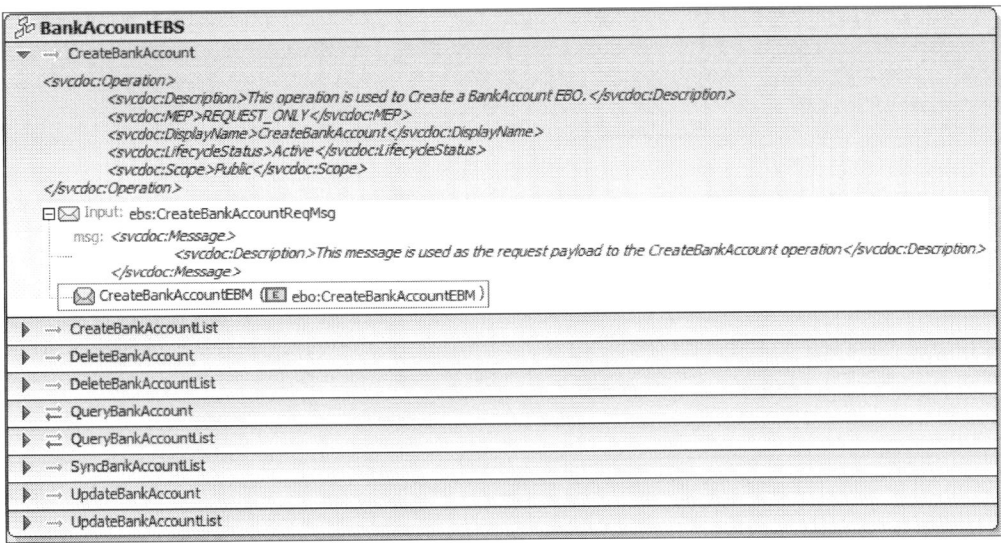

Similar to the `CreateBankAccount` operation, each EBS should have many operations, which depend on the business service that the EBS provides. In our bank account EBS, there are many operations and responses including the `CreateBankAccount`, `DeleteBankAccount`, `QueryBankAccount`, and `UpdateBankAccount` operations. The preceding screenshot also shows a list of operations (requests).

## Role of EBS in AIA

The following are the roles that Enterprise Business Service plays in the AIA approach:

- Receive request EBM from a requester application through requester ABCS or another EBS or EBF.
- Identify and route the request to the required target or Provider Service (typically an ABCS or another EBS or EBF).
- Receive the response EBM from the provider application, such as provider ABCS or EBF or another EBS and routes the response message to the requestor ABCS, EBF, or another EBS.

# Characteristics of EBS

Oracle AIA EBS components encompass some fundamental unique characteristics, which are as follows:

- The EBS component does not predetermine any backend implementation system such as Oracle PeopleSoft, Oracle Agile, or E-Business Suites. It is application agnostic and lies in the canonical layer of AIA.
- EBS basically provides service oriented integration interfaces for your choice of backend systems. It basically plays a mediator between requester and provider systems.
- Each EBS contains various operations, which can be invoked by a requester ABCS, another EBS, or Enterprise Business Flow (EBF).
- EBS always takes the EBM as an input message and gives the output message in the same format.
- Every EBS operation should have a verb-based operation used as an operation identifier, for example, create, query, update, delete, and so on. So whether a service is Synchronized or Asynchronized is defined by using a verb.
- EBS may route the messages to another EBS, EBF, or ABCS based on the routing rules defined in the rules of that operation.

# Structure of the EBS definition

The following diagram will show the sample structure of the Enterprise Business Service. As EBS is based on web services, EBS definition follows the typical structure of WSDL:

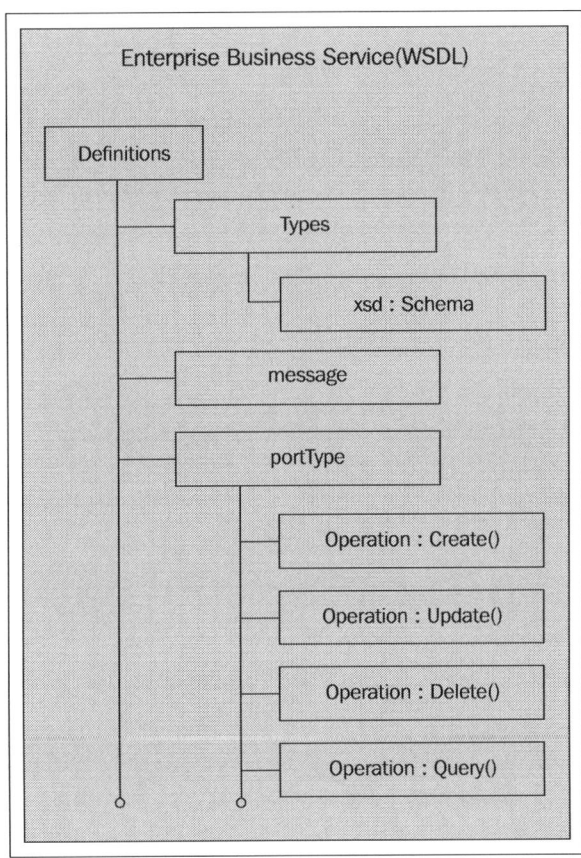

## Definitions element

The element `<definitions>` is the root element of the WSDL. It defines the name of the web service. This element acts as a container of the overall description and includes all other elements. The `<definitions>` elements include the `targetNamespace` attribute. The `targetNamespace` attributes provide reference to the schema being used in the entire web services in messages. An example of the `targetNamespace` is given as follows:

```
<definitions name="BankAccountEBS" targetNamespace="http://xmlns.
oracle.com/EnterpriseServices/Core/BankAccount/V1">
```

## Types element

The `<types>` element is used in the input and output format of the web service operations. In EBS, the input and output messages are in the format of EBM, the `<types>` element imports the reference EBM under its `<xsd:schema>` sub element. The following is an example of the `<types>` element:

```
<types>
  <xsd:schema targetNamespace="http://xmlns.oracle.com/
EnterpriseServices/BankAccount/V1" elementFormDefault="qualified">
    <xsd:import namespace="http://xmlns.oracle.com/EnterpriseObjects/
Core/EBO/BankAccount/V1" schemaLocation="../../../../../
EnterpriseObjectLibrary/Core/EBO/BankAccount/V1/BankAccountEBM.xsd"/>
  </xsd:schema>
</types>
```

## Message element

The `<message>` element is used to describe the data being communicated between service consumers and providers. In the AIA case, the provider is an EBS and the consumer could be an ABCS or a client application that is capable of sending the EBM as a message payload.

The `<message>` element should have zero to many `<part>` elements and each `<part>` element should be mapped with one parameter of input or output message. Each `<part>` element should be matched with a datatype defined in the `<types>` element.

In EBM, the `<message>` element should refer to the definition of the EBO. The following is an example of the `<message>` element:

```
<message name="DeleteBankAccountListReqMsg>
  <part name="DeleteBankAccountListEBM"    element="ebo:DeleteBankAcco
untListEBM"/>
</message>
```

## PortType element

The `<portType>` element is used to combine and build the one-way or request-response operation. The `<portType>` element should act as a container to define multiple types of operations under one web service. Also, a `<portType>` element binds a different format of request and response messages under one service operation.

In EBS, the element `<portType>` contains various operations required under one core business function. The following is an example of the `<porType>` element:

```
<portType name="BankAccountEBS">
<!-- operation support for CreateBankAccount -->
  <operation name="CreateBankAccount">
    <input message="ebs:CreateBankAccountReqMsg"/>
  </operation>
</portType>
```

## One-way operation pattern in EBS

A one-way operation is nothing but a service that can only receive messages. Such web service operation should have only input message format. Therefore, it should only have the `<input>` element. However, Oracle EBS has many one-way operations. The following is an example of the `<input>` element:

```
<!-- operation support for CreateBankAccount -->
<operation name="CreateBankAccount">
  <input message="ebs:CreateBankAccountReqMsg"/>
</operation>
```

In the preceding example, the `CreateBankAccount` operation has only one input message because it will only receive messages from the consumer applications. It never responds back to the consumers. In EBS, most of the create, read, update, and delete (CRUD) operations are one-way operations.

## Two-way or request and response operation pattern in EBS

In request and response model, the web service operation should be capable of accepting input message and also returning response messages. Also, EBS supports different formats of input and output messages. So the request and response operation should have both `<input>` and `<output>` elements. The following is an example of the `<input>` and `<output>` elements:

```
<!-- operation support for QueryBankAccount -->
<operation name="QueryBankAccount">
```

```
    <input message="ebs:QueryBankAccountReqMsg"/>
    <output message="ebs:QueryBankAccountRespMsg"/>
    <fault name="fault" message="ebs:FaultMsg"/>
</operation>
```

The request/response operations should also have fault messages in case of exceptions in the execution. The fault response is generated using the `<fault>` element.

# Exploring Enterprise Business Service Library

Like we explored the physical structure of the EBO and EBM in the previous chapters, we can explore the EBS WSDL definitions from the out-of-box AIA installation. Similar to EBOs, EBSs do have a separate package structure. In a typical installation, an EBS can be located under the `$AIA_Home\AIAMetaData\AIAComponents\EnterpriseBusinessServiceLibrary\` folder. The following screenshot will show the physical structure of EBS groups as directories:

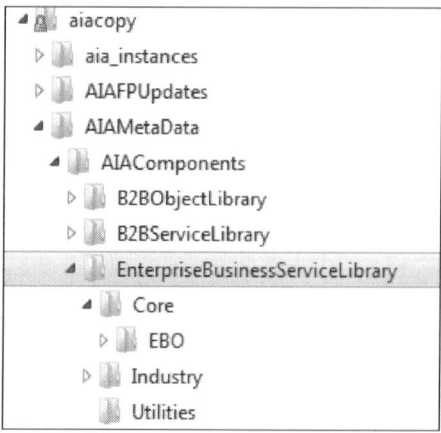

The following points should be remembered while implementing an EBS WSDL. You can validate the sample WSDL provided by Oracle AIA FP under the preceding folder structure (refer to the preceding screenshot).

- Review the operation, EBM, and metadata model, and update the operation according to your requirements.
- Any new EBS should be created as an Activity Service EBS and kept under that folder structure for later design references.
- If you want to create new WSDL, it should be created separately and should not be modified in the existing Entity Service EBS WSDL.

# Types of EBS

Fundamentally, Oracle AIA supports two types of business integration, which are data integration and process integration. Oracle AIA Enterprise Business Services are used to build both data integration and process integration services. Hence, EBS components are categorized as two types of services:

- **Entity type EBS**: The entity EBS is used to share business data as entity objects between enterprise business systems through Oracle SOA infrastructure. The entity EBS is also known as a Data Service because an Entity type EBS is based on CRUD operations EBS.
- **Process type EBS**: The Process type EBS is used to execute a particular business activity or process between enterprise business systems through Oracle SOA infrastructure. It is also known as Activity Service EBS. These are based on complex operations (for example, process and order) defined in Business Processes (EBFs).

The following sections will explain each type of EBS in more detail.

# Entity type EBS

Entity services are predominantly used for standard operations such as create, read, update, and delete by using an Enterprise Business Object (EBO) and its business components. All these standard operations that need to be executed through an EBO come under entity services. That is why every EBO has a counterpart of EBM in order to meet standard operations against business objects. Each standard operation uses corresponding EBM, which represents a specific view of EBO as input and output. So entity service exposes specific operations using EBMs and EBOs.

In Oracle SOA Suite, entity services are exposed as mediator component services with implementation using ABCS. This approach helps to avoid point-to-point integration or direct data source bindings.

We should remember the following points when we use entity EBS:

- Each business entity object should have a corresponding EBS. Hence, all actions to be performed against a business entity should be through the corresponding service operations.
- Basically operations such as create, read, update, and delete operations are common in all the EBSs. There are other specialized operations that exist specific to certain EBSs.
- Entity services always receive request and response messages in EBM format.

*Enterprise Business Services*

The following screenshot shows the typical structural relationship between an EBS, an EBM, and an EBO:

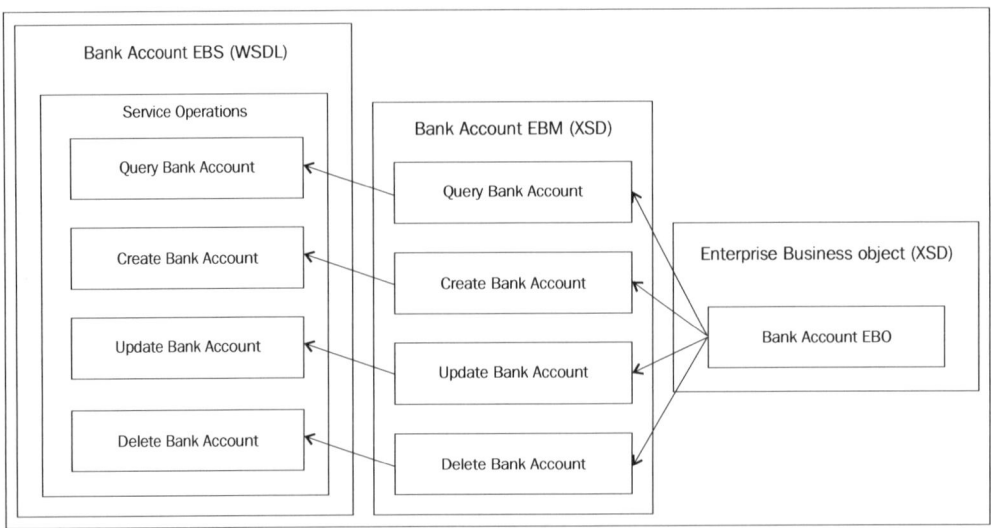

The following WSDL definition shows one of the EBS operations of the BankAccountEBS.wsdl definition. The following WSDL definition will show the CreateBankAccount operation, message, and schema definitions. A detailed definition of BankAccountEBS.wsdl can be located in the AIA instance under the $AIA_HOME/AIAMetaData/AIAComponents/EnterpriseBusinessServiceLibrary/Core/EBO/BankAccount/V1/BankAccountEBS.wsdl folder.

The following code is a sample view of BankAccountEBS.wsdl:

```
<definitions name="BankAccountEBS" targetNamespace="http://xmlns.oracle.com/EnterpriseServices/Core/BankAccount/V1">
<types>
  <xsd:schema targetNamespace="http://xmlns.oracle.com/EnterpriseServices/BankAccount/V1" elementFormDefault="qualified">
    <xsd:import namespace="http://xmlns.oracle.com/EnterpriseObjects/Core/EBO/BankAccount/V1" schemaLocation="../../../../../EnterpriseObjectLibrary/Core/EBO/BankAccount/V1/BankAccountEBM.xsd"/>
    <xsd:import namespace="http://xmlns.oracle.com/EnterpriseObjects/Core/Common/V2" schemaLocation="../../../../../EnterpriseObjectLibrary/Core/Common/V2/Meta.xsd"/>
  </xsd:schema>
</types>

<message name="FaultMsg">
  <part name="AIAFault" element="corecom:Fault"/>
```

```
    </message>
    <message name="CreateBankAccountReqMsg">
      <part name="CreateBankAccountEBM" element="ebo:CreateBankAccountE
BM"/>
    </message>

    <message name="CreateBankAccountRespMsg">
      <part name="CreateBankAccountResponseEBM" element="ebo:CreateBankAcc
ountResponseEBM"/>
    </message>

    <portType name="BankAccountEBS">

    <!-- operation support for CreateBankAccount -->
      <operation name="CreateBankAccount">
        <input message="ebs:CreateBankAccountReqMsg"/>
      </operation>
    </portType>
</definitions>
```

## Process type EBS

Process or activity services do include all kinds of business activities that need to be executed to meet a particular business operation or process. Most of the implementation cases and business activity services are implemented using Oracle SOA Suite component such as Mediator and BPEL. In order to build generic application independent services, EBS has to maintain a generic message data structure as input and output messages to integrate with various backend systems or applications. Process or activity services are basically application-independent operational services. So, a process or activity-oriented EBS requires to pass EBM as an input and generate output in the format of a specific EBM.

A typical example of a Process or Activity EBS is a Shipment Notification EBS, where send shipment notice, advance shipment, sync advance, and shipment notice are processes or activities-related service operations.

The process or activity services are predominantly exposed operations related to business processes. Otherwise it would become an entity service. The following are the fundamental characteristics of process or activity services:

- Each business process or flow has a corresponding process or activity-oriented EBS. All the actions required to fulfill the business process or flow are provided by the EBS operations.
- Process services accept and return messages in EBM format.

# Enterprise Business Services

- Some business operations that are exposed as process oriented EBS are used as cross-functional services. This will institute Enterprise Business Flows to coordinate complex long-lived flows. These flows can interact only with EBS services.
- Process EBS may include more than one EBM as a part of a request or response message.
- There are some cases where process service operation could be a part of the entity service-oriented EBS.

The following diagram represents the diagrammatic relationship between EBS, EBM, and EBO of shipment notification service.

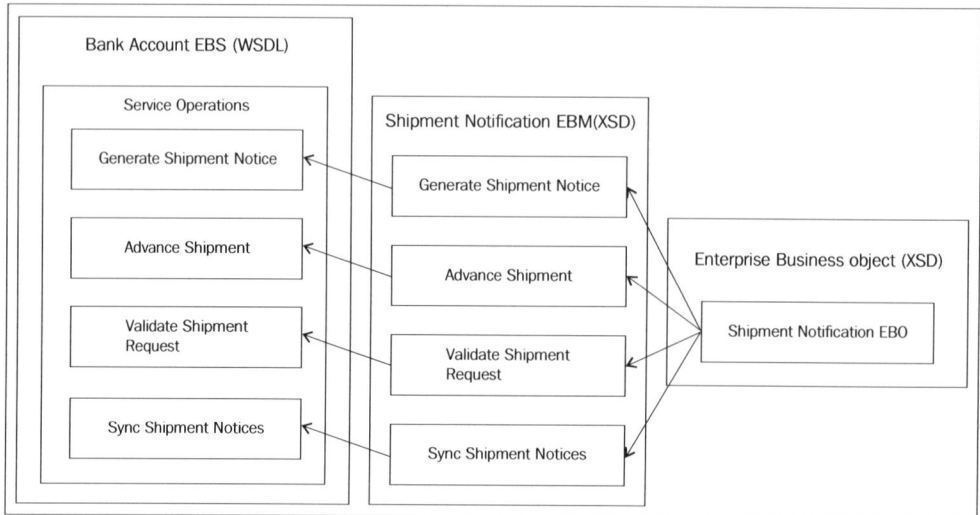

The following is a sample view of the ShipmentNotification.wsdl definition:

```
<definitions name="BankAccountEBS" targetNamespace="http://xmlns.
oracle.com/EnterpriseServices/Core/ShipmentNotification/V1">
<types>
  <xsd:schema targetNamespace="http://xmlns.oracle.
com/EnterpriseServices/ShipmentNotification/V1"
elementFormDefault="qualified">
    <xsd:import namespace="http://xmlns.oracle.com/EnterpriseObjects/
Core/EBO/ShipmentNotification/V1" schemaLocation="../../../../../
EnterpriseObjectLibrary/Core/EBO/ShipmentNotification/V1/
ShipmentNotificationEBM.xsd"/>
    <xsd:import namespace="http://xmlns.oracle.com/
EnterpriseObjects/Core/Common/V2" schemaLocation="../../../../../
EnterpriseObjectLibrary/Core/Common/V2/Meta.xsd"/>
  </xsd:schema>
```

```
</types>

<message name="FaultMsg">
  <part name="AIAFault" element="corecom:Fault"/>
</message>
<message name="GenerateShipmentNoticeReqMsg">
  <part name="GenerateShipmentNoticeEBM" element="ebo:
GenerateShipmentNoticeEBM"/>
</message>

<message name="GenerateShipmentNoticeRespMsg">
  <part name="GenerateShipmentNoticeResponseEBM" element="ebo:
GenerateShipmentNoticeResponseEBM"/>
</message>

<portType name="GenerateShipmentNoticeEBS">

<!-- operation support for GenerateShipmentNotice -->
  <operation name="GenerateShipmentNotice">
    <input message="ebs: GenerateShipmentNoticeReqMsg"/>
  </operation>
</portType>
</definitions>
```

# Understanding the EBS architecture

As it is based on web services standards, EBS operations and definitions are described in Web Service Definition Language (WSDL). EBS WSDL describes the EBS-related business operations, and input and output messages. Oracle Mediator is a widely-used component to build Oracle AIA EBS.

In the AIA-based integration implementation model, EBS plays a critical central service role, which routes the messages to the appropriate target services such as ABCS, EBF, or another EBS. Obviously, EBM is used as a messaging model between the ABCS, EBS, and EBF. This is depicted in the following diagram:

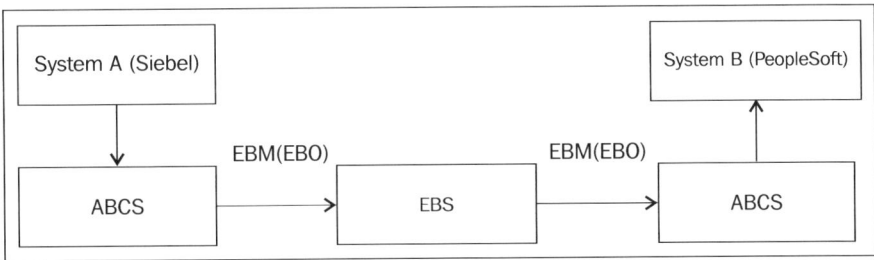

ESB's physical implementation architecture varies depending on the type of the EBS implemented. As we have seen earlier, EBS can be used at entity level services or process level services. We will see the implementation architecture differences in the following sections.

## Architecture for entity services EBS

The following diagram will show the architecture of Entity type ESB and its integration with requester and provider applications:

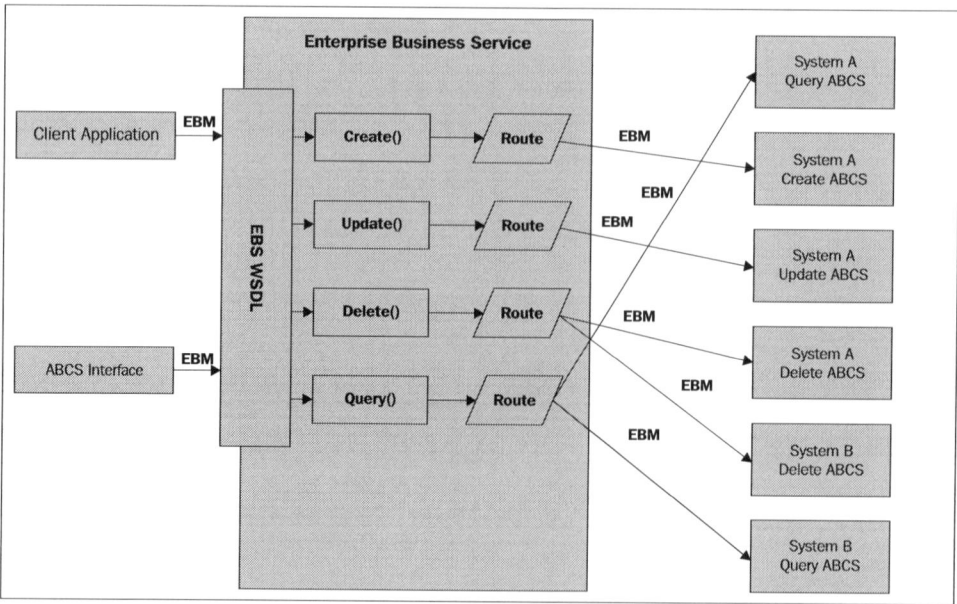

As we have seen earlier, Entity type EBSs are implemented predominantly for data-related operations such as create, read, update, and delete. So the operation that is being exposed by entity EBS is always for data operation. The out-of-the-box AIA FP includes all kind functional EBS with WSDL, which are all useful to fulfill various CRUD operations.

Fundamentally, entity EBSs are used to expose the data operations as services. EBS always receives inputs in the form of EBM. EBM is the business payload, which should have embedded the EBO view for a specific operation. If any application, either ABCS or a client application wants to consume services in the EBS, it should communicate through EBM. If the client application has the capability to produce an EBM message and pass that as a parameter to the EBS, then it can directly consume EBS operations. Such an application does not need to connect through ABCS. Oracle AIA provides default operations for each business function.

However, the implementation should be taken care of by the development team depending on their needs. There are many cases where EBS receives a request from the consumer application, which requires routing to different operations provided by the provider ABCS. The EBS should also communicate with provider ABCS through EBM. Entity EBS always exposes only the CRUD functions as service operations. Fundamentally, Entity EBS does not connect to any other EBS or process directly.

# Architecture for process services EBS

The following diagram presents the architecture of process EBS in the AIA approach:

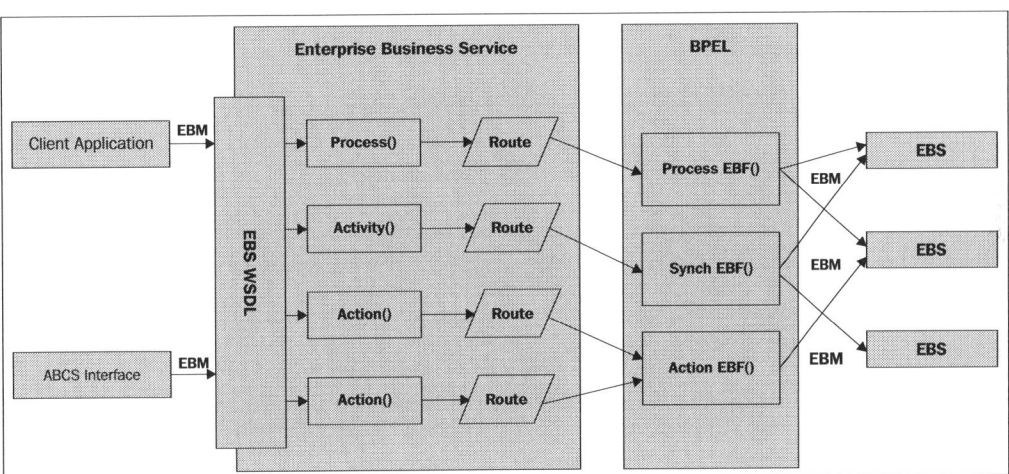

Process type EBS is slightly different from entity service EBS. Process type EBS is designed predominantly for consuming or participating enterprise business process-related integrations. Unlike entity service EBS, process service EBS should not expose database operations as services. This approach is used basically to separate the various layers of SOA Reference Architecture. In the SOA Reference Architecture, data service and process service are separated as different layers. So AIA's two types of EBS approach helps to ensure that we are following such architecture standards as well.

In the Process type EBS architecture, the requester client applications such as ABCS and direct consumer should consume the business operations exposed by the Process service EBS through EBM payload. In this case, the EBM payload should be used to hold the parameters required to execute or participate in the enterprise processes. The operations exposed by process service EBS are more into executing correlated business activity tasks. In order to build process based service, EBS should consolidate the group of business activities as operations. In some cases it should route the messages to other services to validate the request and finally forward the request to the appropriate system.

Finally, the Process type EBS should call the services exposed by BPEL layer to trigger new business process or call another EBS operation directly. That target EBS could be another process service EBS or entity service EBS. The Process type EBS may use EBM while consuming various business processes, however it should use EBM while consuming another EBS. A Process type EBS is mostly the one which connects with an EBF. Entity EBSs do not connect with an EBF.

# EBS Message Exchange Patterns (MEP)

EBS supports multiple operations for meeting various business requirements at a granular level. Each operation is supported by an EBS and should be any one of the following:

- Synchronous request-response pattern
- Asynchronous fire-and-forget pattern
- Asynchronous request and delayed response pattern

The following JDeveloper screen shows the various message exchange patterns supported by AIA Service Constructor process, which are obviously supported by EBS operations:

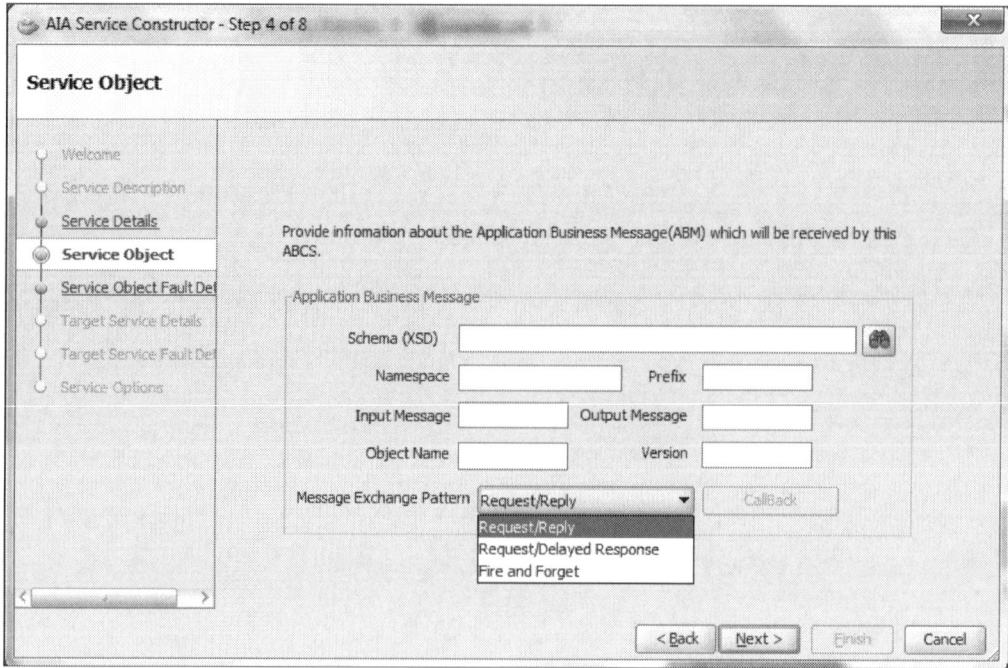

*Chapter 4*

We have to understand that each of these are important while implementing EBS-based integration services.

## Synchronous request and response pattern

**Synchronous request-response pattern** is a well known synchronous communication pattern. In an integration scenario, the requesting application should wait for the response from the provider before continuing further activity. So the requesting application holds its session and state until it receives the response. There is a time-out if the response is not received within the stipulated time. Both the request and response could be in independent message format.

This pattern is very useful in the process and entity service EBSs. Most of the query and reporting functionalities can only be achieved using the request-response pattern. The following sequence diagram will show a simple synchronous request and response pattern:

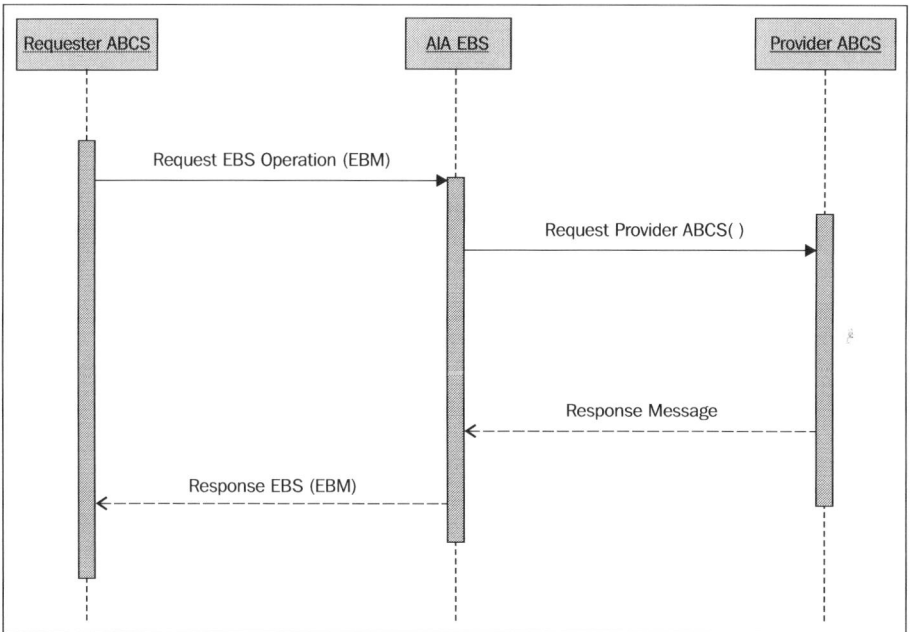

The operation format of the WSDL for the synchronous request-response pattern should be in the following format:

```
<!-- operation support for QueryBankAccountList -->
<operation name="QueryBankAccountList">
<documentation>
  <svcdoc:Operation>
```

```
        <svcdoc:Description>This operation is used to Query multiple
    BankAccount EBOs.</svcdoc:Description>
        <svcdoc:MEP>SYNC_REQ_RESPONSE</svcdoc:MEP>
        <svcdoc:DisplayName>QueryBankAccountList</svcdoc:DisplayName>
        <svcdoc:LifecycleStatus>Active</svcdoc:LifecycleStatus>
        <svcdoc:Scope>Public</svcdoc:Scope>
      </svcdoc:Operation>
    </documentation>
    <input message="ebs:QueryBankAccountListReqMsg"/>
    <output message="ebs:QueryBankAccountListRespMsg"/>
    <fault name="fault" message="ebs:FaultMsg"/>
    </operation>
```

## Asynchronous fire and forget pattern

This pattern is fundamentally a request-only communication pattern. So, it is a kind of asynchronous communication. The requesting application should send messages to the provider service by EBM. The requester application should not expect any response or acknowledgement from the provider application, so the requester application can continue to work on its activities. In entity service EBS, most of the operations are fire-and-forget pattern only. The following diagram shows a simple asynchronous fire-and-forget pattern:

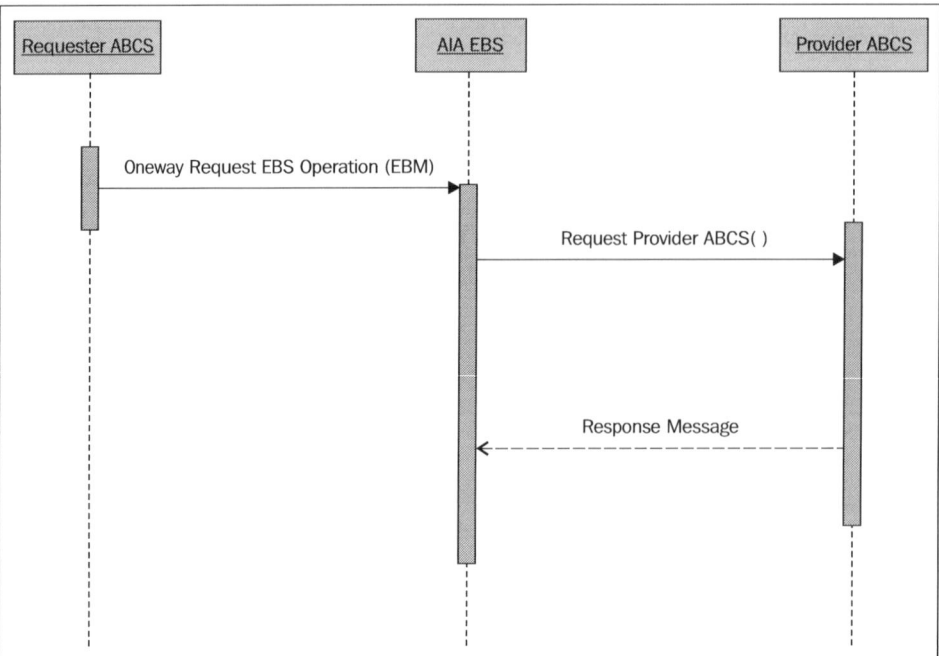

The fire-and-forget operation patterns are useful in executing operations like create, update, or delete scenario. Also, these types of patterns are commonly used in the event notification messaging scenario.

The operations format of the fire-and-forget pattern in EBS should look similar to the following:

```
<!-- operation support for UpdateBankAccount -->
<operation name="UpdateBankAccount">
<documentation>
  <svcdoc:Operation>
    <svcdoc:Description>This operation is used to Update a
BankAccount EBO.</svcdoc:Description>
    <svcdoc:MEP>REQUEST_ONLY</svcdoc:MEP>
    <svcdoc:DisplayName>UpdateBankAccount</svcdoc:DisplayName>
    <svcdoc:LifecycleStatus>Active</svcdoc:LifecycleStatus>
    <svcdoc:Scope>Public</svcdoc:Scope>
  </svcdoc:Operation>
</documentation>
<input message="ebs:UpdateBankAccountReqMsg"/>
</operation>
```

# Asynchronous request and delayed response pattern

This pattern is also based on asynchronous communication approach. In this pattern, the requesting application should send the message as a request and should not wait for the response from the service. However, the requester application should have a separate communication channel for callback. Once the response is ready to serve, it should call the callback to process the response. The delayed response mechanism works in callback mechanism. This pattern is a collection of two asynchronous processes but with a correlation.

In EBS architecture, the EBS should have two operations, one for sending the request and another one for receiving the response from the provider application. Once the EBS receives the request from the requester ABCS, it should route the request to the provider ABCS. Once the provider application is ready to respond, it should call the EBS receive response operation to place the response.

## Enterprise Business Services

The EBS should forward the response to the waiting requester application in a synchronous mode. The EBS sends the correlation and callback context to the provider ABCS to build the delayed communication. This pattern enables handling custom error messages and exceptions especially for the requester ABCS:

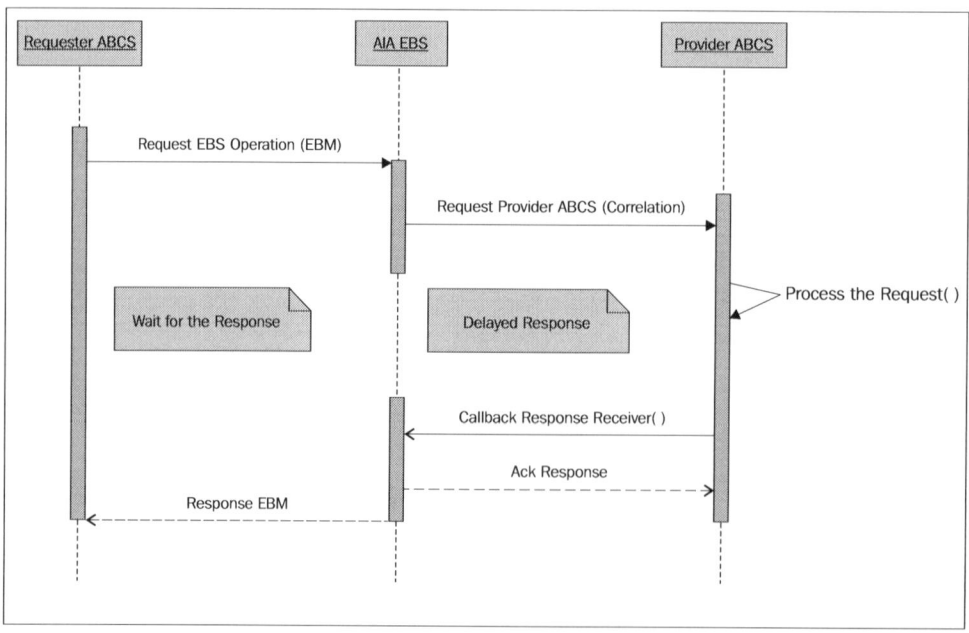

The following sample WSDL operation will show the asynchronous request delayed response pattern:

```
<!-- operation support for CreateBankAccountList -->
<operation name="CreateBankAccountList">
<documentation>
  <svcdoc:Operation>
    <svcdoc:Description>This operation is used to Create multiple
BankAccount EBOs.</svcdoc:Description>
    <svcdoc:MEP>REQUEST_ONLY</svcdoc:MEP>
    <svcdoc:DisplayName>CreateBankAccountList</svcdoc:DisplayName>
    <svcdoc:LifecycleStatus>Active</svcdoc:LifecycleStatus>
    <svcdoc:Scope>Public</svcdoc:Scope>
  </svcdoc:Operation>
</documentation>
<input message="ebs:CreateBankAccountListReqMsg"/>
</operation>

<!-- operation support for CreateBankAccountListResponse -->
```

```
<operation name="CreateBankAccountListResponse">
<documentation>
  <svcdoc:Operation>
     <svcdoc:Description>This callback operation will be used to
provide the CreateBankAccount Response.</svcdoc:Description>
     <svcdoc:MEP>ASYNC_REQ_RESPONSE</svcdoc:MEP>
     <svcdoc:DisplayName>CreateBankAccountListResponse</
svcdoc:DisplayName>
     <svcdoc:LifecycleStatus>Active</svcdoc:LifecycleStatus>
     <svcdoc:Scope>Public</svcdoc:Scope>
     <svcdoc:InitiatorService>BankAccountEBS</svcdoc:InitiatorService>
     <svcdoc:InitiatorInterface>CreateBankAccountResponseEBM</
svcdoc:InitiatorInterface>
     <svcdoc:InitiatorOperation>CreateBankAccountListRequest</
svcdoc:InitiatorOperation>
  </svcdoc:Operation>
</documentation>
<input message="ebs:CreateBankAccountListRespMsg"/>
</operation>
```

# Steps to identify the message pattern

The following points will help to identify the appropriate message exchange pattern while designing EBS:

- Based on the business process requirement from the functional design, identify the message pattern for the EBS operation.
- If the control waits until a response is returned back to the point of invocation, then choose the EBS request-reply pattern.
- This is a synchronous call. In this case, the EBS operation will have input and output messages with a named fault.
- After the EBS is invoked and the requestor does not wait for the reply and continues on, it would be an asynchronous call.
- Check whether the EBS operation results in a response. If we have to correlate the request and the response, use the EBS request delayed response pattern. The EBS will have two `portTypes`, each of them accepting an input message only and each of them belonging to a different port.
- If not needed, then choose the EBS fire-and-forget pattern, and thus the EBS operation will have an input message only.

# EBS design principles

In a typical web service development, there are two approaches that can be followed. They are called as **top-down** approach and **bottom-up** approach. Top-down approach is designing the message schema using XSD and drafting the service contract WSDL by using the schema model and implementing the services from WSDL. Bottom-up approach is creating WSDL by exposing the actual service components. As EBS is based on web services, it supports top-down implementation approach. Hence, Oracle AIA FP comes up with a predefined WSDL for each EBS. The contract description for each EBS is defined in its WSDL.

For business entity EBS implementation, we can use the predefined EBS that is available as a part of the Enterprise Service Library package. It can be located in the $AIA_HOME/ AIAMetaData\AIAComponents\EnterpriseBusinessServiceLibrary folder. For business activity EBS, we can use the TemplateEBS.wsdl definition delivered by Oracle AIA FP.

> Note that the default installation of Oracle AIA FP R3 does not bring the TemplateEBS.wsdl file. We have to request a patch 10255469 from My Oracle Support. This may be fixed by Oracle in future releases. Please check your AIA copy before sending a request to Oracle Support.

The following fundamentals should be remembered while designing and implementing EBS:

- In a synchronous request-response pattern, Enterprise Business Service operation messages are defined in one port type. This kind of operation should have defined the input, output, and fault messages.
- In an asynchronous pattern, EBS operation messages are also defined in one port type; however, it will have only input message format.
- In a delayed response synchronous pattern, there should be two operations, one for sending a request and another one for receiving a response. Each operation should be defined in a separate port type. Response should be the suffix used in this scenario.
- The EBS WSDL should have one port type for synchronous request-response operations and another port type of asynchronous response operations.
- Separate mediator routing service should be considered for port types in asynchronous messaging.
- While designing, consider one EBS for one business function and one application. This helps to manage the independence of each EBS.

- However, one business function may have multiple operations defined in the service contract.
- Each EBS should have covered all the business operations for the corresponding business functions.
- The communication between EBS and ABCS should always be over HTTP; however, if the components are co-located in the same WebLogic domain or JVM it can be considered to have a direct invocation through Oracle SOA Suite components.
- Only if the application does not have the capability to invoke the EBS operation should the ABCS be implemented to facilitate the application to establish communication.
- All services and operations in the EBS should use EBM (EBO) as a messaging payload. However, if the application can understand the EBM, then EBS should pass the EBM payload through response or service call.
- EBS WSDL should have two `portTypes`, one for synchronous and another for asynchronous. There should be two mediator routing services created for each `portType`.

## EBS routing principles

Message routing is one of the fundamental characteristics of Oracle Mediator. EBS requires us to route the input EBM message to the corresponding service provider to complete the operation. Routing rules in EBS are used to decide which request should be routed to which ABCS service provider or target endpoint.

The following principles should be followed while developing EBS routing rules:

- All routing requirements must be implemented in the routing rules of EBS.
- Routing rules should check the target system ID before kick starting the routing process.
- All routing rules should be defined properly and always with specific integration topology.
- Requester ABCS should not define the target system ID but routing rules should always define the target system ID.
- For EBS operation, it should have at least one routing rule. In other cases, every possible target system that EBS connects should go through the routing rules.
- As EBS supports both synchronous and asynchronous integration topologies, routing rules should be defined properly for all the integrations.

- Routing rules are specified in the XPath expression in the mediator routing rules filter.
- One routing rule is for Composite Application Validation System (CAVS) enabling. Routing rule should identify such EBM by checking the EBM header for value of environment code as CAVS.

There are other design points such as Error Handling, Security, Transaction Enabling, and so on, which should also be considered while designing EBS. These Qualities of Service (QoS) components are discussed in detail in later chapters.

# EBS implementation

As we are aware, Oracle AIA integrations can be achieved by using Oracle SOA Suite 11g platform. The EBS component can be developed by using the Oracle Mediator component. Assuming that you are aware of developing various integrations using Oracle SOA suite, the following sections will explain the various MEPs of EBS implementation using Oracle Mediator.

The following points may be helpful before implementing EBS using JDeveloper:

1. Define or identify the abstract WSDL contract between the services (such as the MEP, the operations, the Messages or Business Objects, and exceptions).
2. Create the abstract WSDL in JDeveloper or use an existing one provided by AIA FP EBS templates, making sure you use proper annotations.
3. Import the abstract WSDL into Oracle Mediator, configure the routing rules for the operations, handle the errors, enable CAVS, and deploy it.

## Constructing WSDL for process service EBS

As we have seen earlier, EBS development is a top-down web service development approach. So, first we should have a proper WSDL in order to develop a Process type of EBS. For Entity type EBS, we should use the WSDL provided by Oracle AIA FP as a part of Enterprise Service Library package. The following are the prerequisites to create a WSDL:

The EBM schema model for the EBO schema must be available in the central location or a part of the project structure in JDeveloper. JDeveloper can be used to create Enterprise Business Services from WSDL. So, we need WSDL before starting the EBS development.

WSDL can be designed by using **JDeveloper WSDL Editor**. The WSDL editor requires the XML schema to generate the `portTypes` for the given operations.

1. First open the JDeveloper IDE and create a new SOA application and project. Then we should create a new WSDL file by going through the **Web Service** category and create a **WSDL Document**, as shown in the following screenshot. While defining WSDL, the EBM schema model should be used to generate WSDL `portTypes`:

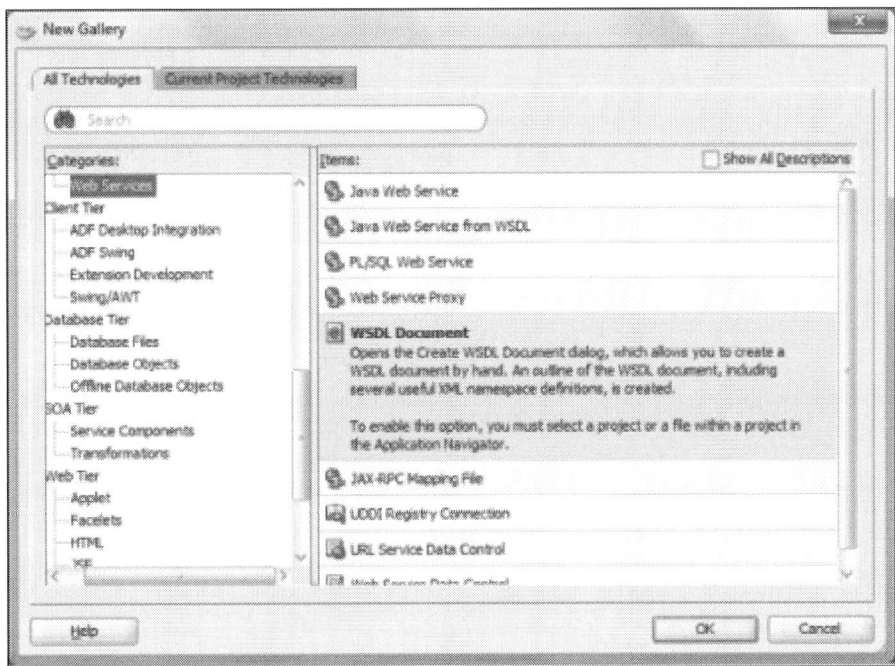

## Developing EBS using Oracle Mediator

Oracle Mediator component is used to route the messages between service providers and external applications. It can also be used for event publishing. Oracle Mediator can perform routing, validating, filtering, and message transformation.

Oracle Mediator component can be used to build EBS solutions. It has been widely used to build EBS components even though there are other technologies supported by Oracle AIA. The following should be executed to develop EBS using Oracle Mediator:

*Enterprise Business Services*

1. Open the JDeveloper IDE and create a new SOA application by selecting **File | New | Applications** (from **Category** pane), and then select **SOA Application**. Enter all the mandatory fields in the wizard. Select **SOA** as **Project Technologies**. Select **Empty Composite** and it will open a new SOA project in the JDeveloper, which is shown in the following screenshot:

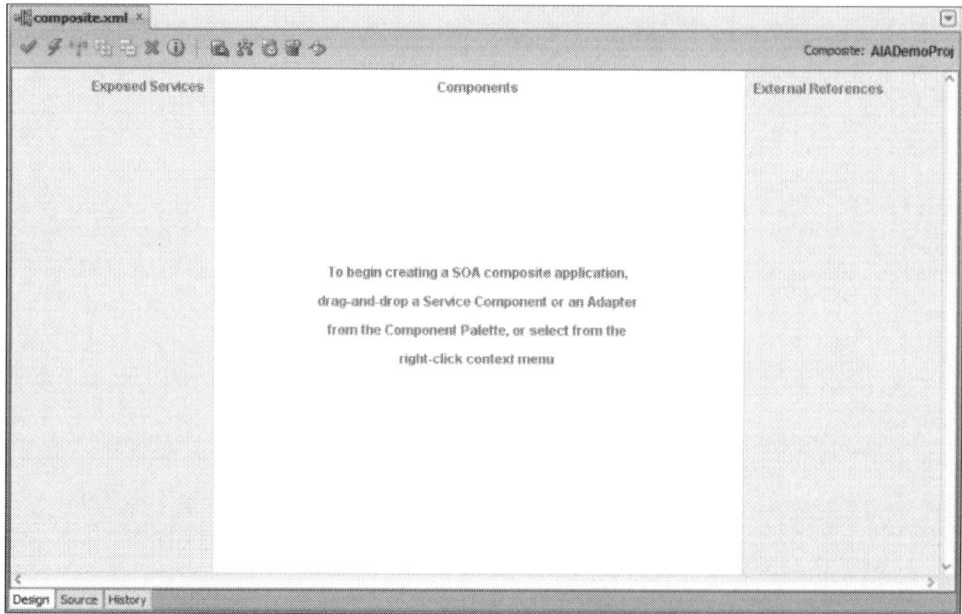

Now the screen should show the **composite.xml** in the design view as shown in the preceding screenshot. If it is not showing in the design view, please change to design view. Now, we have to add the **Mediator Component** in the **composite.xml** to create EBS services and routing rules.

2. Drag-and-drop the mediator from the component palette to the component swimlane of the **composite.xml**, which should pop-up a **Create Mediator** wizard. In that wizard, fill the mediator **Name** field, select the **Interface Definition** from WSDL template, and select the specific WSDL file from the **EnterpriseBusinessServiceLibrary** folder from **AIA_HOME**:

Chapter 4

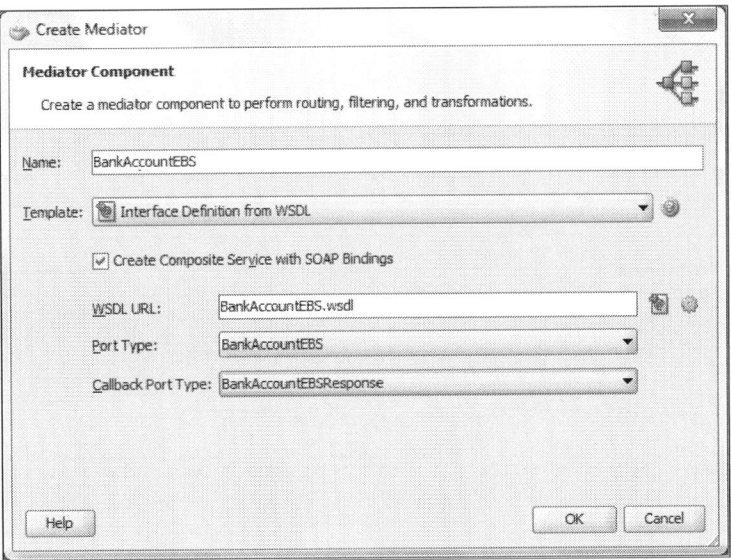

3. Now, we should add provider ABCS Web Service in the external reference in order to route the request received in the EBS to the provider ABCS. So, drag-and-drop the **Web Service** component from the component palette to the **External Reference** swimlane. This should pop-up a wizard and ask for the **WSDL Location**. Add the ABCS WSDL URL in the wizard, which should import the WSDL service references in `composite.xml`. Finally, route the operations from mediator to external reference web service operation:

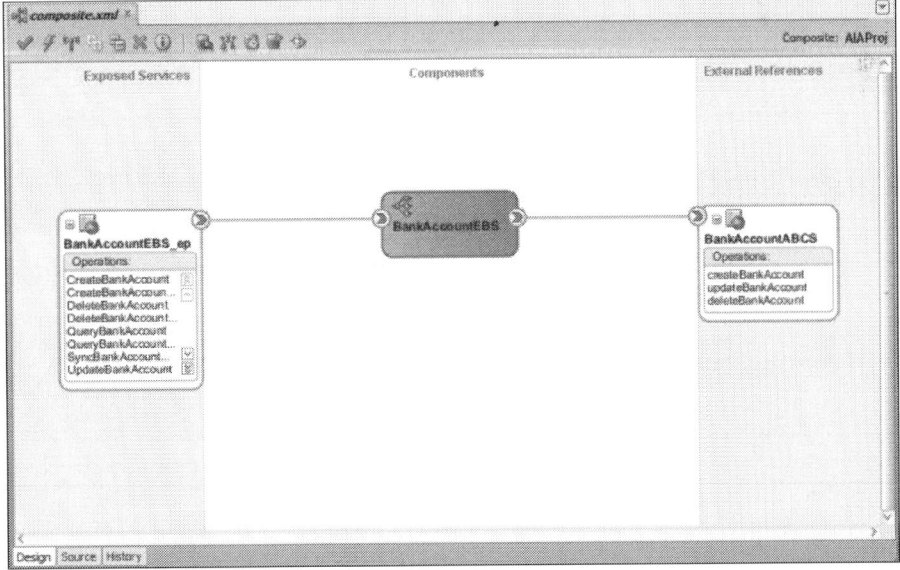

# Enterprise Business Services

> Note that while configuring the external reference ABCS service in the composite, we should make sure that we are configuring the concrete path of the ABCS service URL. However, in a real-time development scenario, we cannot configure the concrete URL of the ABCS service because that may change depending on the environment. It is always a good practice to change the URL references during deployment using custom deployment scripts.

Now, it is time to configure the various validation and routing rules that you would like to implement to meet the requirements. Open the mediator routing window and configure the routing rules shown as follows. It is now ready to deploy:

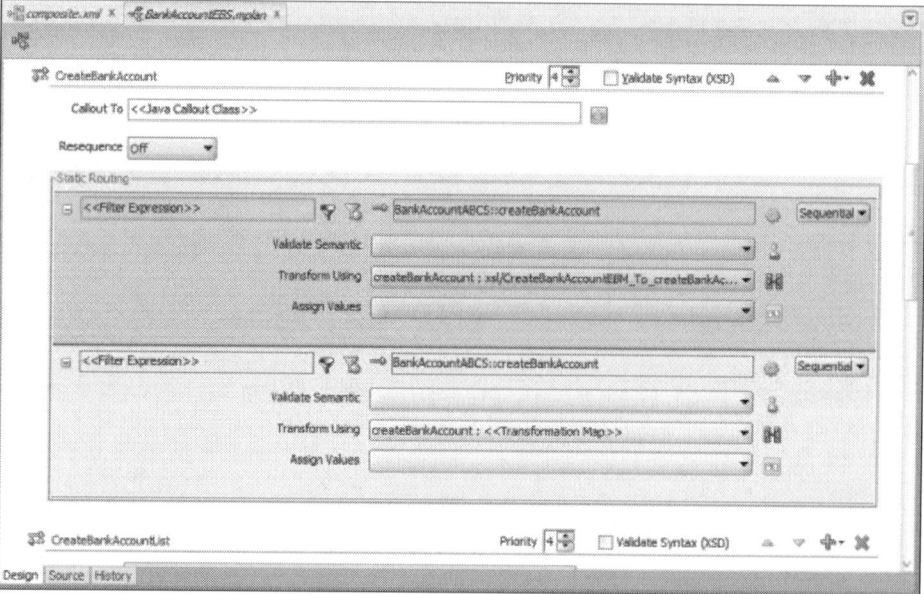

## Developing synchronous request and response pattern EBS

Synchronous request and response MEPs predominantly are used by **Query** operations in the Entity Service EBS. Synchronous request and response pattern also should be developed in Oracle Mediator in a similar way as discussed in the *Developing EBS using Oracle Mediator* section. However, in synchronous request and response, both request and response should be in EBM payload. Mediator routing rules should be defined properly by both request and response route. Also, fault should be properly defined. While implementing using the Mediator, an appropriate operation should be used to create links between the mediator and external interfaces.

The following guidelines should be helpful while developing synchronous request and response MEP:

- While creating a mediator, one mediator should be created for each `portType` in the EBS WSDL. However, if all the EBS operations are either synchronous request-response or fire-and-forget patterns, and exist under one `portType`, then only one mediator can be used.
- If the EBS has more than one `portType` that exists, then maximum number of mediators should be used to build the EBS integration component.
- Always keep the EBS WSDL file in the JDeveloper project folder.
- Always use AIA naming standards as followed in the out-of-the-box AIA FP.
- In fault, the value should be properly defined in the synchronous request and response model. These are depicted in the following screenshot:

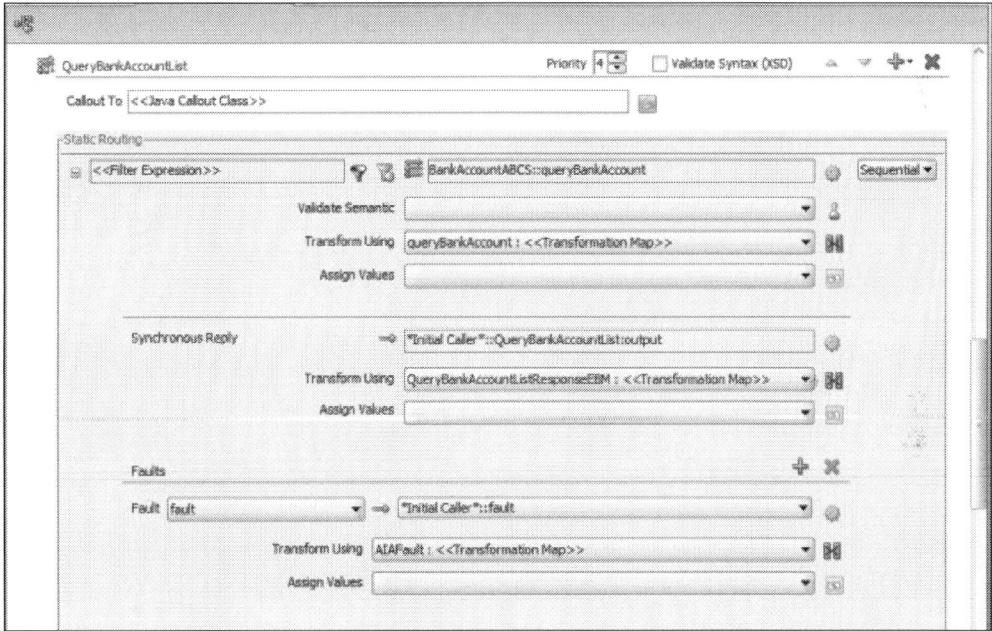

# Developing asynchronous one-way pattern EBS

Asynchronous one-way pattern just forwards the requester's requests to the provider ABCS as enterprise messages. The mediator component should route the requests.

- In the **Mediator Component**, just route the request service to the correct ABCS service provider using one-way routing operation. In this is case, both ABCS service and EBS operation should be one-way operations.

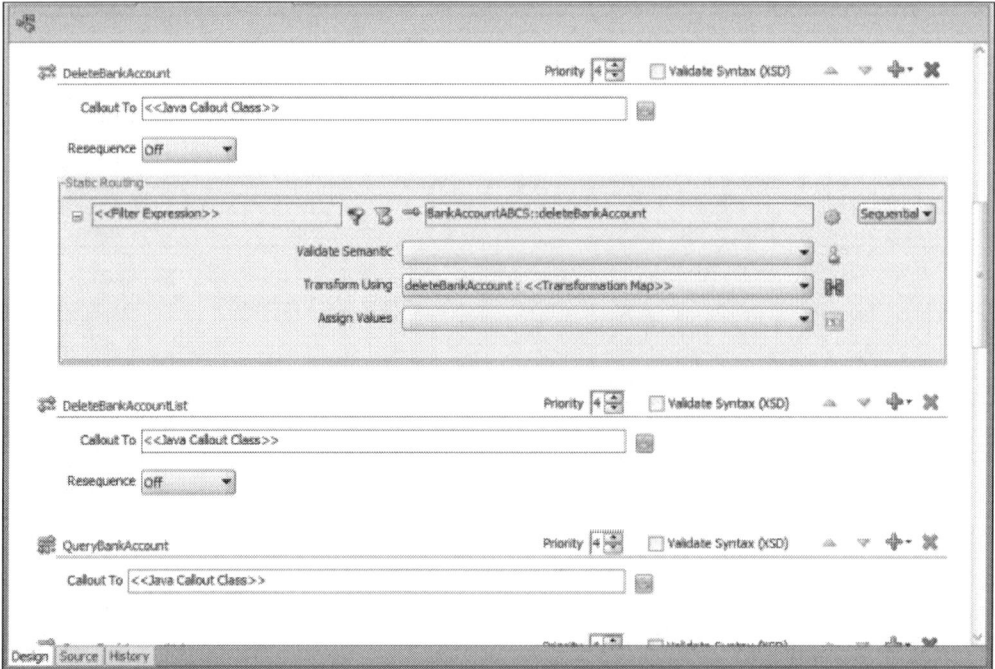

# Developing asynchronous request delayed and response pattern EBS

Developing an asynchronous request and delayed response pattern requires two one-way calls with EBS. The following points should be followed along with steps provided by the *Developing EBS using Oracle Mediator* section.

In the Asynchronous request and delayed response implementation, the following two additional points should be implemented in addition with the *Developing EBS using Oracle Mediator* section.

- The mediator routing service for asynchronous request and delayed response pattern should have two one-way calls with EBS. One is for request and another one for callback of the delayed response.
- For each request, route the requester's request to the corresponding provider services in order to establish connections on both the sides.
- Forward the fault messages in the mediator routing configuration properly for both request and delayed response.
- We must use the EBS WSDL provided by the `EnterpriseServiceLibrary` folder for Entity type EBS and `TemplateEBS.wsdl` file for the Process type EBS.

# Summary

Understanding and developing an EBS component is the most important step in AIA-based integration approach. Oracle's AIA out-of-box-installation comes up with plenty of Entity type EBS WSDL files, which can be used to integrate with any application. However, implementing the Process type EBS is very complex, which requires very good understanding of WSDL and EBS, and good mediator knowledge. We have seen only the core component in the AIA integration architecture. The Application Business Connector Services (ABCS) component plays as a transformer to convert the Application Business Message (ABM) to the enterprise standard format Enterprise Business Message. The next chapter will cover the ABCS architecture, approach, and development using Oracle SOA Suite.

# 5
# Application Business Connector Services

So far we have seen various fundamental components of the AIA architecture such as EBO, EBM, and EBS. In this chapter, we are going to explore another core component of the AIA architecture called **Application Business Connector Services** (**ABCS**). As we have seen in the last chapter, EBS plays a middle role in the AIA approach of integration and it does not directly establish communication with any application or systems until that application can understand EBM. Therefore, it is necessary to have a component that should understand the application-specific messaging format and also communicate with EBS in the EBM format. ABCS establishes communication with application and client systems, and transforms the message formats according to EBM and **Application Business Message** (**ABM**) and vice versa.

In this chapter, we will be exploring the following topics about ABCS:

- Application Business Connector Services in Oracle AIA
- Architecture of ABCS
- ABCS principles and guidelines
- Implementing ABCS using Mediator and BPEL
- EBM to ABM transformation

>  Note that in **Enterprise Application Integration** (**EAI**) and **Service Oriented Architecture** (**SOA**) approaches, transforming messages from one format to another becomes unavoidable. Due to the nature of the different enterprise systems, various transformation logics are being used to transform the message from one form to another form to make it understandable by the target systems. In AIA approach, since ABCS requires to playing a major role in transforming enterprise messages between ABM and EBM format, Mediator, and OSB components of Oracle SOA can be used to achieve the ABCS requirements.

## ABCS in AIA

In AIA integration, ABCS plays the role of exposing application's business function as a service and enabling the EBS to communicate with enterprise applications. ABCS can play two different roles in the AIA integration approach. They are as follows:

1. Requester ABCS
2. Provider ABCS

The provider ABCS will expose the business functions and resources that exist in the various types of enterprise applications. In the canonical data model integration approach, EBS will be used to enable the business functions through the canonical message format. The provider ABCS accepts requests from EBS as **Enterprise Business Message** (**EBM**) or any other client application. Once the request is processed, it will send back the response in EBM or any other supported format. ABCS is mostly a necessary component in integration scenarios as most of the applications have their own language for communication.

The requester ABCS plays a role in the requester side of the AIA architecture. The requester ABCS accepts requests in the form of ABM and transforms those messages as EBM and submits them to the provider ABCS through EBS. The EBS communicates with provider ABCS as EBM model. Once EBS receives the response, it returns back to the requester ABCS and the requester ABCS returns the EBM message as ABM format to the client applications.

In general, ABCS is response for the following in AIA architecture:

- Message validation and support for client applications
- Message transformation according to requester and provider applications
- Enabling of communication channel for client application to access the business functions exposed by EBS either through web service-based or non-web service-based approach

- The provider application side ABCS should expose the application-specific business functions as provider ABCS
- Error-handling and exception messaging
- Security-enabling for the client and applications.
- EBM Header population
- ABCS can also be used for message enrichment during integration

# ABCS Architecture

In the AIA architecture, the fundamental message models are **Enterprise Business Message (EBM)** and **Enterprise Business Object (EBO)**. Any application that should be integrated using the AIA approach should support the EBM and EBO models. This cannot be achieved by most of the applications. So, some intermediate layers of components should enable the enterprise applications to provide business functions as service or to consume services. ABCS facilitates the enterprise applications to achieve the AIA integration approach.

In order to be in compliance with enterprise integration standards, ABCS follows an extended pattern called VETORO, which is based on two integration patterns, as follows:

1. VETO
2. VETRO

**VETO** is a common integration pattern followed by industries for a long time. VETO stands for **Validate, Enrich, Transform, and Operate**. Basically, in the integration environment, different technology and age of applications have to communicate with each other. In order to carry out effective communication, the message being communicated between each application might require verification, enrichment by adding more information, and transformation according to technology or language. VETO has variation that is called **VETRO**.

The VETRO pattern has the entire set of characteristics that VETO pattern possesses. However, VETRO has an additional step in the enterprise integration called **Route**. Apart from message validation, enrichment, transformation, and operations, VETRO has message routing capability. The VETRO pattern is the fundamental approach for **Enterprise Service Bus (ESB)**. The Oracle Mediator completely follows the VETRO pattern.

VETORO is an extended variation of the VETRO pattern. ABCS architecture is based on the VETORO pattern. The VETORO pattern basically has additional operational qualities along with routing.

## Application Business Connector Services

The following diagram will depict the typical role of ABCS in the AIA architecture. In some cases, a single ABCS can accomplish the integration requirements. Let's see each step of ABCS:

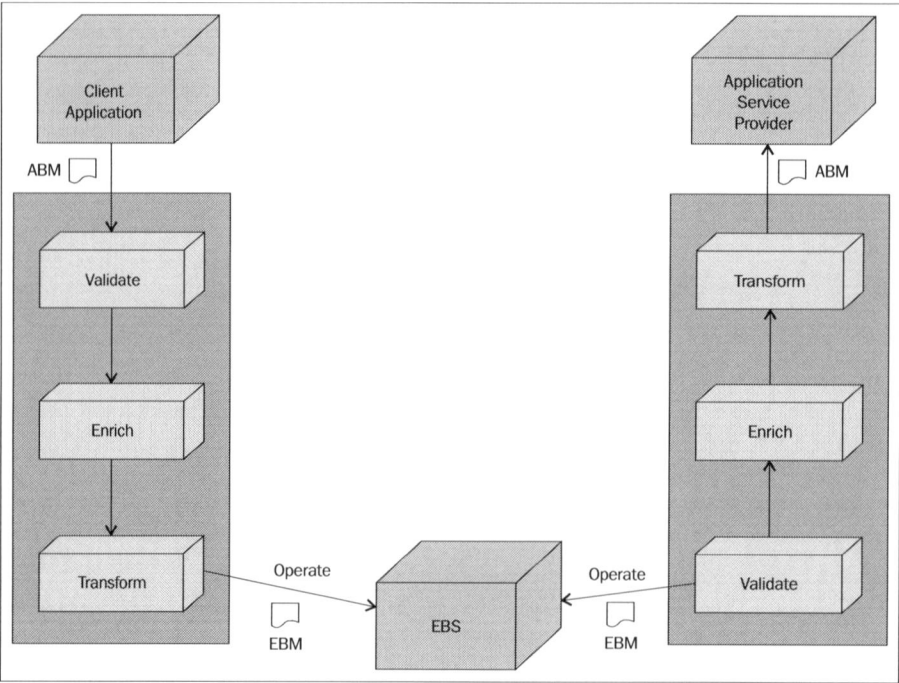

## Validate

In the integration scenarios, communication between two systems plays a critical role. So the communication should be in proper messaging model and valid information in order to successfully complete the data exchange. Every system involved in the integration should ensure that it sends and receives messages in the expected format (or as per the contract). Therefore, validating the received message and data before proceeding with the process or sending to another system is highly critical. ESB architecture facilitates that by default as part of the VETO pattern adoption. As Oracle AIA is based on the VETO pattern, the validation step plays the first step while exchanging messages between client and EBS or EBS and provider application. Some of the common validations are as follows:

- Validate whether the incoming message has well-formed XML
- Validate the version of the message and data integrity
- Check the user credentials in case of secured services even before the message reaches the target EBS

# Enrich

Enrich basically helps to add more relevant data to the message to make it more meaningful for the target application. Enabling enrich step in ABCS is depends on the requirement. In some cases, we may not enrich any incoming or outgoing data in the ABCS.

# Transform

This is another critical step in integration scenarios. Almost every application integration must go through transformation steps. Transformation is basically used to convert the format of the message to another format to meet the target system's expectations. In AIA integration model, client application and provider application communicate with the ABCS in **Application Business Message (ABM)** format. It is ABCS's role to convert the ABM format to EBM format to feed or receive messages using EBS. This approach helps to decouple the application and EBS by handing the VETRO requirements in ABCS.

# Operate

In general, operate basically means communicating with the target or the provider system by invoking the service operations of the target or the provider system. In AIA approach, operate means invoking of the EBS service or other services. Oracle Mediator and OSB have the capability to invoke another service operation without writing web service client code.

# Route

Routing the request to another component is quite common in web application development. When using application integration, routing helps to meet requirements such as message forwarding to another service and business rules. In the SOA world, the routing is handled by Enterprise Service Bus (EBS). In Oracle AIA, the routing step is implemented by EBS (Oracle Mediator or OSB) for different needs. In some cases, ABCS only handles validate, enrich, and transform, whereas EBS handle the routing. Handling routing in the EBS is the best approach rather than building individual EBS for every ABCS service.

Oracle Mediator routing helps to implement content-based routing by using XSL validation and business rules-based routing by implementing the business rules in the composite application.

# Key definitions of ABCS architecture

The following are the key definitions to be remembered while architecting ABCS:

- In AIA architecture, for every service implemented based on EBO, it must be accompanied by the ABCS component to facilitate the participating requester and provider application.
- If the integration is through non-EBO messages (non-canonical pattern), then ABCS should be part of the provider application or requester. So the provider ABCS should accept the EBM request and provide output in the form of response ABM.
- If the ABCS input request is always in EBM, then the output response from the ABCS should be in the form of EBM only.
- Oracle recommends a single ABCS for each action in the AIA architecture, even though ABCS can handle multiple actions.
- If there is a use case where a single ABCS should handle multiple activities, then the input EBM should also accept the action's details that should be performed while processing the request. This also helps to perform transformation, enrichment, and content-based routing.
- In the case of provider applications, if the business functions directly match the required service operations, then ABCS does not need to handle any transformation, but it can act as proxy service. In this case, simple ABCS should just transform the input ABM message format to the EBM format. Oracle Mediator can exactly handle this requirement.
- In case of provider application, if business actions do not match the required service operations, a more fine-grained operation of the provider activities should be exposed by EBS and ABCS should handle the transaction to coordinate the execution with transformation. In that case, Oracle BPEL will be a suitable component to handle the multiple service orchestrations.
- If the application always does not support EBM, then the ABCS should handle the transformation.
- If the provider applications do not support WSDL-based service by default, then other J2CA resource adapters can be used to expose the application functions as service operations. In case of Siebel, PeopleSoft, JD Edwards, Agile, and SAP applications, the Oracle Application adapter will do the interfacing of exposing application functions to the AIA framework.
- Other transport methodologies are XML, SOAP, JMS, and database adapter; **Advance Queue (AQ)** can be used in provider ABCS implementation.

# Design principles of ABCS

The following points will be helpful to make appropriate design decisions while designing different types of ABCS:

- ABCS implementation should be based on ABCS WSDL contract (top-down approach). Therefore, before creating the ABCS WSDL, identify the role of ABCS in the AIA integration.
- If it is a provider ABCS, then identify the EBM schema to be used to transform between ABM and EBM. If the AIA out-of-the-box EBM does not match provider service, then customize or go with non-canonical pattern.
- If it is a requester ABCS, then identify the appropriate EBS and its EBM, and design the transformation mechanism to transform the requester application ABM to EBS input EBM. It is also necessary to identify the EBS **Message Execution Pattern** (**MEP**) to handle the coordination.
- Identify and design the message transportation protocol such as SOAP, JMS, and JCA, but before that we must analyze the capability of requester and provider applications.
- A single ABCS should be able to handle multiple instances or versions of a provider application. At the same time, co-occurrence of multiple versions of the same ABCS should be avoided.
- ABCS should not make any assumptions regarding the target system or to the transport mechanism (SOAP, JMS, native or otherwise).

# Designing ABM Schema

The following design tips should be considered while designing ABM schema model for ABCS:

1. ABM message should be defined at abstract level and encompass all elements required. However, it should not impose frequent development and enhancement of the ABCS components.
2. A better approach is to design ABM schema with multiple reusable components in order to promote reusability of transformation and enrichment.
3. Consider system instance, locale and sender information while designing ABM schema model for requester or provider applications.
4. Always design the ABM schema model as extendable to accommodate future enhancements.

# Developing ABCS

In general, each application (either provider or requester) participating in the AIA architecture must have its own ABCS. Each action of the participating application should have its own ABCS. If it is a request-response pattern, then both request and response should be handled by a single ABCS. In case of request and delayed response pattern, two independent ABCSs should be implemented to handle request and delayed responses, respectively.

Developing ABCS requires a good understanding of the Oracle SOA Suite 11g as Oracle Mediator, Oracle BPEL, and OSB 11g should be used to handle EBM, transformation, and routing. With an understanding that you are aware of Oracle SOA Suite, JDeveloper, and Composite applications, we are going to see the various approaches to building an ABCS.

# Developing ABCS using AIA Service Constructor

AIA Service Constructor is a JDeveloper wizard utility that helps to build the ABCS by generating AIA artifacts and compliance with AIA framework recommendations. It also helps to build appropriate naming standards followed by other AIA components in the AIA architecture.

Before getting into ABCS development using AIA Service Constructor, we must be made aware of the construction phase of the AIA Project Life Cycle (we will see all the phases of the AIA Project Life Cycle in a later chapter). The AIA Service Constructor is used in the construction phase of the AIA Project Life Cycle. The construction phase encompasses four primary sub-phases, as shown in the following screenshot:

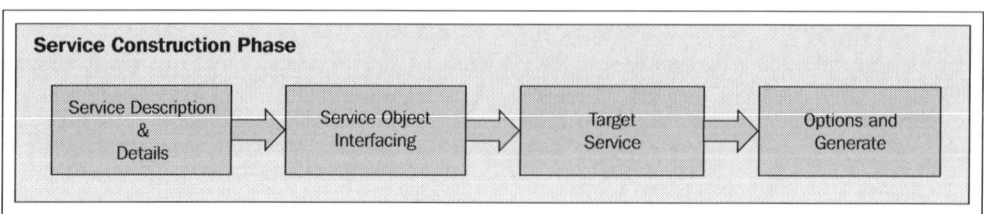

1. **Service Description**: Captures high-level details about components and business activities.
2. **Service Interface**: ABCS message types, input and output approaches to be captured.

3. **Target Service**: Capture service invocation, message and operations that will pass through the ABCS.
4. **Options and Generation** - Add additional options such as fault handling, logging, and finalizes the generation.

The following steps should be executed one-by-one to create an ABCS service solution using the AIA Service Constructor:

1. Run the JDeveloper and create a new application as generic or SOA-based.
2. Now we should create a new projec, "AIA Service Component Project", as shown in the following screenshot:

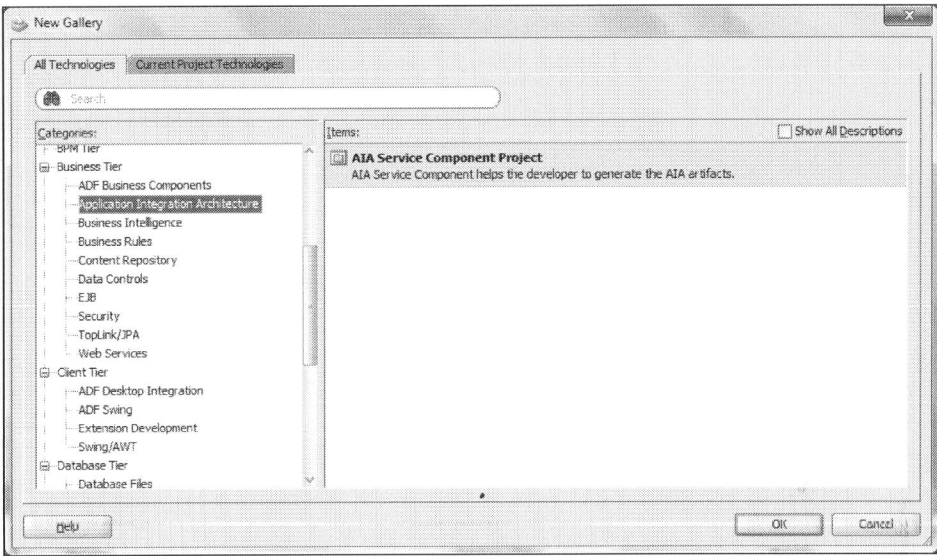

3. Now it should open a welcome screen of the AIA Service Constructor wizard as shown in the following screenshot. Click on **Next** to proceed further.

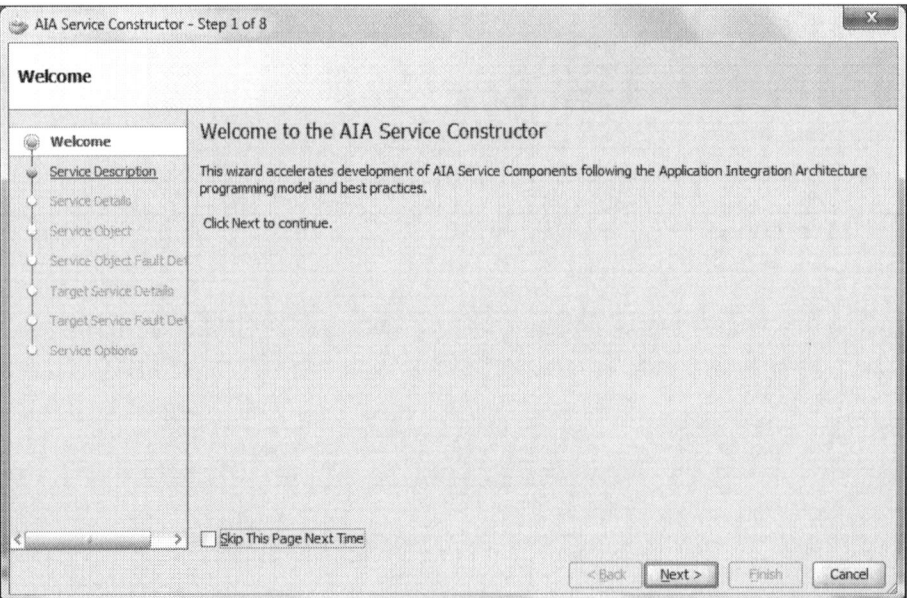

4. Click on **Next** on the welcome screen and it should take you to the **Service Description** screen. The best approach should be first to create the service description in the AIA Project Life Cycle, then import the same using the **Import** button on this screen. Alternatively, we can also import from filesystem. This approach helps to import service artifacts created earlier by the Oracle AIA composite generator.

*Chapter 5*

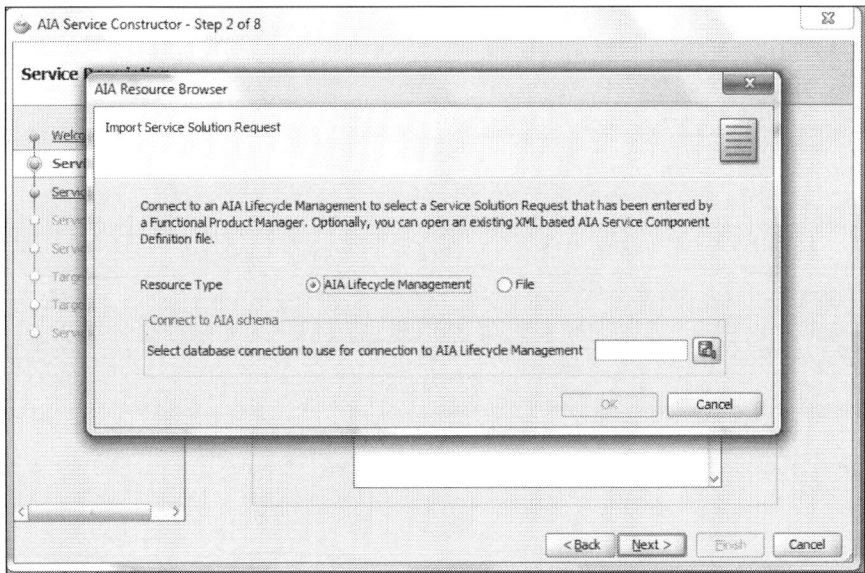

5. After importing the service information from the AIA Project Life Cycle or File, a screen should appear as shown in the following screenshot. Then, click on **Next**.

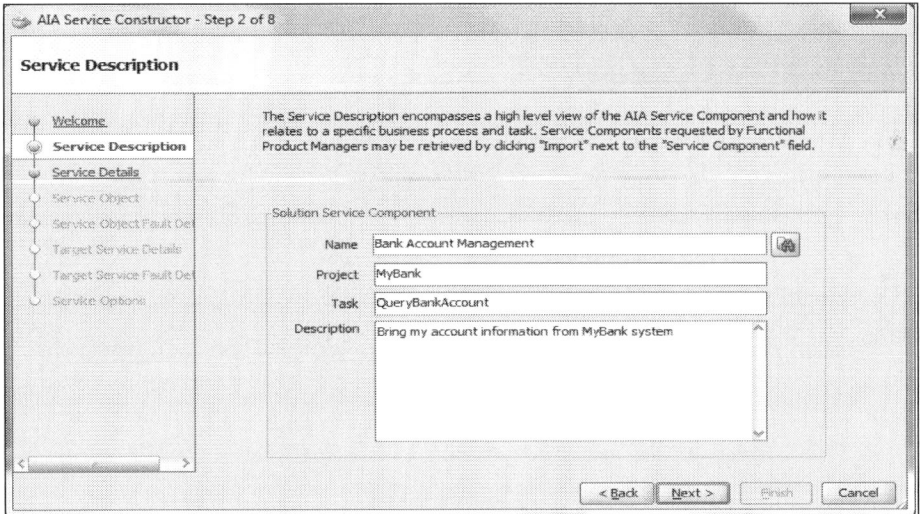

6. The **Service Details** screen is used to capture the associated application (in ABCS, it should be provider ABCS or Requester ABCS) and type of service that should be created in the ABCS. Once entered, click on **Next**.

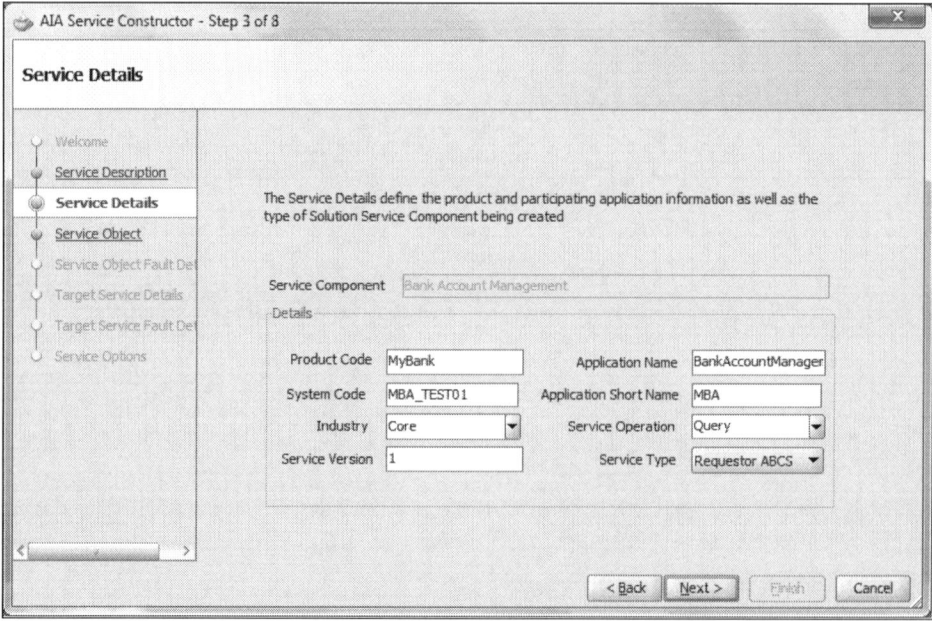

7. The following details should be captured properly in the **Service Details** screen.

    ◦ **Product Code**: Product code is the name of the AIA integration product created in association with applications.

    ◦ **Application Name**: Name of the application being created by using the AIA framework.

    ◦ **System Code**: Application system code or identification being used in the enterprise infrastructure.

    ◦ **Application Short Name**: Short name of the application being developed, if any.

    ◦ **Industry**: The specific industry of the application being developed. If the application is general, then Core can be selected. Notice that it is directly related to the EBO group in AIA installation. EBO is grouped as Core and Industry-specific. AIA PIPs are an industry-specific process flow, developed.

- **Service Operation:** Type of the operation or activity that this specific ABCS associated with. As we have seen earlier, each ABCS should be associated with one activity or operation.
- **Service Version**: Version number of the ABCS.
- **Service Type**: This is where we should define whether this ABCS is for provider or requester. Depending upon the selection, the subsequent Service Object screen parameters will change.

8. The **Service Object** screen is used to capture the service message details. If it is **Requester ABCS**, then it should receive ABM as input from the requesting application so it can invoke the EBS operation. If it is **Provider ABCS**, then it should receive an EBS message as input and communicate with provider application as an EBM object.

9. As we selected the Requester ABCS as the service type in the previous screen, the Service Object screen prompted to enter parameters for ABM. In this screen, we must select the predefined ABM schema model and type of the **Message Exchange Pattern** (MEP).

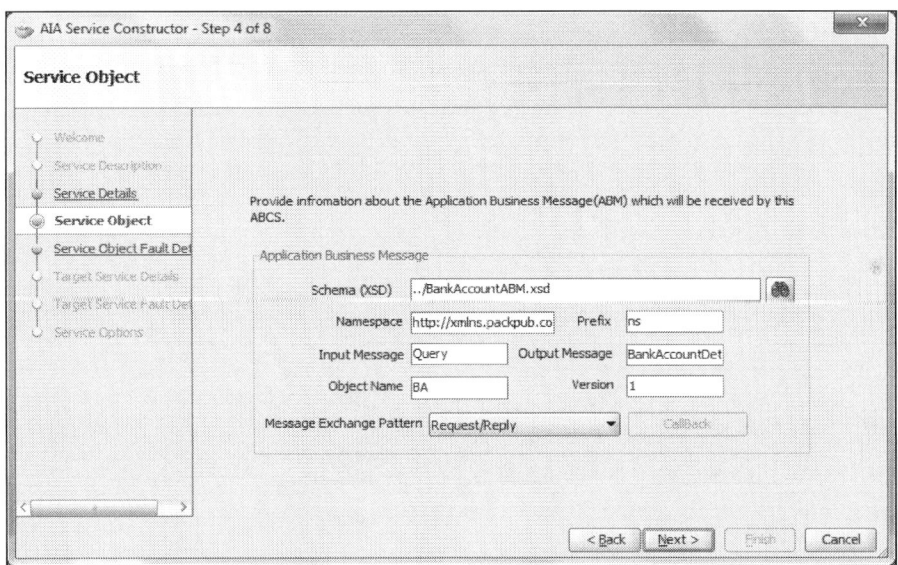

*Application Business Connector Services*

10. The following parameters should be defined in the **Service Object** screen:
    - Schema (XSD): This path of the ABM schema should be located in the field. It is always the best practice to keep all schemas in the JDeveloper project resource path to smoothen the deployment procedures.
    - **Namespace**: Refers to the namespace URL that uniquely identifies the attributes and objects.
    - **Prefix**: Prefix name to associate the attributes.
    - **Input Message**: Name of the input message.
    - **Output Message**: Name of the output message.
    - **Object Name**: Name of the ABM object being used in the integration.
    - **Version**: Version number of the ABM message.
    - **Message Exchange Pattern**: The MEP provided by the service operation. There are three types of MEP being used in AIA. We should select the appropriate MEP from the drop-down list. The call back option will be enabled only if the MEP is selected as Request-Delayed Response.

If the MEP is selected as Request-Delayed Response, then the **CallBack** will prompt to capture an addition callback URL operation, as shown in the following screenshot:

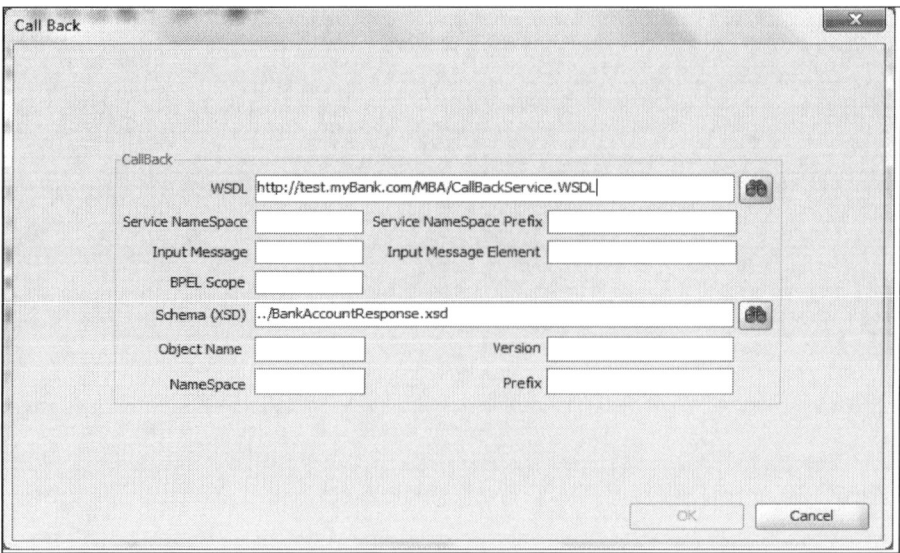

11. The **Service Object Fault** screen is used to capture the fault handling and message format during failure in the integration services. Typically, we should define a fault message for every service. ABCS also requires a fault message schema model to define the ABCS properly. Click on **Next** to proceed further.

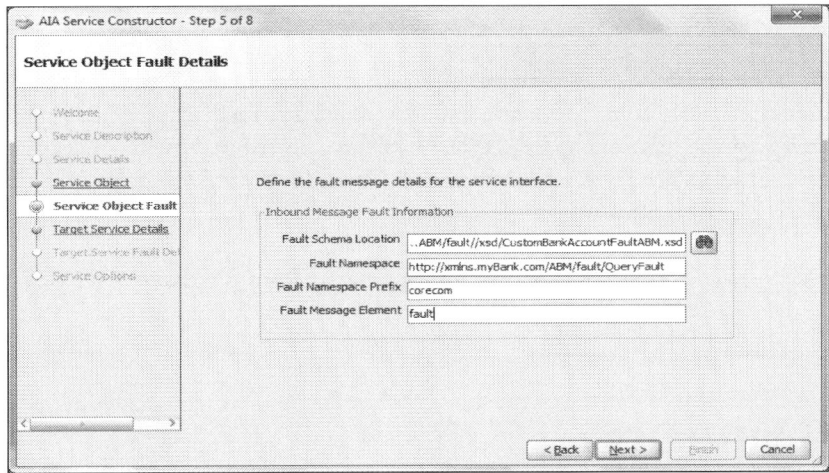

12. The **Target Service** screen is used to capture the target system interface details. If the ABCS is a Requester Type ABCS, then the target system should be Enterprise Service Bus. If the ABCS is a Provider Type ABCS, then the target system should be provider application interface. This screen prompts for parameters depending on the type of ABCS selected in the **Service Details** screen, as follows:

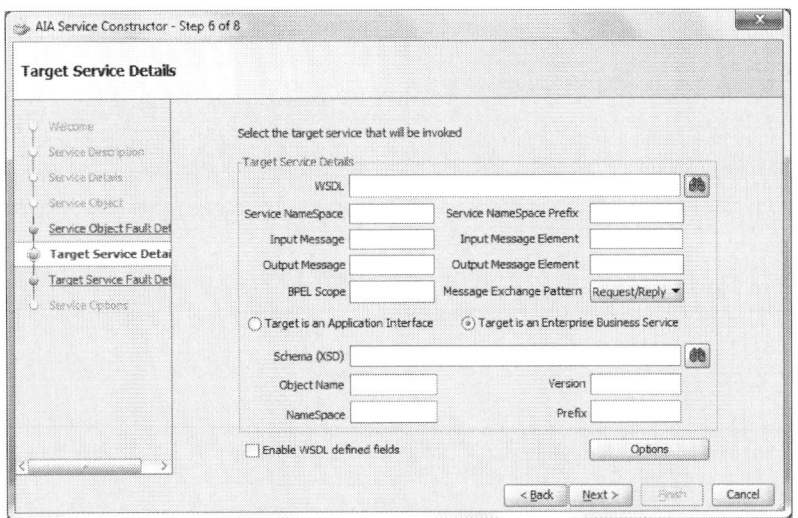

*Application Business Connector Services*

 Note that the Service construct wizard in JDeveloper supports only exposing web service operations and it does not support invoking any JCA adapter directly. So it is always the best practice to expose the JCA adapter operations as Web Service through Mediator, BPEL, or OSB and invoke those services in the AIA framework.

13. Clicking on the button next to the WSDL text field will prompt to select the WSDL that the ABCS should invoke. In the Requester ABCS, it should be the EBS WSDL. In the Provider ABCS, it should be the application interface WSDL or any custom WSDL used to interact with provider application. Then we should select the operation which should be invoked by the ABCS, as shown in the following screenshot:

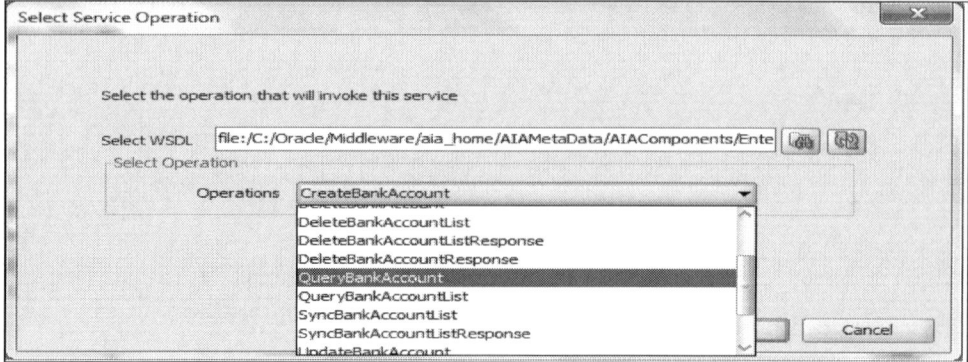

14. Once the target WSDL is selected, it should populate all required parameters in the Target Service Details screen, shown as follows:

*Chapter 5*

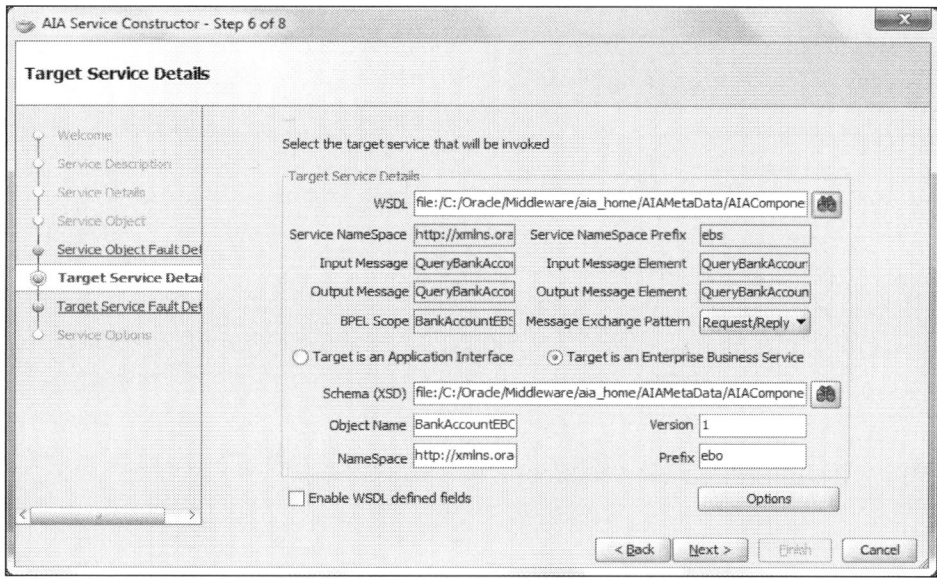

15. If you want to enable additional options such as Enabling CAVS (Composite Application Validation System—we will see in detail about this feature in a later chapter) to create Reference URL and extension, the following screen shows the options of **Target Service Options**:

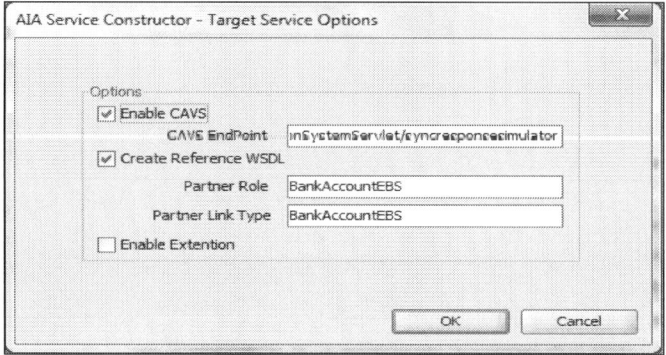

16. The next screen in the process should be **Target Service Fault**. This screen is similar to the **Service Object Fault** screen. The **Service Object Fault** screen is used to capture the fault message model of the ABCS service object. This **Target Service Fault** screen captures the fault message of the Target service. For most of the cases, this screen should be filled by default from the WSDL imported in the previous screen as shown in the following screenshot. Click on **Next** to proceed further.

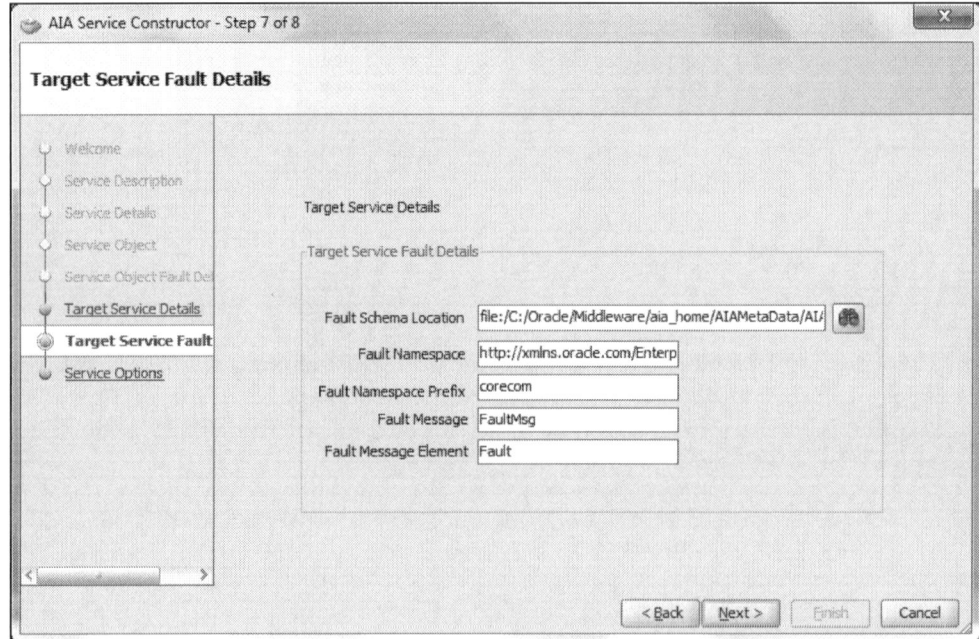

Chapter 5

17. The **Service Option** screen is the last screen in the AIA Service Constructor wizard. In this screen, if we want to add additional target services for the same ABCS service operation, we can do that by clicking on the **Additional Target** button. The **Additional Target Systems** screen is as shown in the following screenshot. Once we added the additional target system, we can complete the wizard by clicking on **Finish** in the **Service Option** screen.

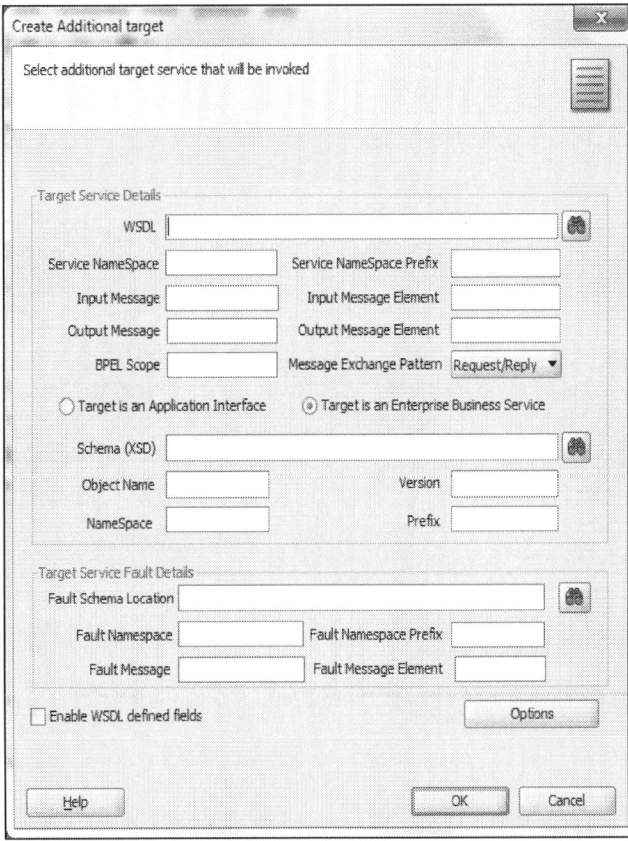

18. Once we complete the AIA **Service Constructor** wizard, it should generate all necessary AIA artifacts and generate the composite application as shown in the following screenshot:

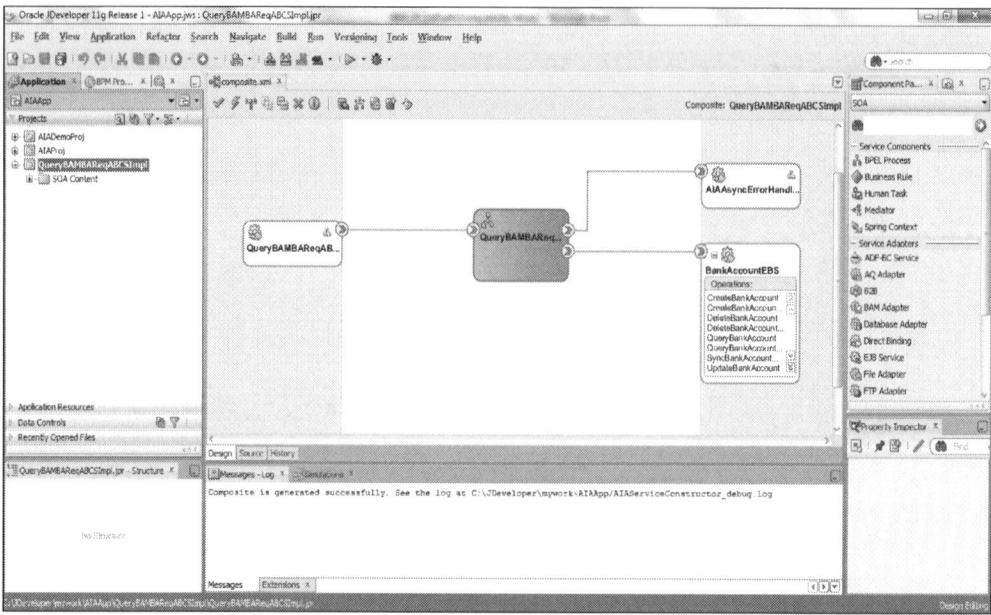

19. Now we have successfully created an ABCS using the AIA Service Constructor. If we watch closely the preceding composite application, then the central component of the composite application is the BPEL process. By double-clicking the central BPEL component, we can open the BPEL to check the process flow built by the AIA Service Constructor. The following image shows the sample BPEL created by the AIA Service Constructor:

*Chapter 5*

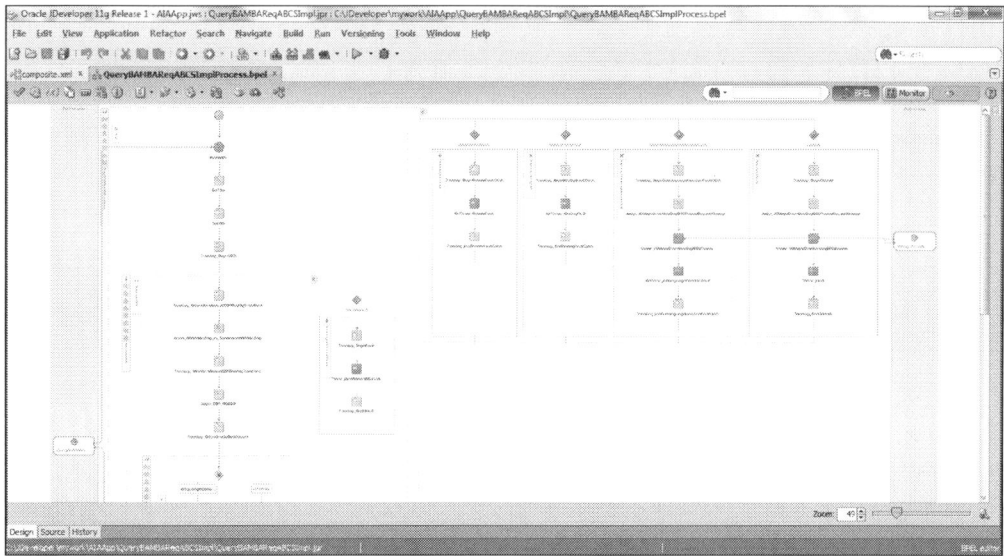

20. We must be aware of the following manual configurations after completing the ABCS constructions using AIA Service Constructor. Most of the points are applicable depending on the type of ABCS generated using AIA Service Constructor, as follows:

    ○ AIA Service Constructor generates ABCS external service invocation in sequence. If we want to change execution in parallel or based on business rules, then we must modify the execution using the Oracle BPEL designer.

    ○ AIA Service Constructor generates ABCS transformation automatically between input and output messages if the target message format type is EBM. Otherwise, it generates mapping at header level. Other business transformations should be done manually using the Oracle BPEL Designer.

    ○ AIA Service Constructor does not support correlation configuration by default for Request-Delayed Response type MEP, which should be configured manually by using the Oracle BPEL Designer.

    ○ As of now, Service Constructor does not support service invocation at multiple times. This should be added manually by copy-pasting the invocation in the Oracle BPEL Designer.

    ○ If the absolute URL of WSDL is not used in the ABCS, then the AIA Service Constructor does not fill up the binding in the composite file under `<reference>`. It should be configured manually.

- All policy-related requirements and configurations should be configured manually or MDS using Oracle BPEL Designer and other JDeveloper utilities.

## Developing ABCS manually using Oracle JDeveloper

The preceding AIA Service Constructor approach helps to build the Provider or Requester type ABCS automatically by providing the necessary data. In this section we are going to build the ABCS by manually building composite application using Oracle JDeveloper.

The following steps should be executed one-by-one to complete the ABCS development using Oracle JDeveloper.

1. In Oracle JDeveloper, create a new SOA composite project. This should create the default composite.xml. Open the composite.xml in the design mode.

2. Now we should add a BPEL component from the component palette to the component swim lane of the composite.xml. The Create BPEL process screen should appear as shown in the following screenshot:

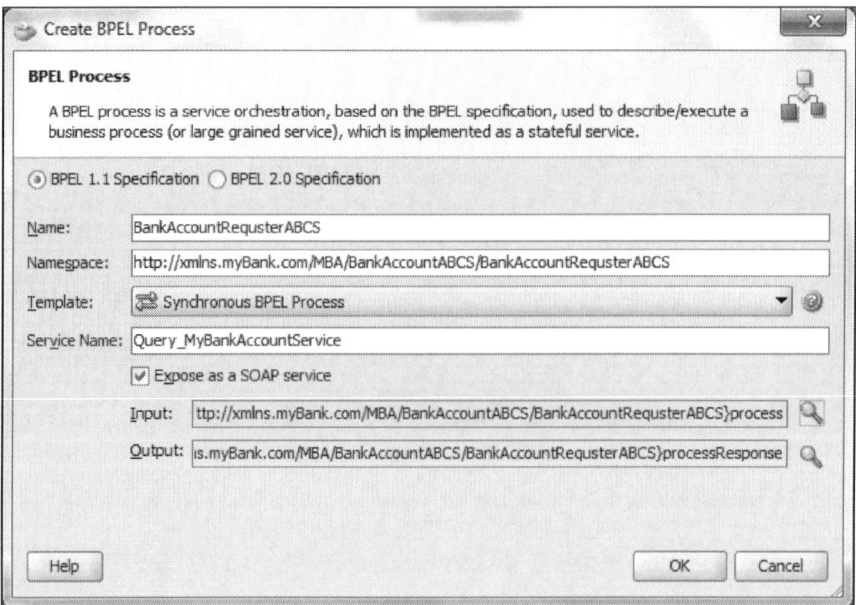

*Chapter 5*

3. In the created BPEL screen, we will enter the following parameters to generate the ABCS service:

    ◦ If the ABCS is Requester Type ABCS, then the input parameter should be configured with ABM input schema file and the output parameter should be configured by selecting the ABM output schema file.

    ◦ If the ABCS is Provider Type ABCS, then the input parameter should be EBM schema model and the output parameter should be output EBM schema model to facilitate the EBS to invoke the provider ABCS operation.

    ◦ The template parameter is nothing but the Message Exchange Pattern supported by the ABCS. The template parameter drop-down should provide option to select MEP pattern supported by AIA. In addition to that, we can also select the WSDL created manually for the ABCS Service, which will import all the operations, input, and output attributes automatically.

    Once the BPEL component is added in the ABCS `composite.xml`, the JDeveloper should appear as shown below:

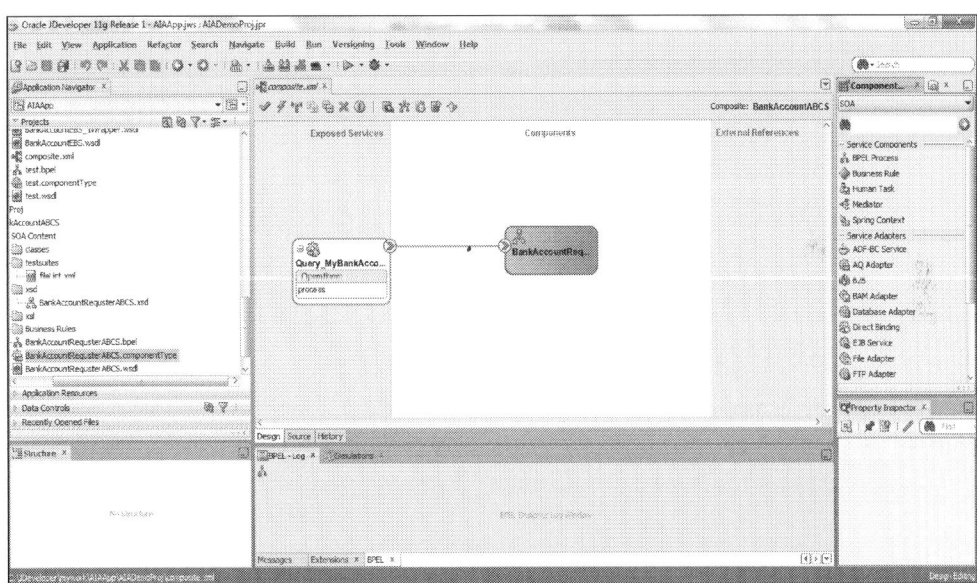

4. Now we should add the external web service reference in the External Reference swim lane. If it is Provider Type ABCS, then the external web service should be Application Integration Interface, JCA Adapter Web Service, or any service that is participating in the AIA integration. If it is Requester Type ABCS, then the external service should be EBS WSDL.

*Application Business Connector Services*

5. Now to import the external web service reference in the `composite.xml`, we should drag-and-drop the Web Service component from the Component Palette into the external reference swim lane. This action should prompt Create Web Service screen. The Provider gives all necessary parameters in the screen as shown in the following screenshot:

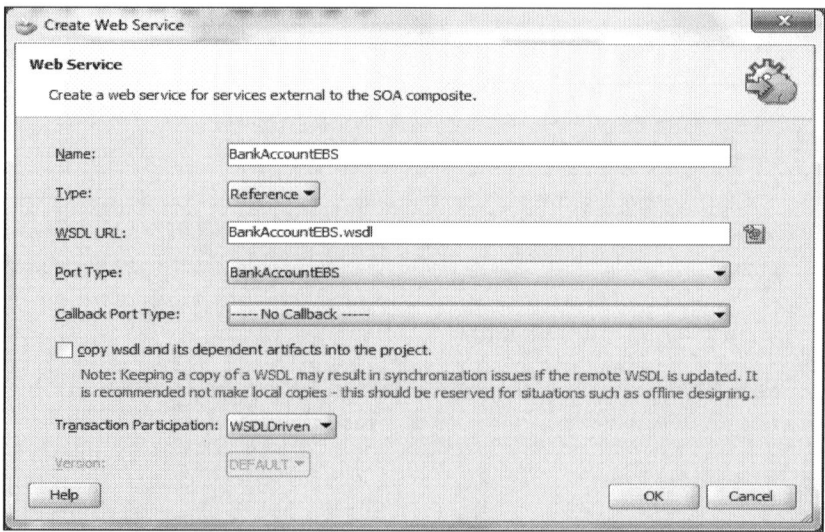

6. Once we configure the external web service in the `composite.xml`, we should create a wire between the BPEL component and the external web service component, as shown in the following screenshot:

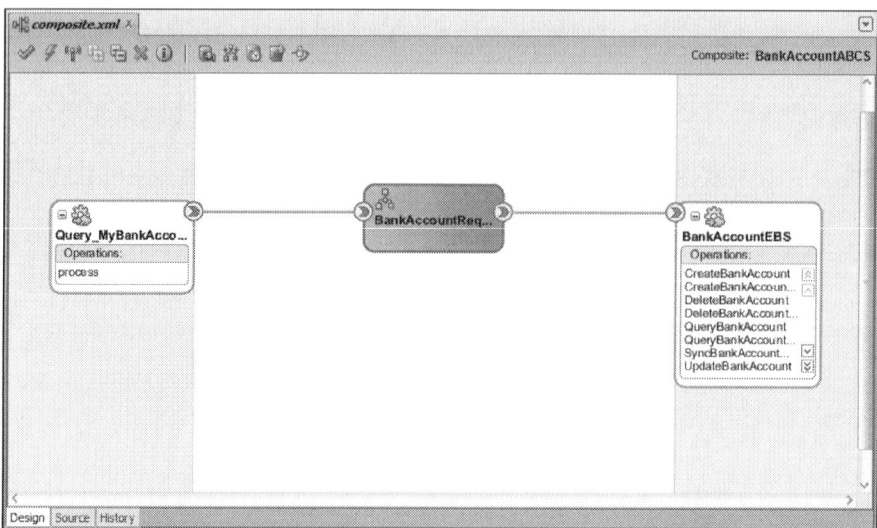

7. Now we should create invocation, mapping, and transformation between the ABCS (BPEL component) service and provider services. We should open the BPEL in the BPEL Designer and add the invoke and assign objects in the process flow, as shown in the following diagram (sample process flow):

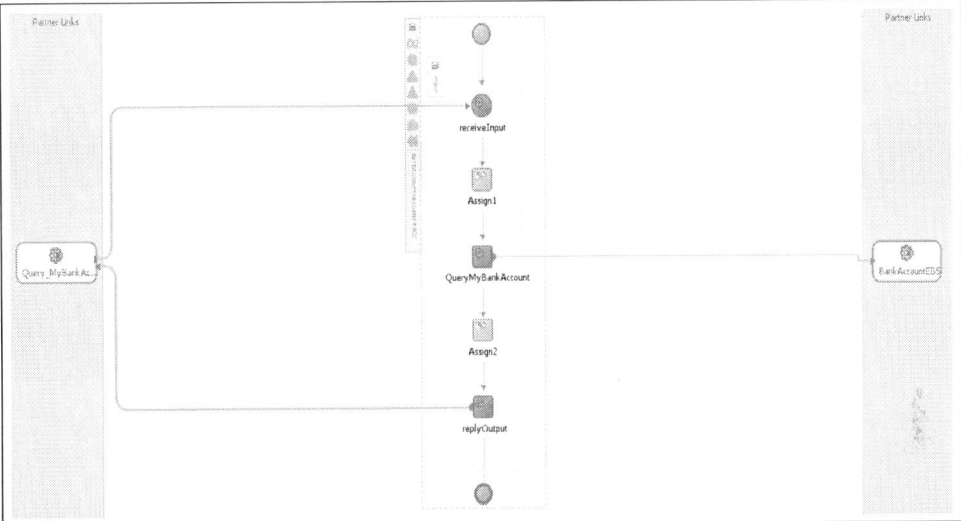

8. Now we should add the fault, exception handling and all other notification-related services in the business process flow to meet various requirements and standard compliances.

If any type of ABCS build uses this approach, then we can implement message enrichment, transformation, error handling, extension, multiple call, and parallel process manually and more comfortably.

Note that the ABCS construction and transformation can also be achieved using Oracle Service Bus 11g, which requires a different kind of approach. Additionally, Oracle Service Bus can be used to build EBS components. You can refer to www.oracle.com for further details.

# Briefly about extending ABCS using Custom Code

Both Requester Type ABCS and Provider Type ABCS have the capability to invoke custom code during execution. ABCS supports extended calls during the request and response pattern and during fire-and-forget pattern.

ABCS can pull the custom code in the following circumstances:

- Before executing the transformation from ABM to EBM in the Requester ABCS implementation
- Before invoking the EBS operation in the Requester ABCS implementation
- Before transforming the message from EBM to ABM in the response in the Requester ABCS
- Before invoking the callback response in the Request and Delayed Response pattern
- Before the transformation from the EBM to the ABM in the Provider ABCS
- Before invoking the Application Interface in the Provider ABCS implementation
- Before the transformation from ABM to EBM in the response to Provider ABCS
- Before invoking the EBS callback response in the Provider ABCS

The extension option in the ABCS is very useful while customizing the previously delivered ABCS and should also be followed for a new ABCS so as to make it more customizable.

# Summary

In this chapter, we have seen ABCS Architecture, types of ABCS, ABCS role in AIA, and various development approaches. The combination of ABCS and EBS provides a loosely-coupled, message-independent, and service-oriented integration approach. Even though we have seen the end-to-end integration approach between applications through EBS and ABCS, we still have to understand how to achieve business processes using AIA integration framework. The next chapter will elaborate in more detail about Enterprise Business Flow and its approach.

# 6
# Enterprise Business Flow

In the IT world, business flow or process means execution of various business tasks in a sequence or non-sequential mode to meet a specific business goal or objective. The modern IT architecture and technologies help to build the workflow and business processes as parts of the system to ensure that business users are following the process defined in the enterprises.

In the last chapter, we learned about Enterprise Business Services and its role in the AIA. Some of the business process scenarios require process or integration flow. ABCS and EBS are predominantly playing a role of message transformation and communication. Therefore, a list of Enterprise Business Services may not be enough to meet the process requirements. We may also need to build certain integration processes to meet process-related needs. AIA has come up with the **Enterprise Business Flow** component that helps to build the process implementation by coordinating multiple business services or EBSs. In this chapter, we are going to understand the following topics about Enterprise Business Flow:

- Overview of Enterprise Business Flow
- EBF architecture
- Building Enterprise Business Flow
- Business use case for EBF

## Overview of Enterprise Business Flow

Before we go into the details, let us see some basics about business flow. **Business flow** means executing related business activities to meet a common business objective or goal. Commonly, business flow is also known as business process. In IT context, business flow or process encompasses executing related activities through related or non-related systems in a structured approach. In the Oracle AIA context, EBF is an orchestration mechanism that implements a single operation but coordinates a set of multiple tasks and participates with multiple services.

# Common characteristics of Enterprise Business Flow

The following are some of the characteristics of Enterprise Business Flow:

- EBF are cross-functional business flows that establish a relationship between EBS activities.
- EBF enables to build processes by leveraging existing capabilities from multiple applications.
- EBF involves integration between systems by consuming EBSs and does not involve human workflow.
- EBF is about implementing the EBS kind of service by consuming other EBSs.
- Each EBF should have one or more corresponding EBS.
- All actions performed by EBF should be a part of the EBS operation.
- EBF can only invoke or be invoked by another EBF or EBS. It never communicates with an ABCS directly. EBF encapsulates business logic amongst several participating applications. The AIA framework tries to minimize changes to the business logic artifacts while allowing the participating applications to keep changing. This can be done only if the EBF does not communicate with the ABCS directly.
- EBF can be invoked by other applications, requester ABCS, or another EBS.

**Business Process Execution Language (BPEL)** is a preferred technology to build business processes. In AIA, BPEL helps to build the asynchronous coordination in EBS. In addition, Oracle Service Bus is widely-used to build synchronous or one-way coordination among EBSs.

# EBF architecture

In the AIA architecture, EBS helps to expose the application functions as services using common framework components such as EBO and EBM. Exposing EBS as services may help client and application systems to interact with the provider application. However, it may not be enough in the enterprise infrastructure. While building enterprise-level solutions using AIA, there should be a variety of process requirements. AIA helps to build the processes or workflow requirements through Enterprise Business Flow.

Again, business flow means executing related business activities to meet a specific business goal. In AIA architecture, Enterprise Business Flow helps to build business flow/processes by composing multiple EBS services to meet a specific business process integration goals. Enterprise Business Flow itself can act as an EBS service, which will accept EBM as an input request and reply with EBM as a response. Alternatively, it can also build to accept non-canonical input requests and responses. If EBF is designed to process EBM schema as a request/response, the consumer should be another ABCS component or client application, which can communicate in EBM format. As EBS supports messaging in EBM format, EBF should invoke EBS and pass the EBM format as a request. EBF may not include human workflow in its processes since the context of the AIA is all about application integration. An EBF design becomes essential when an EBS operation translates into a complex operation that can span across EBOs.

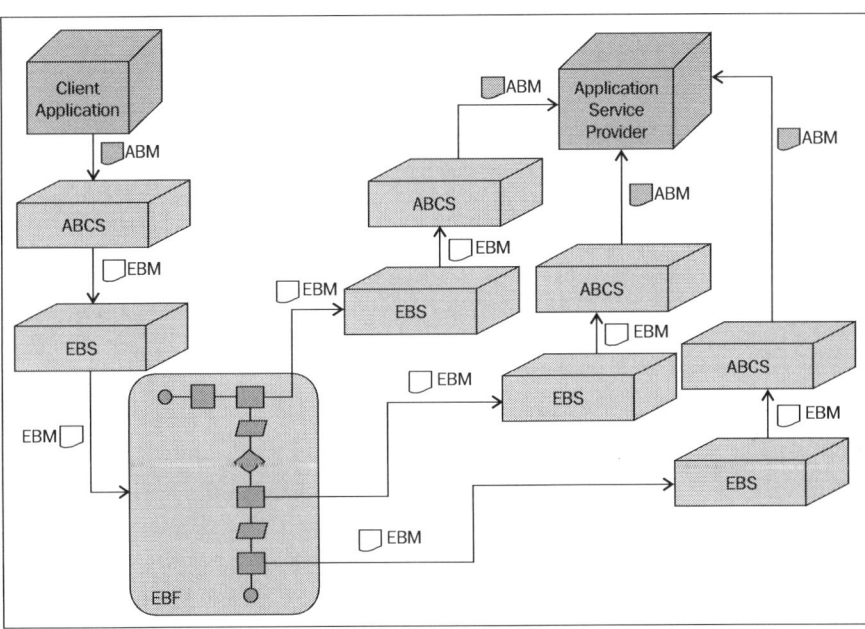

The preceding diagram shows the typical structure of the EBF in the AIA architecture. In the previous chapters we have seen the communication between requester application and provider application through requester ABCS, requester EBS, provider ABCS, and provider EBS. In order to build the business processes, EBF should compose multiple EBSs to build the process flow. In the preceding diagram, the EBF comprises of three EBSs to build the process flow. As the preceding diagram shows, EBF can process the EBM as input request and response.

If the EBF is designed to process EBM as requests and responses, ABCS or the client application can invoke it, which can process an EBM scheme. The major difference between EBS and EBF is that EBF is predominantly for process orchestration by consuming various services; whereas, EBS is for enabling the services in a standard message format such as EBM.

For better understanding let us walk through a real-time business scenario.

# Building Enterprise Business Flow

Developing processes flow or business flow requires identification of the list of services to be invoked through Enterprise Business Flow, then defining the service contract for the process flow, and finally building the process flow logic.

## Identifying service contract for EBF

As per AIA standard, EBF also should follow the top-down implementation approach. Therefore, the service contract should be defined before implementing Enterprise Business Flow. However, before that we should identify the use case for the EBF candidate. There are five steps that we must follow to implement the service contract for EBF, which are as follows:

1. Identifying the business process candidate from the given requirement is the potential first step.
2. Identify the message exchange pattern for the given identified process candidate so that the EBF satisfies the requirement.
3. Find the related Enterprise Business Message (EBM) scheme that can be used to define the request and response of the EBF. Sometimes, custom EBM or non-canonical EBM may be required to complete the given business process.
4. Construct the WSDL service definition for the EBF based on the identified MEP and EBM. JDeveloper can be used to design the WSDL for the given EBF.
5. Build the EBF by assembling the existing Enterprise Business Services through the BPEL service. In some cases, we may need to create new services to complete the business process requirements.

## Identifying the EBF candidate

Identifying the potential EBF candidate from the enterprise infrastructure requires extreme knowledge in the domain and business model. In the SOA world, the top-down approach implementation is widely accepted because this approach helps to implement the current enterprise business model in the architecture solution.

Similarly, top-down approach helps to identify the EBF candidates. In the EA world, one of the Enterprise Architecture (EA) domains is called as Business Architecture, which may help you to identify the potential business processes to implement in the enterprise infrastructure. The business architecture and business models help to identify the need for integration with the existing system architecture, which will help to identify the process or workflow. Alternatively, if we already defined the Enterprise Business Services, it is easy to compose the list of services to build the process model. In AIA context, EBF should be selected when there is a need of combining multiple EBS to meet a specific requirement or integration process—also, if there is a need for combining multiple EBOs that can be achieved by implementing an EBF.

# Creating the service contract for an EBF

The following steps should help you to build the EBF WSDL service contract using Oracle JDeveloper:

1. Open the JDeveloper, create a new application, and create a new SOA project. It should create an empty composite, shown as follows:

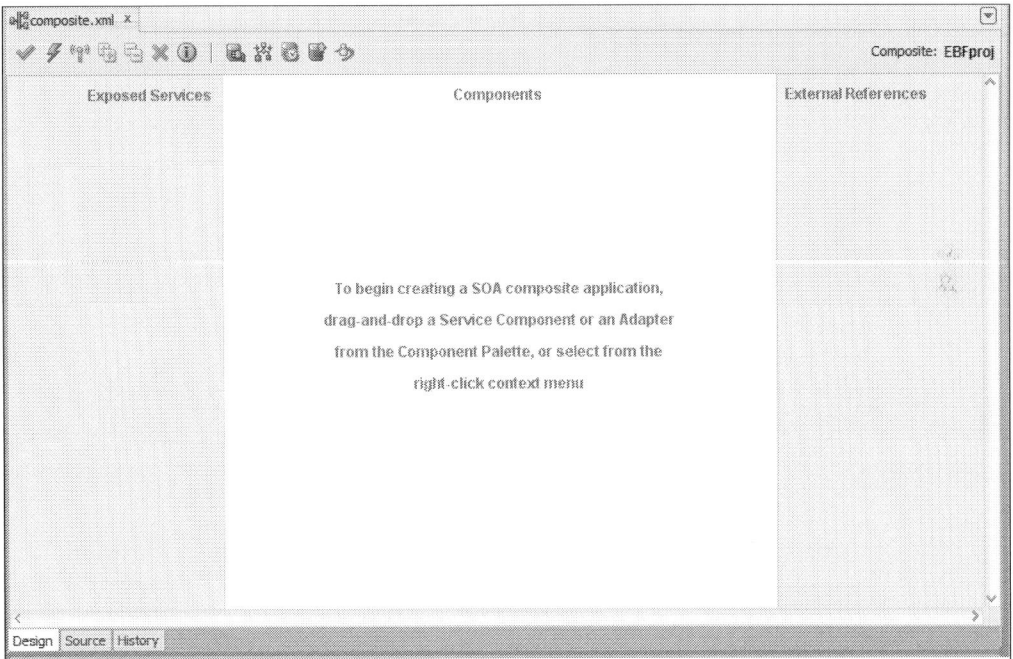

2. Now, create a new WSDL by selecting WSDL document from the **All Technologies** tab from the gallery:

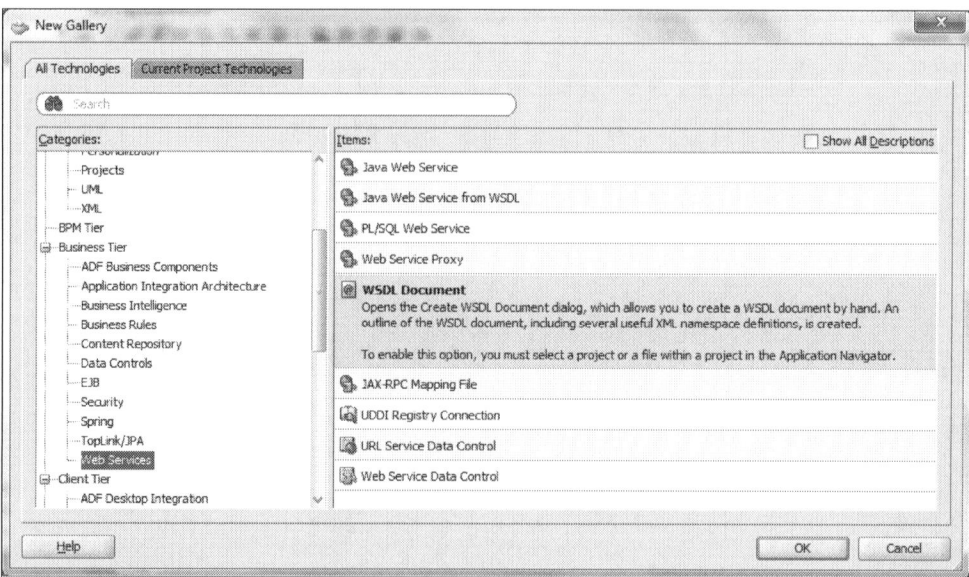

3. Once the WSDL document is created with proper AIA naming standards, it should appear in the WSDL design layout, shown as follows:

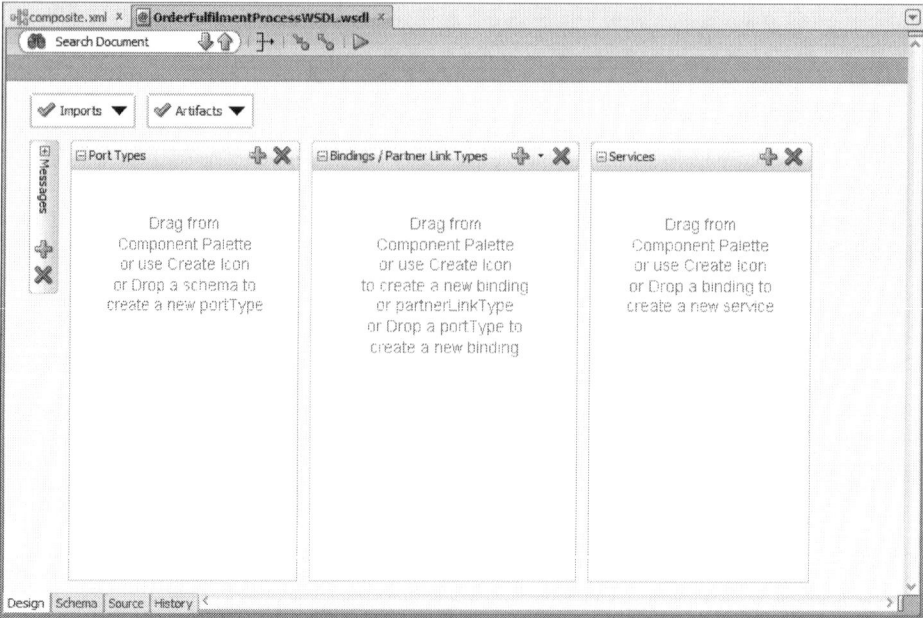

4. If the custom input and output schema is already designed for the given scenario then drag-and-drop the schema into the **Port Types** pane to create the component message model.

5. Alternatively, you can drag-and-drop the existing EBM schema (if that schema does solve your process requirement) in the **Port Types** pane to create the `PortType` and continue to build bindings, service, and so on. The constructed WSDL should look similar to the following screenshot:

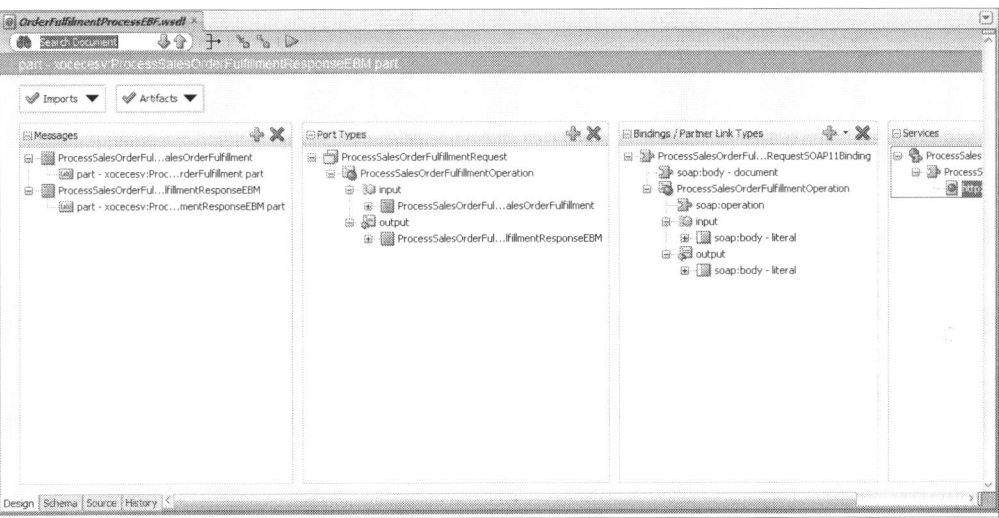

## Building EBF as BPEL Service

So far, we have been successful in the creation of the WSDL for the EBF process scenario. Now, we have to develop the business process flow by composing multiple valid EBSs using Oracle BPEL. Oracle BPEL is a primary tool, which is a part of Oracle SOA suite and helps to build business processes by composing multiple services available in the enterprise infrastructure.

Using Oracle BPEL, we can build EBF as synchronous message processes or asynchronous message processes. The simple logic is that if the service is blocked until a response is returned to the invoking point, it should be a synchronous service call. If the invoking point does not wait for the response and continues to exit, then EBF implementation should be an asynchronous call. Either way, it should be properly defined while designing the WSDL service contract for the given EBF.

*Enterprise Business Flow*

Now, we should follow the following steps to build the EBF using Oracle BPEL. As we already created the application, project, and WSDL in the JDeveloper, we will continue with the same structure. Otherwise, you will have to create a new application, an SOA project, and WSDL as per the preceding section:

1. Open the composite in the JDeveloper designer mode. The screen that appears should look similar to the following screenshot:

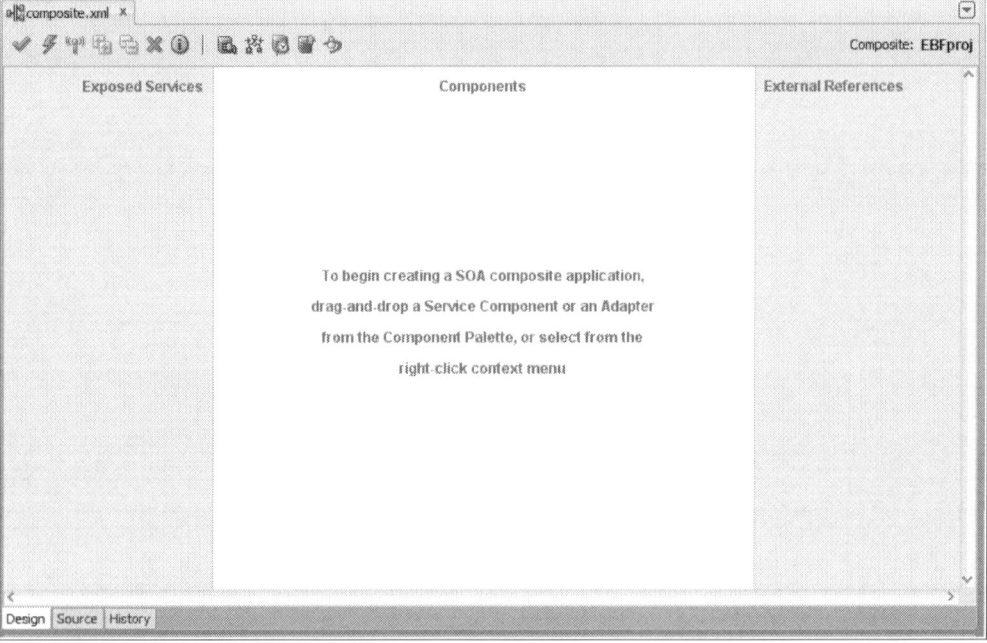

2. Now, drag-and-drop the BPEL component from the **Component** palette to the **Component** section of the **composite.xml**. It should trigger the **Create BPEL Process** window, shown in the following screenshot.

3. If we have already created WSDL for the EBF using EBM, then we should select **Base on a WSDL** from the **Template** drop-down. Otherwise, we should select either one of the MEP calls from the drop-down:

*Chapter 6*

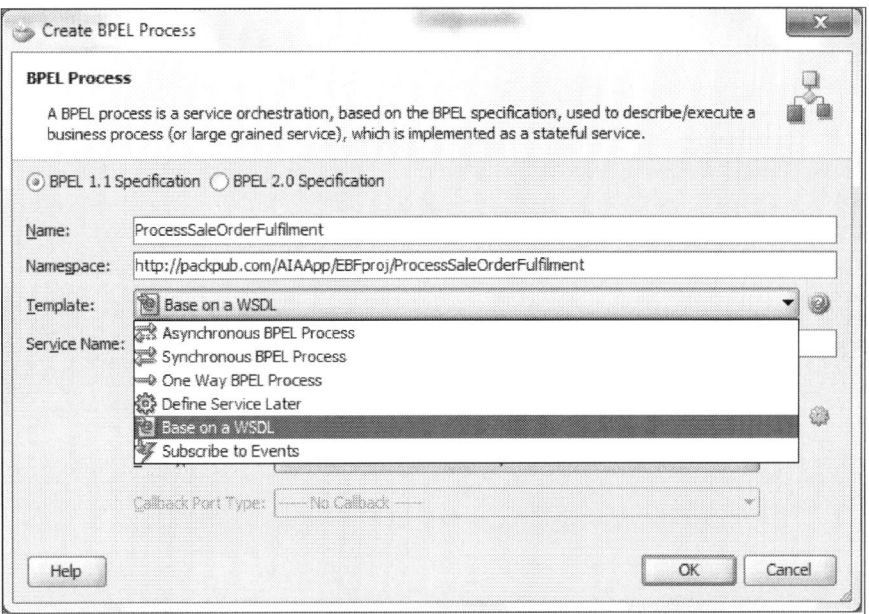

4. Once the BPEL is created in the composite with WSDL, it should appear in the composite, as shown in the following screenshot:

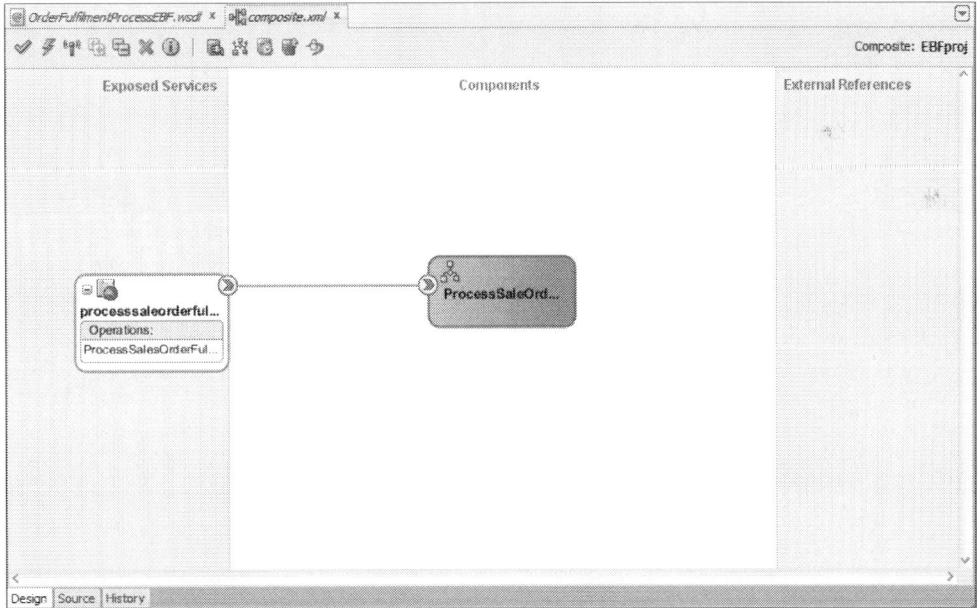

5. Now, we have to import the reference EBS services in the **External References** side of the composite to establish a connection between BPEL and external services. So, drag-and-drop the **Web Service** component from the **Component** palette to the **External References** side of the composite, which will trigger the **Create Web Service** window, which is shown as follows:

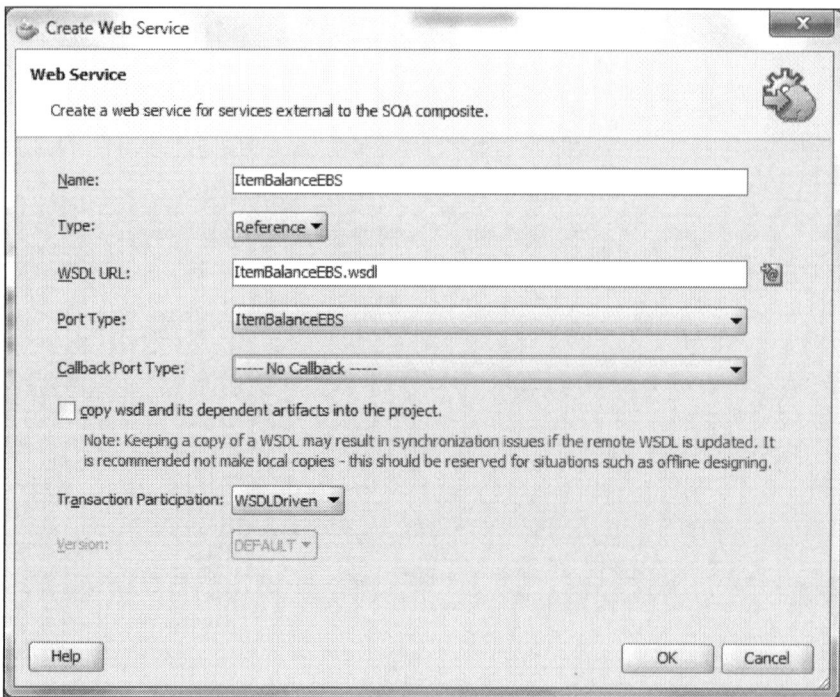

6. In order to configure all the parameters, include the WSDL URL. The WSDL URL should refer to the concrete URL (runtime service endpoint URL) of the EBS WSDL. This will import and generate necessary components in the composite application.

7. Once the EBS WSDL is imported into the composite, we should create the wire between the BPEL component and external reference component using a drag-and-drop of the link, shown as follows:

Chapter 6

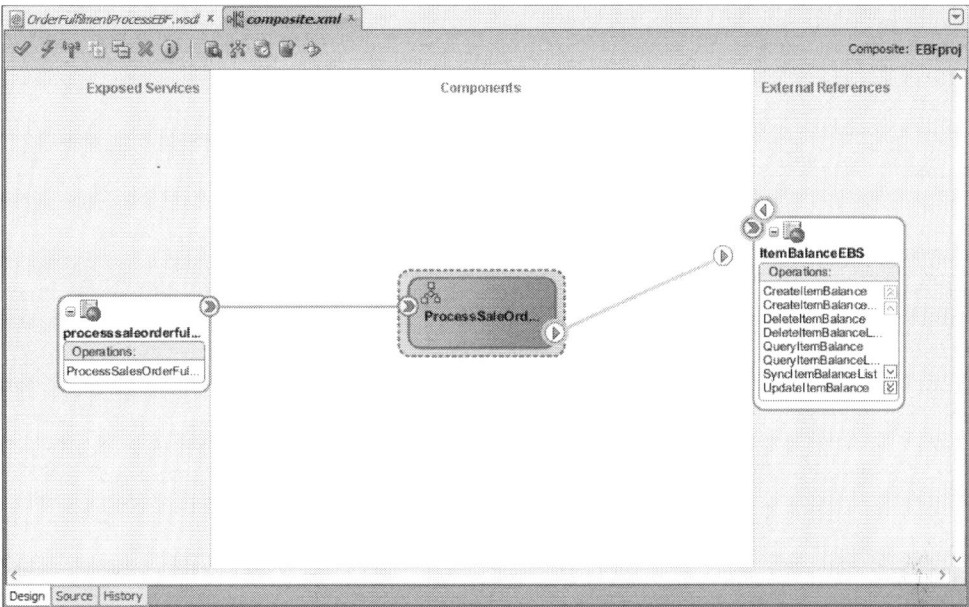

8. Once the wire is created between BPEL and the external service reference (EBS), carry out the steps 10 to 12 repeatedly in order to create connections with all necessary EBSs. The final composite may look similar to the following screenshot:

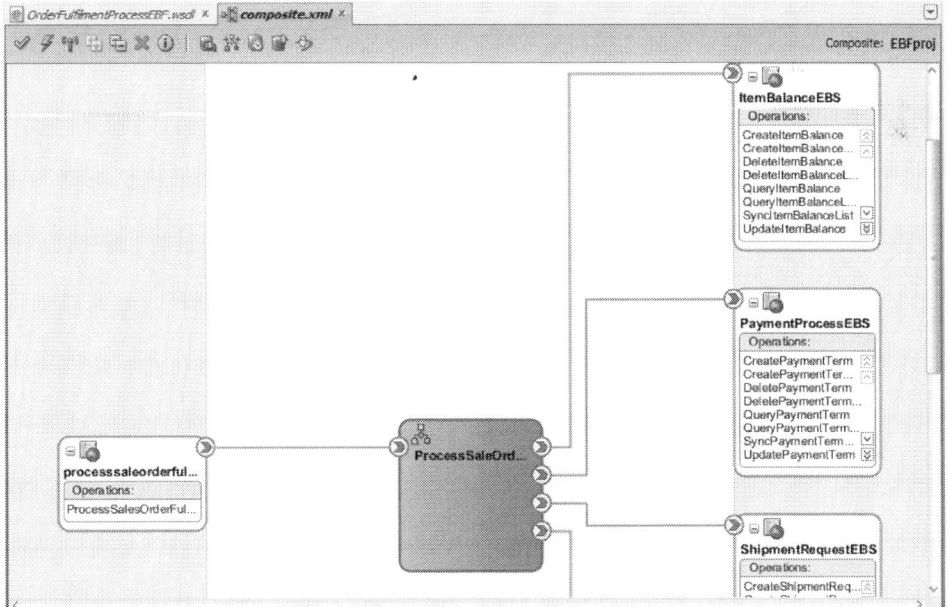

9. Until now, we have imported and created the connection between EBF WSDL, BPEL, and external EBS references. Now, we have to build the process flow in the BPEL to make the invocation between BPEL and EBS components as per the process requirement.

10. Open the BPEL process flow by double-clicking the BPEL component from the composite view. The initial process should appear as follows:

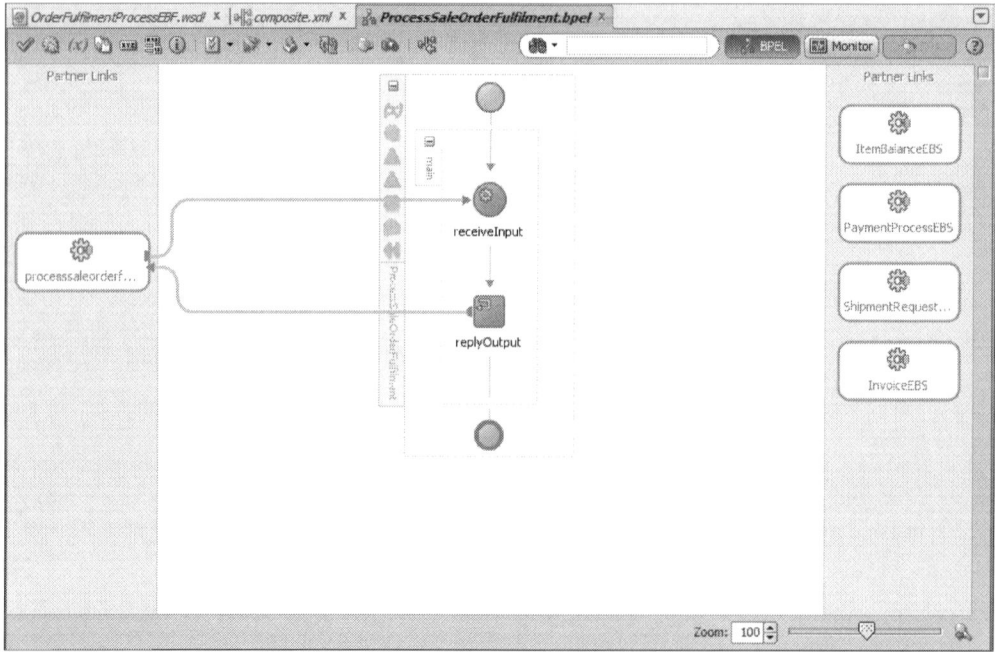

11. Build the requirement process by invoking the operation from the various EBSs as per the business process requirement and approach. Once you have completed the BPEL process, it may look similar to the following screenshot:

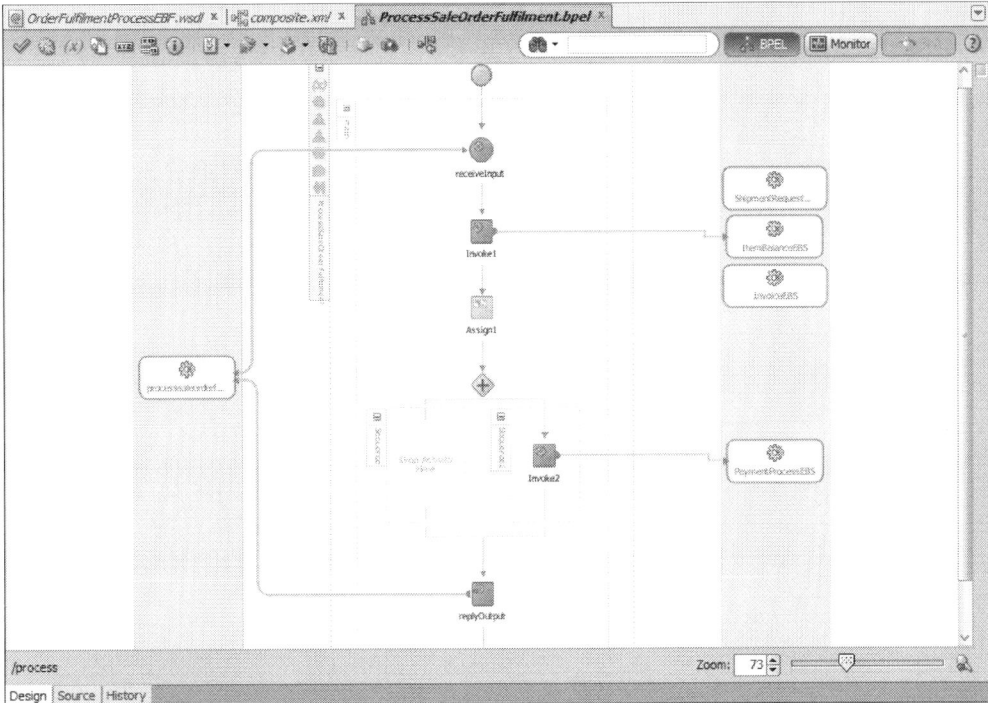

12. Now, we have successfully built the Enterprise Business Flow by composing multiple EBS operations to meet the integration business process.

# Business use case for EBF

The simple and common use case for business process is an order fulfillment scenario. In addition, it is easy to understand for those who are new to the business process. So, let us take order fulfillment as our use case here. In the order fulfillment scenario, an order is placed in the integration system, and the system does all the validation and processes automatically. The idea is to reduce the human intervention or manual entries in order to move the data from order management system to order systems to make sure the order is processed quickly.

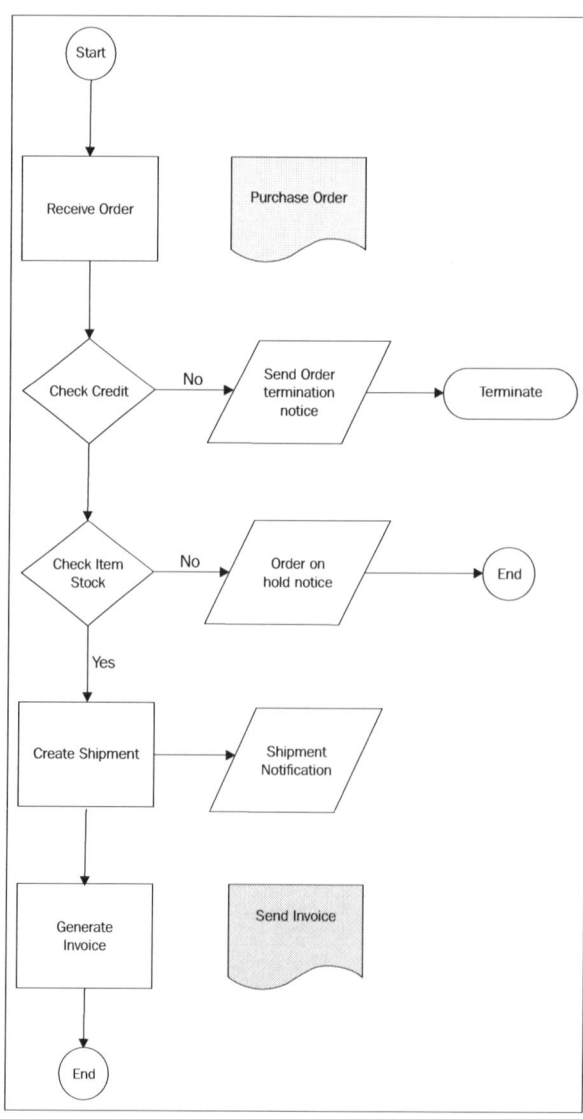

The preceding flow chart shows the simple version of order fulfillment, which is common across industries. In the process, the first step is to receive an order, then validate the customer credit, and process the payment. Once the payment is successful, validate the stock, create a shipment, and generate an invoice order and shipment. If there is any customer query or credit issue, terminates it as an invalid order, and send a notice to the customer about the order termination. If there is a shortage of stock in hand, then hold the order and notify the customer, so the orders on hold can be retriggered later by another process, once the stock is available. The following diagram shows the architectural view of the EBF for the requirement:

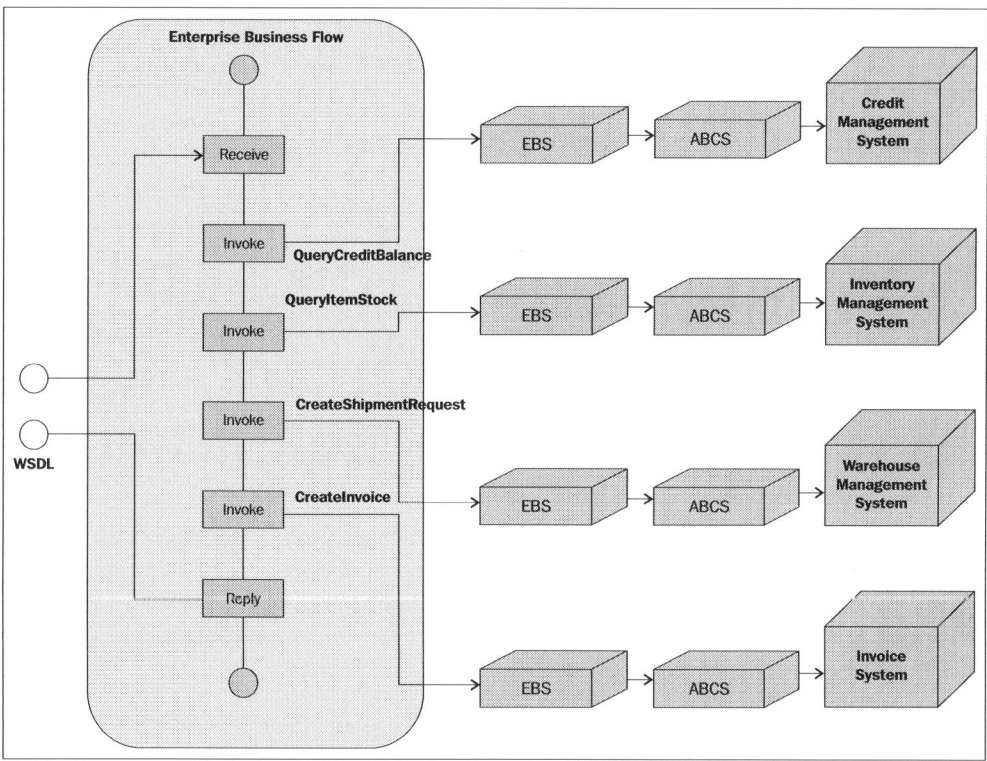

Now, the preceding architecture model should be built using Enterprise Business Flow. As we have seen in the preceding sections, we should build the required WSDL for the EBF and build the process flow using Oracle BPEL process designer. While designing the process flow, we should consider error handling and other messaging as well. The build solution should look similar to the following Oracle BPEL process:

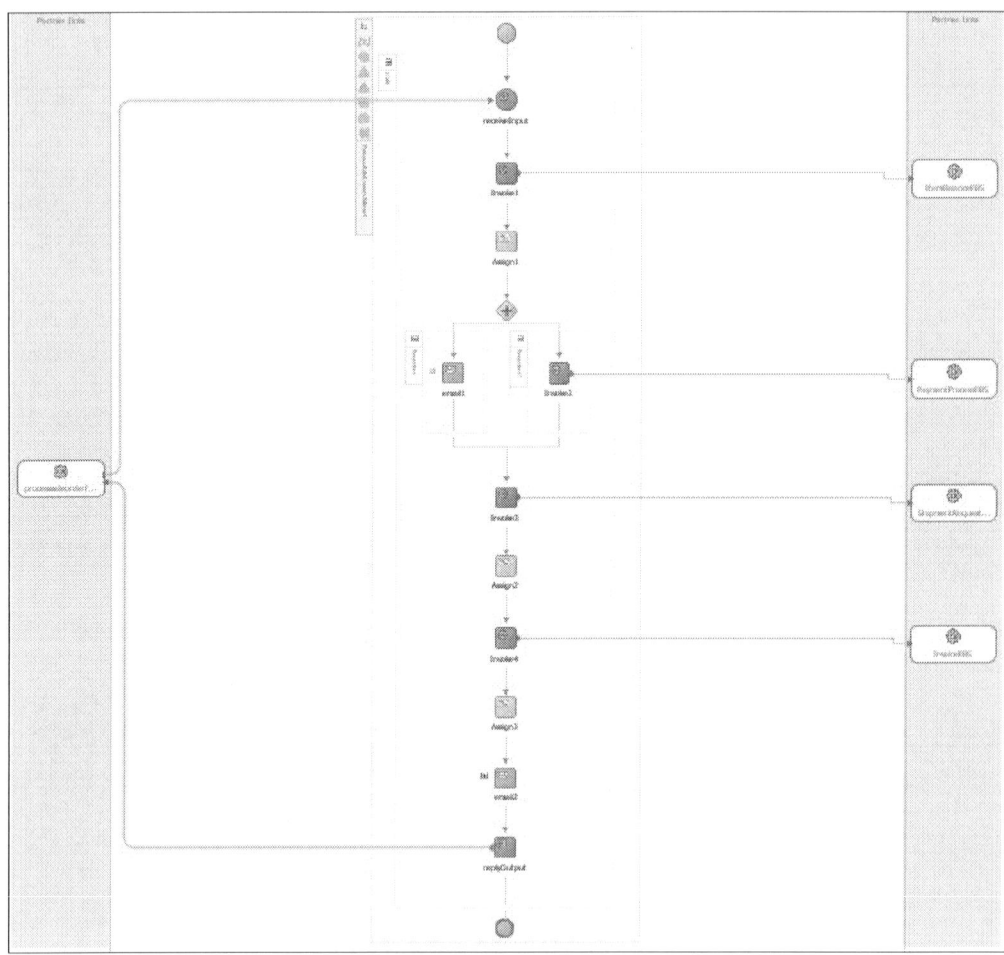

# Summary

In this chapter, we have seen the important features of AIA framework, which help us to achieve the process requirement by composing existing EBS assets. We have also seen characteristics of EBF, building various MEP types of business processes by using the Oracle BPEL process and EBS external services. However, apart from designing and developing AIA integration solution, we should also be aware of some other best practice approaches defined by AIA. The following chapters are going to explain version management, error management, patterns, and so on.

# 7
# AIA Security

So far, we have learned to build integration solutions using the Oracle AIA approach. However, just building an integration component or process does not completely fulfill the enterprise needs. Security is one of the important requirements that every enterprise integration solution must address—especially when exposing the services outside the enterprise network such as partner access, external hosting site, and so on.

Securing enterprise data and communication is also important to ensure data integrity while transferring over the wire. In this chapter, we are going to learn various security measures that Oracle AIA supports. We are going to explore and learn the following topics in this chapter:

- Levels of security implementation
- Security in Oracle SOA Suite
- Implementing security in AIA
- Securing ABCS

## Levels of security implementations

AIA components are built on top of fusion middleware, which supports a variety of security implementation through **Oracle Web Service Manager** (**OWSM**). Before exploring OWSM in detail, we need to understand a few fundamentals about security.

In general, security implementations can be applied in the integration processes at three levels such as data, access control, and transport mechanism:

- Transport level security
- Message level security
- Access control level security

We must understand some of the key differences between each level of security implementation in order to apply appropriate security measure for specific needs.

## Transport level security

In any type of integration, we must use some transport mechanism to transfer the data over wire. TCP, SOAP, HTTP, Message Queue (MQ), FTP, e-mail, and folder sharing are some of the common transport protocols and mechanisms, which are used to transfer data. When the data is confidential, it is obvious that we must take some kind of security mechanism to ensure that the data transferred over wire is secure. Hence, transport level security implementation is required when data confidentiality and integrity are important.

In a typical integration, securing the communication between source and target systems can be achieved by using Secure Socket Layer (SSL) mechanism. SSL provides a mechanism to secure the connection between source and target systems by allowing the systems to share and identify each other's identity. Once an identity is authorized by both systems, the secure layer of connection is established between the systems and all the data being transferred through that channel is encrypted. Only the intended recipient of the channel should be in a position to read the encrypted data.

## Message level security

Transport level security only ensures that data transferred from one point to another point is encrypted and secure at transport level. However, it does not ensure the security of data that is transferred over multiple layers and while application system generates that data. Message level security ensures end-to-end data security in addition with SSL features. It helps to secure the data from source generation to target processing stage. Hence, data transfer over various levels of intermediate layers is secure. Message security mechanism will enforce that messages are digitally signed and encrypted, so that only an authorized recipient can process the encrypted data using a secure key.

Message level security is highly appropriate if confidential data has to be transferred over message queue, FTP, folder sharing, and e-mail.

## Access control level security

This is all about providing resource access control to certain known recipients. Access level security is appropriate in service-based integration scenarios such as web service and HTTP-binding. Access level security can be implemented by defining the user group, users, and role-based privileges.

Based on the access level provided, the consumer or client application may get access to different levels of service resources. However, access control level security is all about providing access to the integration services but it does not enforce transport level security and message level security.

# Security in Oracle SOA Suite

As Oracle SOA Suite is based on SOA principles, by default Oracle SOA suite provides flexibility to separate the service layer from logical layer. There is a high possibility of implementing a variety of security models. Some of the security models supported by Oracle SOA are as follows:

- Authentication by verifying the identity of invoker
- Authorization to control various levels of resource access
- Privacy and data security by XML encryption
- Data integrity by using digital signature and cryptography

Oracle SOA suite provides efficient approach of implementing security in the service infrastructure using Oracle Web Service Manager (OWSM). OWSM provides functionality to define the security policies and applies those policies to the service component in order to enforce the policies. This approach helps the integration architect and development team to focus on achieving the functional requirement rather than security. At the same time it provides complete control to the enterprise security owners to implement the security as per the corporate IT policies.

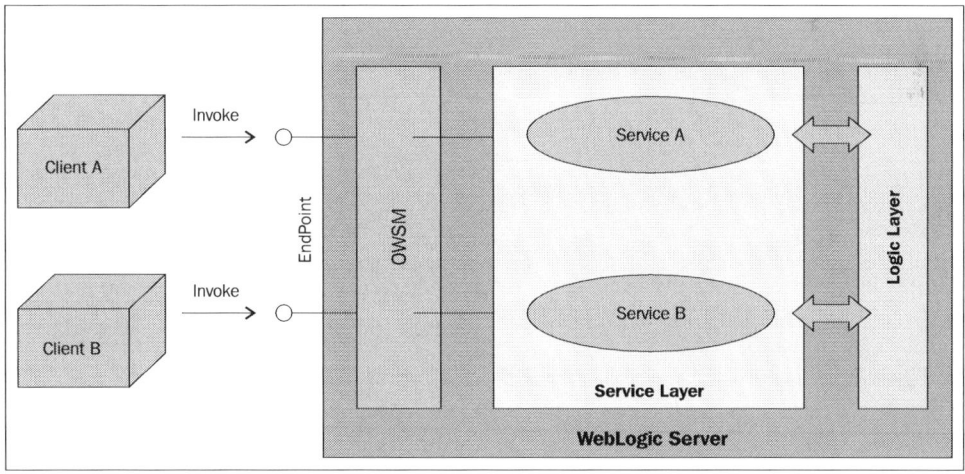

AIA Security

The preceding diagram shows the typical approach of OWSM in the service infrastructure. Once the security policies and security is configured in the enterprise service infrastructure, every invocation call from the client application will be intercepted by OWSM. Actually, the OWSM will validate the identity of the consumer against the security policy applied for that service either in the form of security tokens or digital signature. As the policy enforces OWSM, it collects the events and generates reports on the OWSM web screen.

> Note that Oracle SOA Suite 11g comes up with completely re-architected OWSM as a part of the WebLogic Server platform. In earlier versions of the Oracle SOA suite, OWSM was a separate standalone component.

# Implementing security in AIA

As Oracle AIA approach is fundamentally using Oracle SOA Suite components to build integrations, AIA supports all security approaches supported by the Oracle SOA Suite and OWSM. In addition, OWSM has predefined policies, which come with out-of-box Oracle SOA installation.

> Note that the Oracle AIA recommends implementing security policies and implementations separately through a declarative approach by using OWSM during deployment. It also recommends implementing the Web Service security rather than simple transport level security such as SSL.

The following sample architecture diagram will show the security implementation applied in both the requester side and the provider side of AIA model:

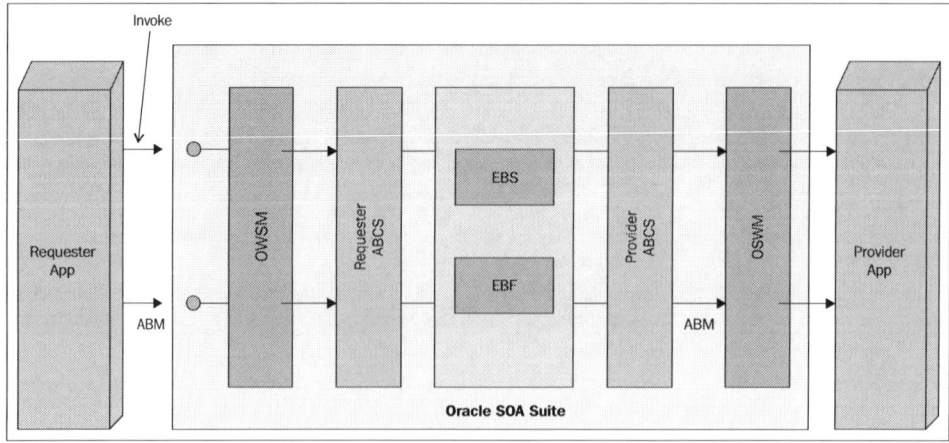

Oracle AIA recommends applying security in all the layers of services such as ABCS and in transport adapter services if any. In the diagram structure, the requesting application that connects to the requester ABCS should pass the security requirements to get access into the services. The OWSM plays as interceptor, which intercepts the requests coming from the requesting application to the requester ABCS and validates the security requirements, only if the security pass through OWSM allows the requesting application to make use of services available in the requester ABCS. The same security credentials are forwarded to the provider side of ABCS to get access into the provider application. The following are the security requests that the OWSM interceptor can handle; however, it is based on the level of implementation:

- Authentication request
- Authorization request
- Integrity
- Confidentiality
- SSL

Assuming that AIA integration is enabled for WS-Security, it requires adding the security parameters in the SOAP header. Based on the type of security such as authentication, integrity, and encryption, the SOAP header should carry the security parameters in both requests and responses. The following code snippet is the sample SOAP header for username password type WS-Security:

```
<wsse:Security env:devone="1">
  <wsse:UsernameToken wsu:Id="UsernameToken-QZUTlfISrMtw12">
    <wsse:Username>weblogic</wsse:Username>
    <wsse:Password Type="http://docs.oasis-
      open.org/wss/2004/01/oasis-200401-wss-username-token-
        profile-1.0#PasswordText">admin</wsse:Password>
  </wsse:UsernameToken>
</wsse:Security>
```

## Securing AIA services

Securing AIA services requires a systematic approach to make the security implementation smooth and standard. The following is the most common approach that we must follow:

1. First, we must identify the type and level of security required for our AIA infrastructure. Sometimes, security requirements might come as a part of the non-functional specification. Sometimes, it may be part of the functional requirement. Oracle AIA recommends using WS-Security for authentication, encryption, and integrity.

2. Oracle AIA comes with a predefined set of security policies, which we can apply as a global security policy in all services. Some of the predefined security policies are a perfect blend of different security models. We may have to select the appropriate combination based on the requirement.

3. The next step would be attaching the policies to the AIA services by using OWSM. OWSM provides easy configuration options to apply the security to the services based on custom or predefined policies.

4. In some cases, we may have to change the predefined security policies to meet the requirements. Configuring policies would be the next step if required.

5. Finally, validate the security implementation by invoking the services through service client or CAVS.

> Oracle AIA recommends that applying security in all AIA services may slow down the performance of the integration. If performance is one of the success criteria, then apply security to AIA services that are consumed outside of the corporate network and secure corporate network.

Oracle AIA services are out-of-the-box secured. If security is not a major concern then enable the security at appropriate levels.

Oracle AIA uses eXtensible Access Control Markup Language (XACML) as structure to exchange access control requirements between requester and provider applications. XACML is a declarative policy language defined in XML that describes interpretation of the policies. XACML context mechanism is recommended by AIA for exchanging access control information.

> Note that if you are new to XACML, you must have some basic understanding of the WebLogic context to execute security calls with the AIA services. This book does not cover the fundamentals of XACML. We recommend reading the **Oracle WebLogic** security administration guide for better understanding.

## Applying predefined policies to AIA services

Oracle Web Service Manager has a set of predefined policies. Depending upon the security requirement, we may use the existing predefined policies. The following steps will help you to attach the security policy for an AIA service from a set of predefined policies existing in OWSM:

*Chapter 7*

1. As OWSM 11g is part of the WebLogic Enterprise Manager 11g, we must start the AIA WebLogic instance and log in to **Enterprise Manager 11g**, as shown in the following screenshot:

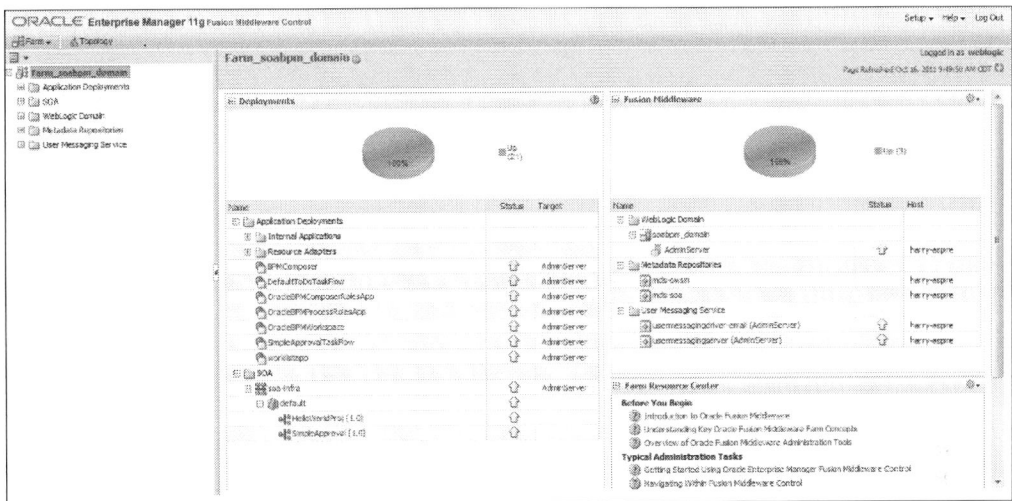

2. Select the **AIA Service [1.0]** package that you have deployed in the server, and select the **Policies** tab, as shown in the following screenshot:

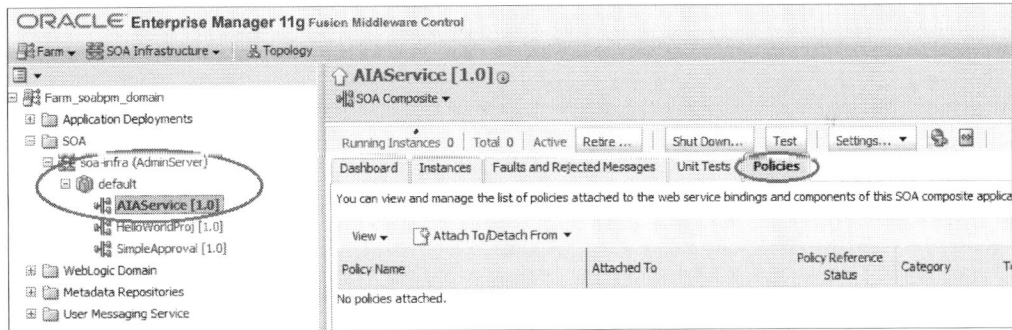

[ 149 ]

3. Now, select a process from the **Attach To/Detach From** drop-down menu. This helps to apply the policy in the process level instead of service endpoint. Depending upon the requirement you may apply policies at the service level, the process level, or the global level:

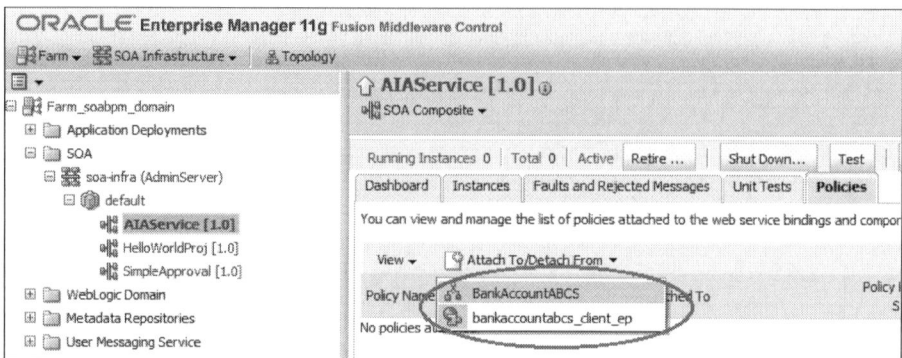

4. Once you select the process or service endpoint, it should pop-up a new window, shown as follows. In that window, you can find the list of available policies including predefined policies:

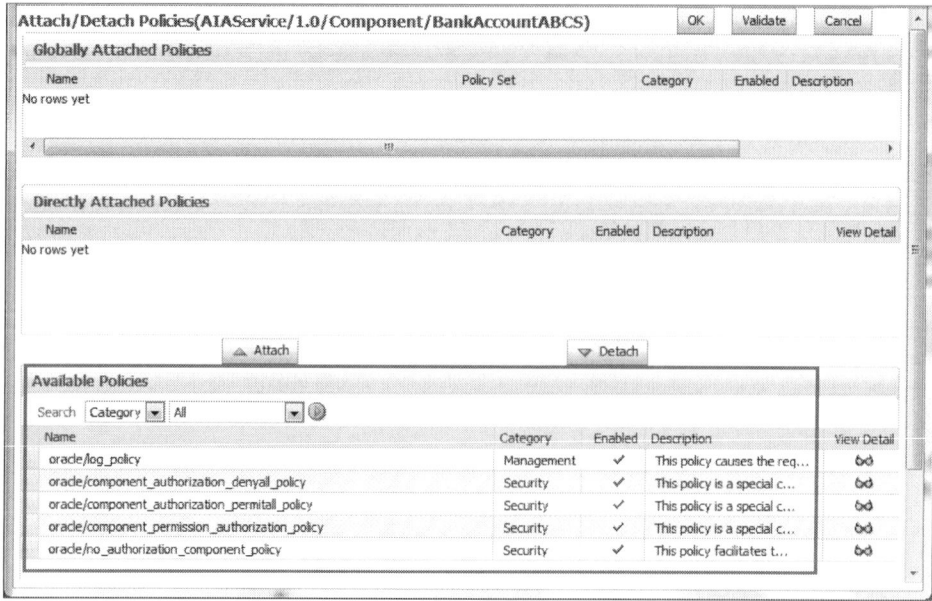

5. Now you can apply the required security policy depending upon the requirement. Select the policies one by one and click on the **Attach** button on top of the policies list. This will attach the policies with services shown, as follows:

Chapter 7

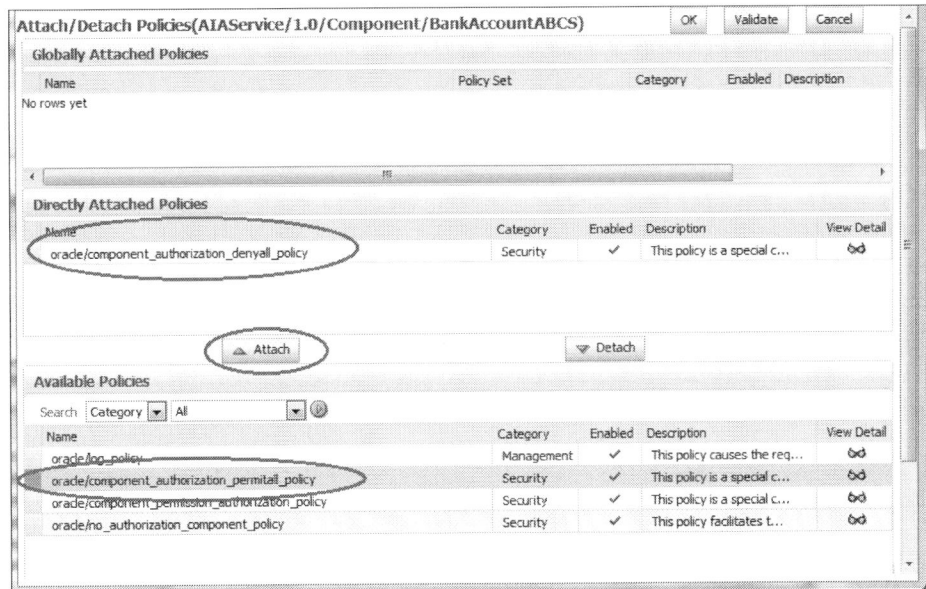

6. Once you have attached all required policies to the services, click on the **Validate** button on the top of the screen to validate the security attachment. If it is successfully validated it should display an information box showing that **Validation is successful**:

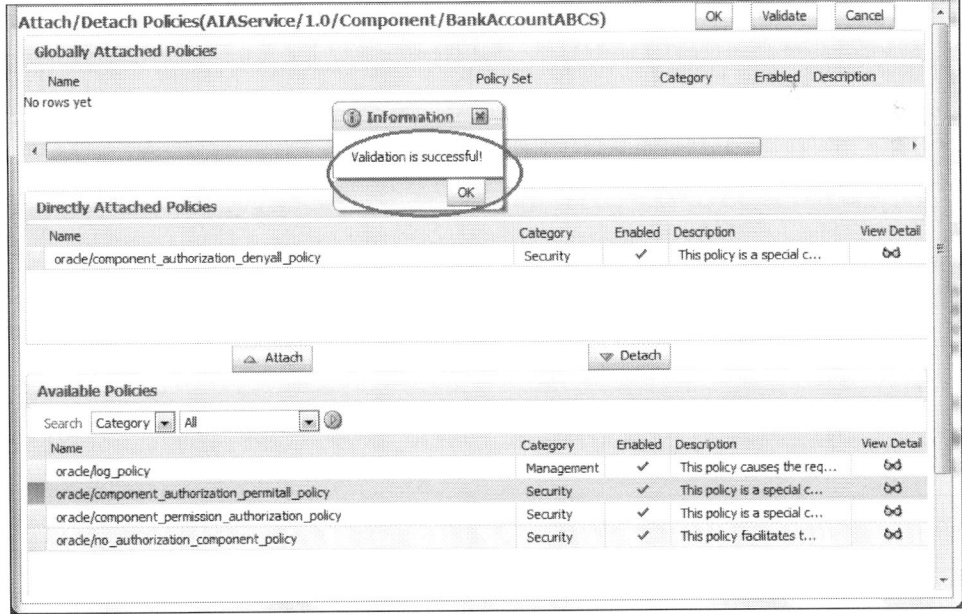

7. Once validated, click on **OK** to close the window. Now security policies are attached to the service endpoint.

# Securing ABCS

In the AIA approach, securing ABCS is the recommended approach as ABCS is interacting with the requester application and provider application. In the AIA security context, applying uniform security in all the requester and provider application levels will bring a more standardized way of exchanging security credentials across infrastructure. Executing security credentials from requester ABCS to the provider ABCS through EBS and EBF requires a process:

- We must transform the application security context into standard format in requester ABCS.
- Once it is transferred to the standard format, it should propagate the standard security context from requester ABCS to provider ABCS through EBS and EBF.
- Finally, transform back from the standard security format to application security context to facilitate the application understanding.

Applying security in the ABCS is a two-step approach. We must apply security in the requester ABCS and provider ABCS services. There are some fundamental points we must be aware of before starting work on the ABCS security. In order to apply security in the requester ABCS:

- In most of the cases, the requester application might not follow the standard defined in the XACML. So, the requester ABCS should map and transform the application authorization information in the XACML format.
- The requester ABCS should always call the security services with application information in XACML to receive the standard authorization. This approach also helps to standardize the security implementation at a global level.
- Once the authorization is received from the security services, the requester ABCS should insert the authorization information in the EBM header as part of the request while calling the EBS services.

Similar to the requester ABCS, the provider ABCS also should handle certain standard processes to facilitate the interaction with the provider application. The provider ABCS should call the security services in the standard authorization format, but receive the request in the XACML format. In order to facilitate the provider applications, the provider ABCS should send the security information in the application-specific format if the application does not support XACML.

ABCS security implementation might change depending upon the message exchange pattern followed in the ABCS services. We must select the appropriate security approach depending upon the pattern.

>  Note that too many security restrictions may slow down the performance of the service and make it difficult for legacy or older systems to consume the services. Oracle recommends limiting the security implementation to the services, which are access and data-critical.

Also, Oracle recommends that you should avoid security for services that are internal to the integration systems and if the consumer is another service or process.

## Summary

We have touched some fundamental information that we must understand while designing and developing the AIA approach of integration. In this chapter, we learned the types of securities applicable to AIA services, applying security policies from OWSM, and ABCS security. In the next chapter, we are going to explore the version management approaches required to manage the AIA components during the development and maintenance phases.

# 8
# Versioning

In the previous chapters, we learned about various AIA components required to develop the AIA integration processes and services. In this chapter, we are going to understand schema, and service versioning and management that are important to establish the mature practice of managing enterprise integrations. We are going to explore the following in this chapter:

- Importance of version management
- Web Service versioning
- AIA versioning

## Importance of version management

In a modern enterprise world, the system functions and processes continue to change in alignment with business demands, change requests, and bug fixes. It is very important that IT has to change quickly in accordance with enterprise business expectations. Version management and control is an important practice followed by software development groups in order to control the changes of documents and program code. Over a period of time, various version management approaches were followed by various industries. Now in the revolution of Web Service and **Service-Oriented Architecture (SOA)**, version management becomes more complicated. Due to architecture complexity, Web Service and SOA application implementations require a different approach for effective version management and change control management. The real success of Web Service and SOA is in the hands of the consumer consumption. Therefore, we need to understand the service version management approach before we get into AIA versioning.

## Services version management

Before we jump into AIA versioning and techniques, we must understand the importance of version management and web service versioning. In the IT industry, every IT professional must have exposure and experience in managing the versions of each deliverable including application code. However, web services version management requires a slightly different approach.

Service version management is a little tricky compared to than the traditional application version management. In application version management, it is always one version of the application that will be deployed and will be used by the user community. Therefore, it is easy to force the user community to make use of the latest version. However, in the SOA approach, multiple versions of the services are required to be supported in order to provide backward compatibilities support to the consumers. In addition, it is a limitation to force the consumer applications to upgrade according to the latest version of service upgradation.

In the SOA design pattern, Canonical versioning patterns help to provide backward compatibility support to the service and message model, which helps to minimize the impact in the consumer community.

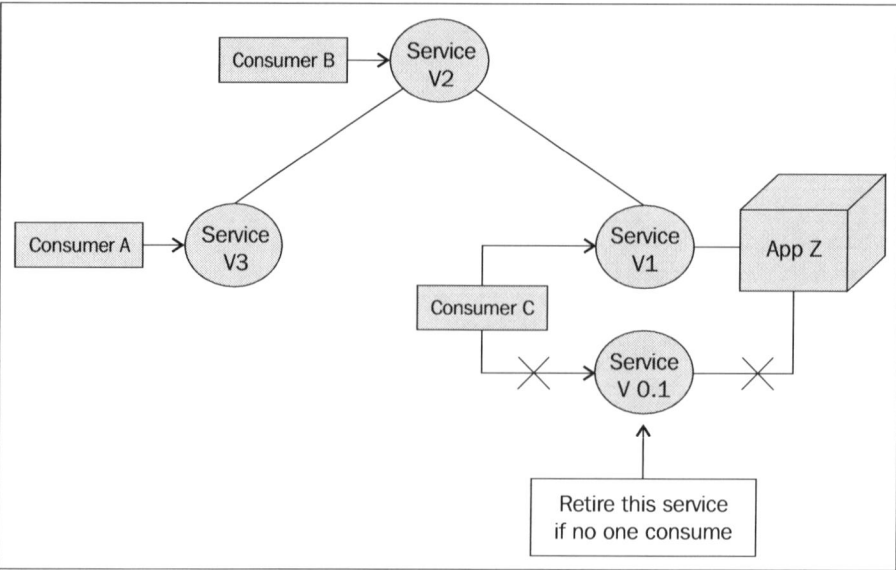

The above diagram represents one of the approaches followed to provide continuous support to the consumers' community in previous versions of the services. Assume that an application Z provides service which is consumed by various service consumers applications. The initial version was V0.1, and over a period the application service contracts are modified, which results in versions such as V1, V2, and V3. Consumer A upgraded to version V3 and consumer B to V2, respectively. Once Consumer C updated the consumption from V0.1 to V1, no consumer is now using the V0.1. It is a perfect time to retire the service of V0.1 from the deployment. Similarly, once Consumer C upgrades to V2, service contract V1 will be retired. This approach provides independence to the consumer to follow its own lifecycle.

In order to differentiate the various versions of the service contract, the approach that industries follow is to include the version numbering in the contract namespace definition, as follows:

```
targetNamespace =
  "http://ns.example.org/Enterprise/App/[Integration Name]
  /v[Version Number]"
```

The creation and implementation of newer versions requires versioning standardization and governance. Therefore, this approach requires effective discovery and repository mechanism to maintain various versions of the service's contract.

As Oracle AIA is based on an Oracle SOA suite infrastructure, Oracle AIA supports to managing various versions of service definitions, service contract descriptions, and message scheme models as best practices.

## AIA versioning

Oracle maintains versioning in the AIA components such as **Enterprise Business Objects** (**EBO**), EBM, ABCS, EBF, and EBS. In order to make it backward-compatible and continue support to existing AIA customers, AIA came up with all its previous versions of components. Therefore, we must choose an appropriate version of the EBO, EBM, or EBS to make it work with existing AIA integration solution or a new solution. Before getting into exploring EBO and EBS versioning, we should understand the versioning approach followed by Oracle AIA. AIA versioning enables the SOA artefacts to evolve over a period of time.

## AIA versioning approach

Oracle AIA manages different versions of EBO and EBS components to provide backward support compatibility. In detail, Oracle AIA out-of-the-box approach brings major and minor versions of EBO and EBS components. In AIA, each EBO and EBS has its own release lifecycle, so each object has its own versioning that might be used by different versions of other components. The EBO version numbers are not aligned with any of the Oracle application or product releases. For example, Oracle AIA does not release newer versions of EBO and EBS components whenever a newer version of Oracle Enterprise Business Suite is released. However, Oracle AIA releases support both older and newer version of Oracle EBS functions and newer version of EBS functions. Therefore, this approach allows limiting the application's dependencies and continuous growth of each individual component.

Each Oracle AIA version number comes with a combination of major and minor version numbers. The major and minor terminologies are used to refer to the characterizations of the changes only. The first portion of version number always shows the major version number and the second portion of the version shows the minor version number, as shown in the following screenshot:

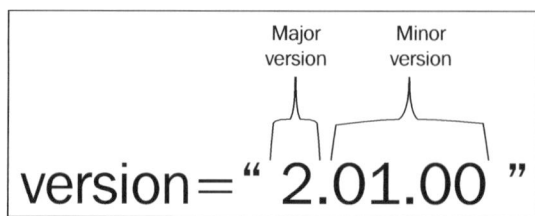

Oracle AIA defined certain standards for releasing major and minor versions of AIA components. The following points would trigger the major release of Oracle AIA EBO and EBS components:

- If there is any change in the meaning or semantics of components
- The addition of new mandatory components that cannot be avoided during messaging
- Removal of any existing mandatory component that triggers changes in the messaging
- Change in the sequence of the content or schema model
- Change in the data types of any attribute or element

Similar to major versioning, there are certain points that might trigger a change in the minor version number, as follows:

- Adding any optional component such as element or attribute in the existing schema or service model
- Extending enumeration
- Change or removal of initialization, sequence of approach, and so on
- Fixing of bugs
- Language enhancements

Each single major version a of schema model such as EBO must undergo several iterative changes that force a change in the minor version number. A major version of EBO contains changes that make it impossible to support prior releases. Therefore, the consumer application may not work with new releases of a version that requires modification. That means the consumer application built against major version such as 1.0 will work with changes in the minor numbers of the major release such as 1.1, 1.22, but cannot work with version 2.0. Let us understand a little more about AIA schema (EBO/EBM) and service (EBS) versioning standards.

## Schema (EBO/EBM) versioning

Oracle is one of the biggest business application providers. Based on many years of experience in various business domains, Oracle has built business objects specific to each domain and business function that meet a variety of enterprise businesses. Such business objects form EBO components in AIA. However, each EBO is undergoing continuous growth and is fine-tuned through adding and removing contents, and changing semantics or elements of the EBO according to specific business needs. EBOs are predominantly modified to meet product enhancements, bug fixes, and to support new technologies and languages.

In AIA, each EBO has its own namespace element. This gives an advantage to the EBO components to maintain their own release lifecycle. The namespace of the EBO should be in the following format:

```
http://xmlns.oracle.com/EnterpriseObjects/Core/EBO/
   [ObjectName]/v[Version Number]
```

*Versioning*

Now we have to explore the physical structure of the EBO components in the AIA installation to identify the release versions:

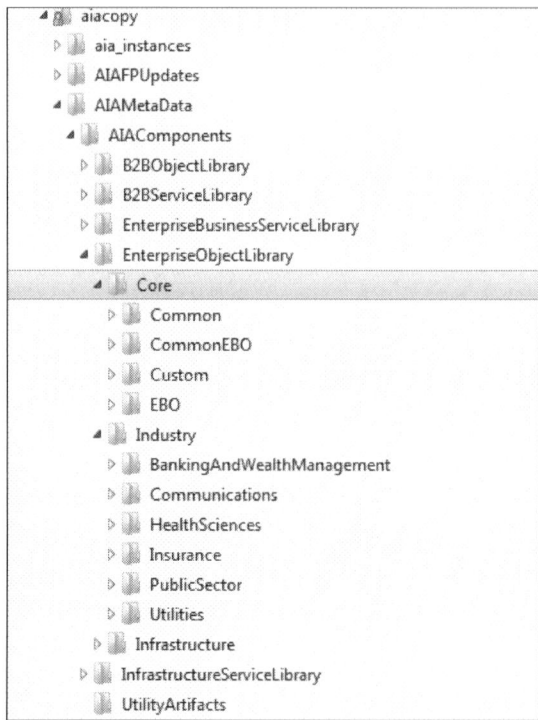

Go to the `$AIA_HOME/\AIAMetaData\AIAComponents\EnterpriseObjectLibrary\Core\EBO` folder. This folder should have all the EBO and EBM components separated by business functions in folders under the name of each particular business function.

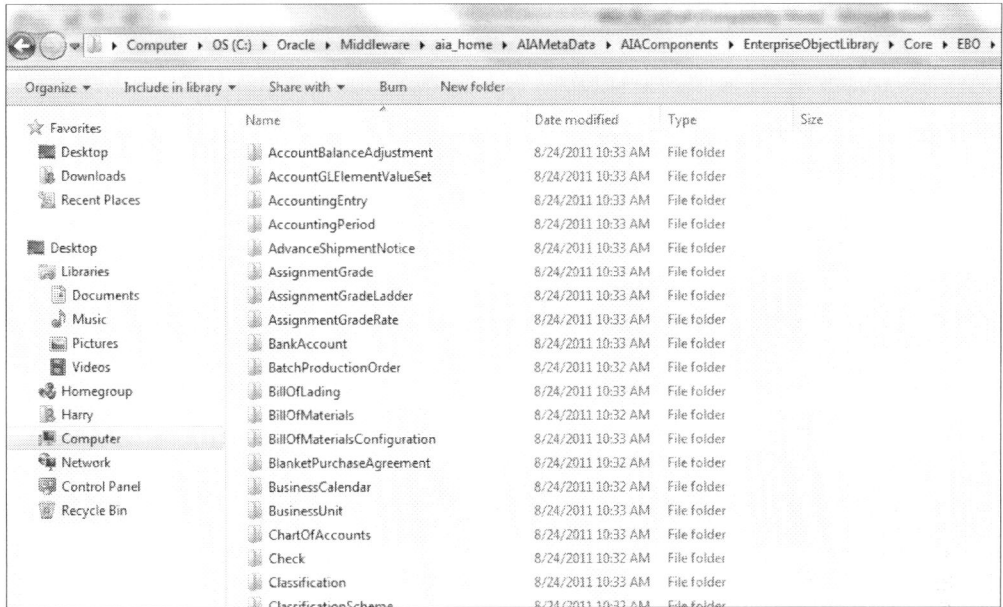

If we open any one of the folders from this place, we could see the subsequent folders in the name of the version number such as in the preceding screenshot. If a particular component does not have more than one version, then only the one version of the folder should exist. For example, if we open the `AccountBalanceAdjustment` folder, we should see two subfolders in the name of V1 and V2. This shows that `AccountBalanceAdjucement` objects are available in two versions, that is, version 1 and version 2. If we open the latest version folder from here, we should see both EBO and EBM objects.

Open any one of the EBO object files in the editor application, in which the first portion of the element must show the namespace and version number, as shown in the following code:

```
<xsd:schema
  xmlns:corecom="http://xmlns.oracle.com/EnterpriseObjects
    /Core/Common/V2"
xmlns:coreaccountbalanceadjustmentcust="http://xmlns.oracle.com/
    EnterpriseObjects/Core/Custom/EBO/AccountBalanceAdjustment/V2"
  xmlns:corecomcust="http://xmlns.oracle.com/EnterpriseObjects
    /Core/Custom/Common/V2"
  xmlns:corecomEBO="http://xmlns.oracle.com/EnterpriseObjects/
    Core/CommonEBO/V1" xmlns:xsd="http://www.w3.org/2001/XMLSchema"
    xmlns:svcdoc="http://xmlns.oracle.com/Services/Documentation/V1"
    xmlns="http://xmlns.oracle.com/EnterpriseObjects/Core/EBO/
    AccountBalanceAdjustment/V2"
```

```
    targetNamespace="http://xmlns.oracle.com/EnterpriseObjects/Core
    /EBO/AccountBalanceAdjustment/V2" elementFormDefault="qualified"
    attributeFormDefault="unqualified" version="2.01.00"
>
```

In the preceding schema definition, the `targetNameSpace` attribute should hold the EBO reference namespace and version number. If we notice from the above schema, then the version number specified as `"2.01.00"`. This includes the major version number as `"2"` and minor version number as `"01.00"`.

Furthermore, from the preceding schema definition, if we refer to the `xmlns:corecomEBO` attribute, then that should refer to the version 1 of `commonEBO` component. This is because even though this EBO component belongs to a major version of V2, it does refer the `commonEBO` of version 1. Additionally, EBM always refers to the major version of the EBO component.

## Services (EBS) versioning

Similar to EBO versioning, AIA maintains versioning in the EBS libraries as well. AIA also allows upgrading the EBS versions through various criteria similar to EBO. Any change in the interface definition and implementation could force an upgrade in service contracts that leads to the creation of a new version of the EBS.

As we have seen earlier, co-locating multiple similar EBS services in the same domain is possible through the maintenance of different versions. Deploying multiple versions of the same business services allows the application consumers to use any one of the versions, which serve their needs. In addition, this approach helps to deploy a new version of services in the enterprise that does not immediately force the consumer to switch to the newer version. This approach helps enterprise integration solutions to maintain their own development lifecycle.

It is time to explore the physical structure of the EBS component in the AIA installation to identify the release versions.

Go to the `$AIA_HOME/\AIAMetaData\AIAComponents\ EnterpriseBusinessServiceLibrary\Core\` folder. This folder should have all the EBS components separated by a business service function in folders.

*Chapter 8*

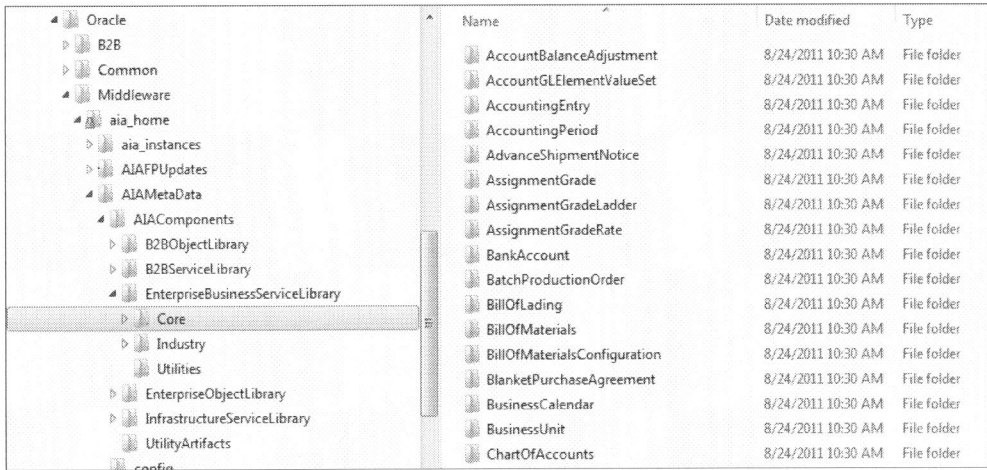

Open any one of the EBS WSDL file in the editor application, in which the first portion of the element must show the namespace and version number, as follows:

```
<definitions
xmlns="http://schemas.xmlsoap.org/wsdl/"
  xmlns:xsd="http://www.w3.org/2001/XMLSchema"
  xmlns:soap="http://schemas.xmlsoap.org/wsdl/soap/"
  xmlns:svcdoc="http://xmlns.oracle.com/Services/Documentation/V1"
  xmlns:corecom="http://xmlns.oracle.com/EnterpriseObjects/Core
  /Common/V2"
 xmlns:ebo="http://xmlns.oracle.com/EnterpriseObjects/Core/EBO
   /AccountBalanceAdjustment/V2"
xmlns:ebs="http://xmlns.oracle.com/EnterpriseServices/Core
   /AccountBalanceAdjustment/V2" name="AccountBalanceAdjustmentEBSV2"
   targetNamespace="http://xmlns.oracle.com/EnterpriseServices
   /Core/AccountBalanceAdjustment/V2">
```

From the preceding namespace definition, if we notice the `targetNamespace` declaration, it should show the version number as V2. This WSDL contract definition is the latest version of the `AccountBalanceAdjustment` function. Therefore, if there is any major change in the message EBO and EBMs that should help to upgrade the integration services to major versions.

## ABCS versioning

AIA out-of-box installation includes all the versions of EBO, EBM component, and the latest version of the service contract (EBS). However, ABCS will be designed and built during the implementation by the development group. Therefore, Oracle suggests guidelines to manage similar versioning mechanisms in the ABCS as well. The following points are provided as guidelines to be followed while implementing and managing ABCS:

- Maintain new service with version suffix in the name of the composite and service components
- The target namespace in the ABCS service WSDL should represent the version number similar to EBS
- Maintain ABCS version numbering independent of the application version number
- Concurrent version number should be avoided especially while two or more teams implement similar ABCSs
- ABCS should not have multiple version incompatible contracts among versions
- The application systems should not adopt more than one version of similar activity through a specific role (requester or provider)
- ABCS should not have more than one service with different business logic, but the same name
- In sequence, a change made to ABCS without changing the version suffix should support backward-compatible
- Oracle supports using Oracle Enterprise Repository as central discovery repository to maintain and manage different versions of ABCS effectively

## Summary

As we all know, version management is one of the best practices that we should follow as part of the software development lifecycle. From the AIA point of view, version management is a key approach which helps to build a completely independent release lifecycle for each integration component and provides service backward compatibility and availability. In this chapter, we learned about how Oracle AIA manages versioning control in EBO and EBS components and its advantages. The next chapter is about design patterns, which is important while designing the AIA integration implementation.

# 9
# AIA Design Patterns

Design patterns are proven solutions for commonly-occurring problems in software engineering. Design pattern solutions are not a finished product or code which can be deployed in the infrastructure of an enterprise, but they are solutions in the form of descriptions. Fundamentally, design pattern solutions are a software programming language independent solution. However, most of the language-specific frameworks and products support the implementation of design patterns effectively. Design pattern solutions help to implement the solutions for commonly-known problems without putting any effort in research or trails runs. The most efficient software design approach includes identification of the appropriate design patterns to avoid common problems. Design patterns are grouped based on the nature of the common problem and solution mechanisms.

Similarly, there is variety of patterns defined for common issues in the area of integration solution. Oracle AIA is the best of breed of framework that supports different communication patterns during integration, which simplify the implementation. In the previous chapters, we have seen some of the patterns as a part of development steps. In this chapter, we are going to see little more about various patterns supported by Oracle AIA Foundation Pack 11g R1.

Oracle AIA FP provides design pattern solutions in the following areas:

- AIA message processing patterns
- AIA assets centralization patterns
- AIA assets extensibility patterns

We will walk through every pattern which belongs to each of the preceding categories. The following sections will cover the issues, solutions, and architecture approaches.

# AIA message processing patterns

The message processing patterns are related to the communication channel and protocols, which help to implement a specific format of the communication model. In a typical web application, request and response is the common communication pattern that is used. However, integration solutions require different formats of communication as the communication between these systems are independent of system functionalities. AIA message processing pattern covers the following communication pattern models:

- Synchronous request-response pattern
- Asynchronous fire-and-forget pattern
- Asynchronous delayed response pattern
- Guaranteed delivery pattern

# Synchronous request and response pattern

**Synchronous request-response** communication model is a very common pattern in the web world that everyone may have come across. In a typical web technology, we request the query from the web server and wait for the response from the server. Unless the server responds, we do not proceed to the next task (except for timeout scenario). Once the server processes the request, it prepares the response and sends it back to the requester. This model is commonly known as synchronous request and response model.

Similarly, in the integration world, the integration between two systems may happen as a synchronous request and response model. Synchronous request-response pattern is commonly used in the area where the client application requires the responses immediately and the client application can hold the process until the response comes back.

The following block diagram will show a typical synchronous request-response communication model:

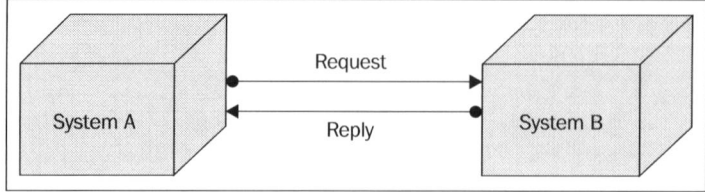

In general, native query operations are request-response type communications. An Oracle Siebel CRM solution may query customer details from an Oracle PeopleSoft system. When one application sends a query to another application, naturally the requesting application is expecting a response immediately, so it has to hold its status until the response comes. Thus, the AIA approach of the synchronous request-response model should look similar to the following diagram:

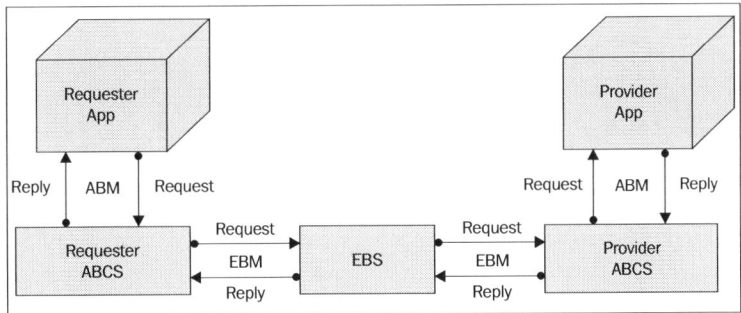

In the preceding architecture model, the requester application queries information from the provider application. The request communication traverses through the requester ABCS to EBS to the provider ABCS, finally reaching the provider application. Once the provider application transforms the request, the response comes back through a similar route and reaches the requester application. The requester application should wait until it receives the response.

In AIA framework, most of the query operations are synchronous request-response method only. In the AIA EBS model, if we open the `BankAccountEBSV1.WSDL` file, we can see the `QueryBankAccountList` operation as a synchronous request-response model.

```
<!-- operation support for QueryBankAccountList -->
<operation name="QueryBankAccountList">
<documentation>
<svcdoc:Operation>
<svcdoc:Description>This operation is used to Query multiple
  BankAccount EBOs.</svcdoc:Description>
<svcdoc:MEP>SYNC_REQ_RESPONSE</svcdoc:MEP>
  <svcdoc:DisplayName>QueryBankAccountList</svcdoc:DisplayName>
    <svcdoc:LifecycleStatus>Active</svcdoc:LifecycleStatus>
<svcdoc:Scope>Public</svcdoc:Scope>
</svcdoc:Operation>
</documentation>
<input message="ebs:QueryBankAccountListReqMsg"/>
<output message="ebs:QueryBankAccountListRespMsg"/>
<fault name= "fault" message="ebs:FaultMsg"/>
</operation>
```

Oracle AIA recommends using the synchronous request-response service in all composite applications where the query processing mechanism is required. AIA also recommends co-locating the dependent services in the same infrastructure to eliminate the performance overheads.

# Asynchronous fire and forget pattern

**Asynchronous fire-and-forget** or **request only** pattern is uncommon in web application architecture, but widely used in mechanisms in the previous generation of integration. Message-oriented integration architecture is commonly adopted by the asynchronous communication pattern to handle large volumes of messages at higher processing rates.

In asynchronous fire-and-forget pattern, the requesting application should continue the processing after submitting a request to the provider application regardless of whether the provider application performs that request immediately or not. This approach helps to decouple the relationship between the requester and provider applications. Ultimately, the requester and provider applications should have the capabilities to produce and consume those messages independently. Asynchronous fire-and-forgot patterns are widely used in the financial companies, stock market, and telecom industries where the data is shared across enterprises without any dependency. The following diagram will show the common synchronous fire-and-forget mechanism in integration architecture:

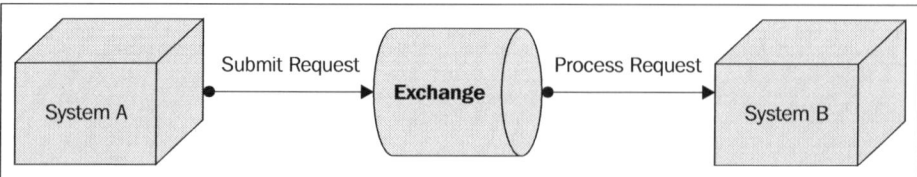

In the preceding architecture, the exchange could be anything from a filesystem to a Message Queue (MQ) server. Typically, JMS and MQ-based broker architecture is used widely in this scenario. Specially, a queue-based mechanism can hold large volumes of messages and at the same time guarantee message delivery.

In the AIA approach, Oracle recommends using message queue mechanism with database or file-based persistence to implement fire-and-forget pattern. For example, in a typical e-commerce scenario, customers and partners place orders on the online systems, which should to be transferred to the backend application to process the orders. As there is a high volume of transfer in the decouple mode, the most appropriate solution will be to implement a message queue to capture the orders.

Once the orders are placed in the message queue, these messages can be processed by the backend systems at anytime. Customers and partners should be directed to place orders in the message queue. This approach will help to capture the orders without any interruption.

The following diagram will show the highly detailed message queue model between various AIA components:

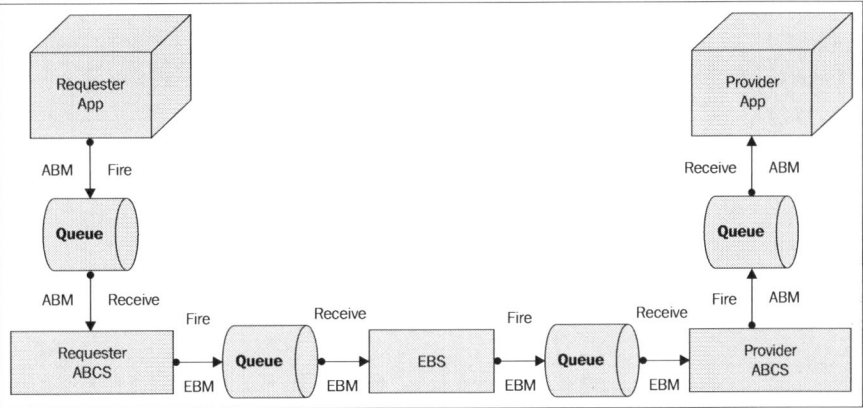

The preceding architecture shows the extensive use of queue mechanism in each layer of the AIA approach to decouple the dependencies between each layer. In this approach, the requester application should fire the request to the queue in the form of ABM. The requester ABCS should fetch the message from the queue, transform it into the EBM format, and place it in the next queue for EBS. The EBS should fetch the message from the queue and fire the same in the provider ABCS queue. The provider ABCS should fetch the message from the queue and fire it into the provider application queue in the format of ABM. The provider application should receive the message and process it. In this approach, we cannot expect the provider application to respond back. However, this approach will slow down the entire process, so message processing performance expectations should not be a requirement. The following operation is an example of the fire-and-forget pattern:

```
<operation name="UpdateCurrencyExchangeList">
<documentation>
<svcdoc:Operation>
<svcdoc:Description>This operation is used to Update multiple
CurrencyExchange EBOs.</svcdoc:Description>
<svcdoc:MEP>REQUEST_ONLY</svcdoc:MEP>
<svcdoc:DisplayName>UpdateCurrencyExchangeList</svcdoc:DisplayName>
<svcdoc:LifecycleStatus>Active</svcdoc:LifecycleStatus>
<svcdoc:Scope>Public</svcdoc:Scope>
</svcdoc:Operation>
```

```
        </documentation>
        <input message="ebs:UpdateCurrencyExchangeListReqMsg"/>
    </operation>
```

It is highly recommended that each component that dequeues the message from the queue should be within the same transaction. Queue mechanism will always dequeue the message from the queue until the transaction succeeds. This helps to ensure the messages have been delivered to the target system properly.

# Asynchronous delayed response pattern

**Asynchronous delayed response** pattern can be applied when synchronous communication is not feasible. In a situation, when an application provider requires more time to process a request, it is obvious that the requester application may end up in a disconnection or time-out. Such situations require asynchronous delayed response approach.

The following diagram will show the communication between two applications in an asynchronous delayed response pattern:

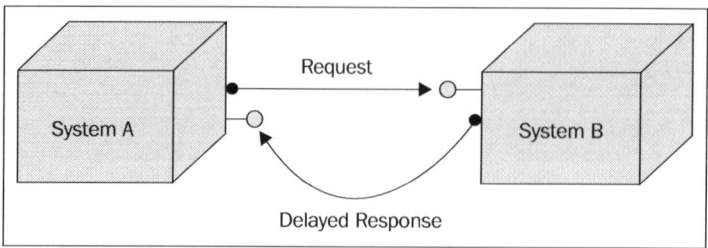

The requester system should invoke the service of the provider system but does not expect the response and continues to next task. The provider system receives the request and processes it. Once the process is complete, it invokes the callback service of the requester system to submit the response. In the delayed response pattern, participating applications should provide service to call back.

The same approach can be implemented in AIA. Oracle AIA recommends implementing this pattern when a requesting application submits a request to the integration layer along with callback address as part of metadata Web Service Addressing (WSA) in the message.

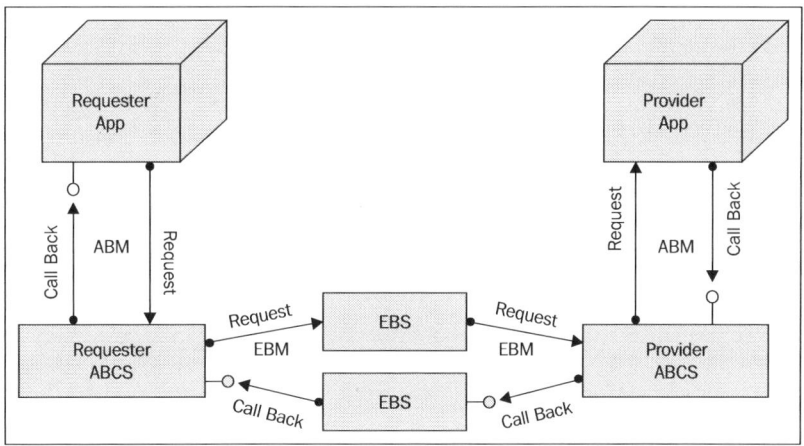

The preceding architecture diagram shows the integration approach using asynchronous delayed response pattern. In this architecture, the requesting application sends a one-way request to the requester ABCS in the form of an ABM. The requester ABCS transforms this request into the EBM format and submits the same to the EBS. The EBS sends a request to the provider ABCS. The provider ABCS transforms the message into provider ABM format and submits it to the provider application service. Once the provider application completes the process, it should call back the provider ABCS service to send back the response. The provider application should handle the message correlation while invoking the provider ABCS service. The provider ABCS should invoke the EBS (a separate one to handle response), which in turn invokes the requester ABCS service. The requester ABCS should invoke the callback service of the requester application. Each participating component should handle the message correlation using correlation identity. The following operation is the sample EBS operation that supports asynchronous delayed response pattern:

```
<operation name="UpdateAccountBalanceAdjustmentListResponse">
<documentation>
<svcdoc:Operation>
<svcdoc:Description>This callback operation will be used to
   provide the UpdateAccountBalanceAdjustment
      Response.</svcdoc:Description>
<svcdoc:MEP>ASYNC_REQ_RESPONSE</svcdoc:MEP>
<svcdoc:DisplayName>UpdateAccountBalanceAdjustmentListResponse
   </svcdoc:DisplayName>
<svcdoc:LifecycleStatus>Active</svcdoc:LifecycleStatus>
<svcdoc:Scope>Public</svcdoc:Scope>
<svcdoc:InitiatorService>AccountBalanceAdjustmentEBSV2
   </svcdoc:InitiatorService>
<svcdoc:InitiatorInterface>UpdateAccountBalanceAdjustmentResponseEBM
```

*AIA Design Patterns*

```
        </svcdoc:InitiatorInterface>
    <svcdoc:InitiatorOperation>UpdateAccountBalanceAdjustmentListRequest
        </svcdoc:InitiatorOperation>
    </svcdoc:Operation>
    </documentation>
    <input message="ebs:UpdateAccountBalanceAdjustmentListRespMsg"/>
    </operation>
```

Oracle AIA recommends using two operations in the same EBS to handle two separate requests, one for request and another one for delayed response request (callback). Both the operations should be independent and atomic. When we talk about a callback request, we need to talk about the WS-Addressing standards that are used to define the callback URL. In asynchronous delayed response pattern, the callback URL is highly important as it can receive the response at a later stage. WS-Addressing specifies to include the callback URL in the header of the original request.

## Guaranteed delivery pattern

In a real world business scenario, delivery of a message to the appropriate systems is considered one of the important criteria. For example, in the e-commerce world, each order placed by a customer is considered as an important entity that should properly reach in the backend system and processed appropriately. Business cannot accommodate a single failure in the order of flow between applications. How do we handle such issues in the integration world? Guaranteed delivery pattern is a solution for this issue.

The following diagram will show the message queue model between each component that is needed to push the message to another system:

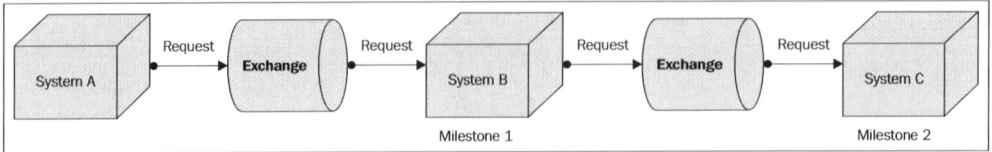

In integration scenarios, where the message has to reach several systems to complete one business process, it requires a guaranteed delivery pattern. The preceding diagram shows the simple guarantee mechanism used to handle the multiple stages of message delivery. Each target system is considered as a milestone, with an aim that the message should reach the final milestone. If it fails any one of the milestones due to any reason, the process stops at the previous milestone, so that it can be triggered again to reach the final destination. Queue-based messaging mechanism is widely used for this scenario.

Oracle AIA recommends using the milestones as logical stages in an end-to-end integration. For example, in an integration scenario where multiple components (composite application, business rules, service components) of Oracle SOA suite are involved to meet a business process requirement. Similarly, in AIA approach we may have to follow the logical milestone stages to identify the message delivery guarantee.

The following diagram represents a simplified approach of implementing a guaranteed delivery pattern in the AIA approach:

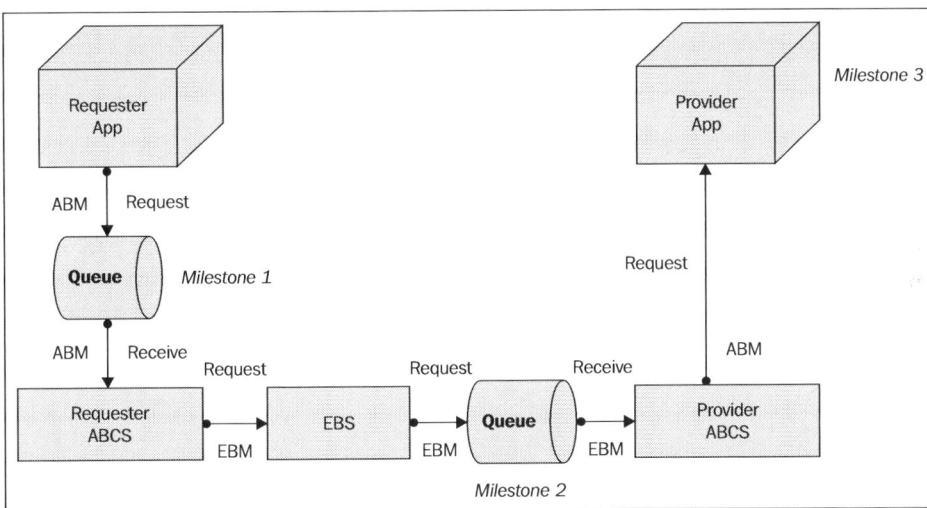

As per AIA standards, the end-to-end transaction will be separated as three milestones and considered as two transactions. When the requesting application's requests reach the first queue, it is considered as **Milestone 1** completed. Therefore, the requesting application delivery responsibility has ended in that stage and it will be relieved from the transaction. The requester ABCS fetches the message from the queue, transforms it, and submits it to the EBS. Subsequently it delivers the message to the second-level queue where the **Milestone 2** has ended. If there is any service unavailability during that transaction, the processes roll back the transaction so that the message continues to exist in the **Milestone 1** queue. If the **Milestone 2** has succeeded, the provider ABCS should fetch the message from the queue and submit it to the provider application in the format of ABM. If there is any service availability issue in the provider application level, the transaction initiated by the provider ABCS will be rolled back, so that the message continues to exist in the **Milestone 2** queue. Therefore, the fundamental approach is to move the message stage by stage without losing the message.

# Other message processing patterns

Apart from the previous pattern, there are other patterns which have extended functions from the previous four patterns. We will see them briefly in the following sections.

## Service routing pattern

This pattern helps to identify the target system services dynamically. The decision of invocation is based on either content or logic. In the previous four patterns, the requester application had to bind the service invocation with the target system's service. If there is a situation when the requesting application has to invoke another instance or region of the target service, it may not be possible. Therefore, the service routing pattern helps to identify the service location of the target system, which eliminates the tight binding of interface exchanges. The dynamic binding and message routing to the target system could be based on content or any other logical decision.

The following diagram shows the request routing model in the AIA approach:

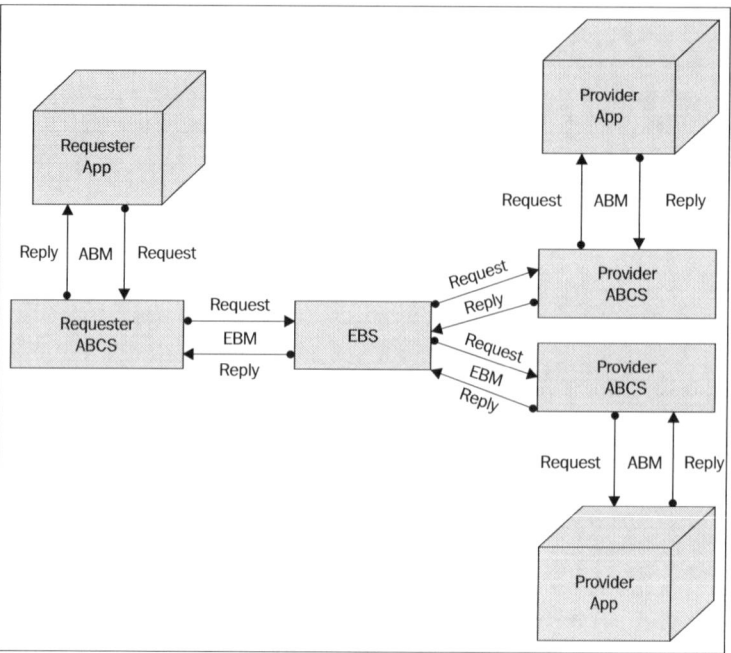

AIA recommends externalizing the dynamic routing decision from the process to identify the right service provider for the actual request of the application. The decision logic can be incorporated in the routing mechanism. The Oracle Mediator component may be used to build the dynamic routing logic.

## Competing consumers pattern

This pattern is related to process-improvement and high availability. In the asynchronous fire-and-forget pattern, AIA recommends using queue mechanism to handle a large volume of messages. However, that approach may lead into an issue such as the queue may become a storage mechanism if the consumer does not process the messages at the same rate as the publisher. In queue mechanism, the throughput of the publisher and consumer application should be balanced to make the queue lightweight and hence, lead to a better performance.

In order to resolve the mentioned issues, Oracle AIA recommends to use multiple consumer processes to publish the messages for provider application to meet the maximum throughput and performance. The multiple consumer or listener processes should run in parallel to consume the messages at a high processing rate. In the Queue (point-to-point channel) approach, even though multiple listeners or consumers are configured to run in parallel to process the messages, each consumer will not get the same messages. Hence, this helps to avoid duplicate message distribution. In addition, Oracle recommends to use this approach with a **queue** and not with **topic** (publish-subscribe channel) because topic will deliver the same messages to all the consumers.

This approach should only be applied if it is required to handle a large volume of messages using the AIA approach.

# Asset centralization pattern

AIA's **asset centralization pattern** will help to avoid duplicate or redundant data models and service contracts. In enterprise-wide integration, implementation using the Oracle AIA approach may generate multiple service contracts and data models. This will lead to confusion in identifying the right service contract for the right scenario. Therefore, AIA recommends to build central asset repository using Oracle Enterprise Repository (not part of the Oracle SOA suite and AIA) where data model and service contracts can be stored.

Asset centralization pattern suggests some of the following standard approaches to avoid redundancy in data models and service contracts.

# Data model centralization

In the AIA approach, the service contract and transformations in the application may require similar data that leads into data redundancy. In addition, a change in data model is very difficult to implement and verify.

*AIA Design Patterns*

AIA recommends separating the data model from service contracts and physically storing it in a central repository (such as, an enterprise repository), which can be referred to during design and run-time. Therefore, EBO, EBM, and ABM should be stored in the central repository in structure.

## Service contract centralization

In a typical real-time implementation, service contract may include descriptions for various service operations. However, during implementation, the development will happen at the operational level, which will result in creating multiple artifacts using the same service contract.

AIA recommends that service contract should be separated from the physical location and kept in a central repository. Therefore, the central repository can be referred to during the development. AIA recommends maintaining the EBS, ABCS, and other supporting services in a central location.

## Asset extensibility patterns

AIA asset extensibility patterns describe how to manage the extended AIA components in a uniform approach. As we have seen in the previous chapters, out-of-box AIA comes up with default schema and messaging models for various business domains. However, during implementation it may require to modify the components such as EBO, EBM, EBS, and EBF to accommodate specific requirements. It is not a recommended approach to modify the out-of-box EBO and EBM components.

## Extending EBO/EBM

AIA recommend extending the EBO and EBM to accommodate more elements to meet the business requirements. AIA comes up with custom a folder where all the custom components can be placed. The custom components of EBO and EBM have an extension placeholder called Custom at the end of the schema. The custom data types and elements can be added under this custom section in the schema. The following code is an example of a custom component:

```
<!-- ================================================== -->
<!-- ===   AccountBalanceAdjustment Custom Components ==== -->
<!-- ================================================== -->
<xsd:complexType name="CustomAccountBalanceAdjustmentEBOType" />
<xsd:complexType name=
  "CustomAccountBalanceAdjustmentStatusHistoryType" />
<xsd:complexType name="CustomAccountBalanceAdjustmentTaxType" />
```

## Extending EBS and ABCS

Similar to EBO and EBM, the customer may require extending the delivered AIA solutions at a later point of time to accommodate changes in the services or logics. If we modify the existing solutions during the maintenance phase, it may require a lot of effort to validate the changes and deployments. Instead of modifying the existing solution, if possible, extend the solutions. This would reduce the risk and make the extension much faster.

AIA recommends handling the need by introducing various extension points during service implementation. AIA thus recommends four logical extension points. They are pre-processing ABM, post-processing ABM, pre-processing EBM, and post-processing EBM. Similar to extending an ABCS, an Enterprise Business Service (EBM) can also be extended to include additional operations and message format. Extending EBS requires us to customize the default EBS WSDL to include additional operations and message models. It also recommends allowing the customer to enable or disable the previous four-point locations based on the customer's preference.

## Extending EBF and transformation

There is always a possibility that the customer may wish to extend the EBF and the transformation logics in a way similar to EBO, EBS, and ABCS. AIA recommends extending these business processes at logical entry points. However, it does not recommend any four-point extension locations. The number of extensions for EBF depends on the implementation model. AIA recommends having extension points at the beginning of the process flow and at the end of the process flow.

Similar to EBF, transformation is another important component that requires changes very often. Many a times, a customer wishes to add or modify the elements in the transformation logic. Customers can modify the existing XSL to meet the modification requirements or extend the transformation model. AIA recommends using the XSD `Import` command in xml schema definitions to accommodate the custom templates that include the custom transformation elements.

# Summary

In this chapter, we learned that the design patterns help to avoid some of the common issues that may occurs during AIA implementation. More than implementation and meeting customer requirements using AIA, it is important to design the solution that is most efficient and scalable.

We saw the synchronous request-response messaging pattern and a sample AIA service operation format, asynchronous fire-and-forget messaging pattern and a sample AIA service operation format, and service routing approach, asset centralization, and its extensibility.

In the next chapter, we are going to learn about various error-handling approaches in the AIA framework and how AIA exception handling framework will help you to build the exception handling mechanism for various integration models.

# 10
# Error Handling and Logging

A well-designed business system should be able to handle various error scenarios that it may encounter during execution. In order to make such a system, we should identify the potential risks that the system may encounter, and instruct or design the systems to manage such risks in a specific approach called error handling. Usually, in user-application systems, the system will capture the input feeds, validate the feeds, capture the exception, and respond back to the user with a proper message. However, in the systems integration scenario, when feeds are triggered by systems, there is a high possibility of system errors, communication errors, and data errors. As integrations are mostly between systems, and the user may not directly interact with integration solutions, it is compulsory that the system should handle such situations and recovers from the fault. In addition, such issues should be notified to the system's owners for fine-tuning and correction.

**Service Oriented Architecture (SOA)** provides enormous flexibility to handle the error scenarios and notifications regardless of systems and functions. It is also good practice to implement the error handling and notification services as part of the enterprise services to handle the system exceptions in a standard approach. When we design SOA reference architecture, we must consider the error handler and notification services as part of the solution design.

Oracle AIA provides a framework and the best approach to handle the integrations between applications. As the error handling is important to succeed in integration, AIA also provides framework to handle exception and error scenarios. In this chapter, we are going to learn about the following topics:

- Fault handling in BPEL
- AIA error-handling framework
- Fault handling in AIA
- Enabling and disabling error notification
- Error logging approaches

# Fault handling in BPEL

Before we get into fault handling in the AIA approach, we must understand the fault handling approach in Oracle BPEL. Fault represents error conditions in the web service or process layers. In BPEL terms, fault handling allows BPEL processes to handle error condition and exceptions that occur while invoking the external services or data handling. BPEL fault handlers define the reaction that BPEL should take when external invocation fails due to unexpected responses.

There are two categories of faults:

1. Business faults.
2. System faults.

## Business faults

Business faults are related to application errors and exceptions that occur when the information being processed is not in the expected format or standard (for example, if the one of the mandatory data fields is null such as invoice number). Similarly, business faults may also occurs if the invoking service responses back with fault responses. `FaultHandlers` using `FaultName` and `FaultVariable` can catch all business faults.

For example:

```
<faultHandlers>
  <catch faultName="ns1:nameoftheFault" faultVariable="faultVar">
    <! Implement the action/>
  </catch>
</faultHandlers>
```

In BPEL, faults that are thrown by throw activity will be handled by a catch block using fault handlers. In the catch block, the error can be notified to the process administration group through user and e-mail notification mechanism. In general, business faults may happen locally or remotely. The process should handle both kinds of fault situations.

In BPEL, if any business error happens within process, such as data validation, it should be captured and thrown by the throw activity. Such throws should be captured by the catch block and invoke an error notification service to handle the notifications. The fault input to the error notification should be in fault schema model.

If the invoking external service responds back with a fault message, then the Oracle composite application should capture the responses using composite fault policy. The following image shows the typical error-handling approach followed in the BPEL process:

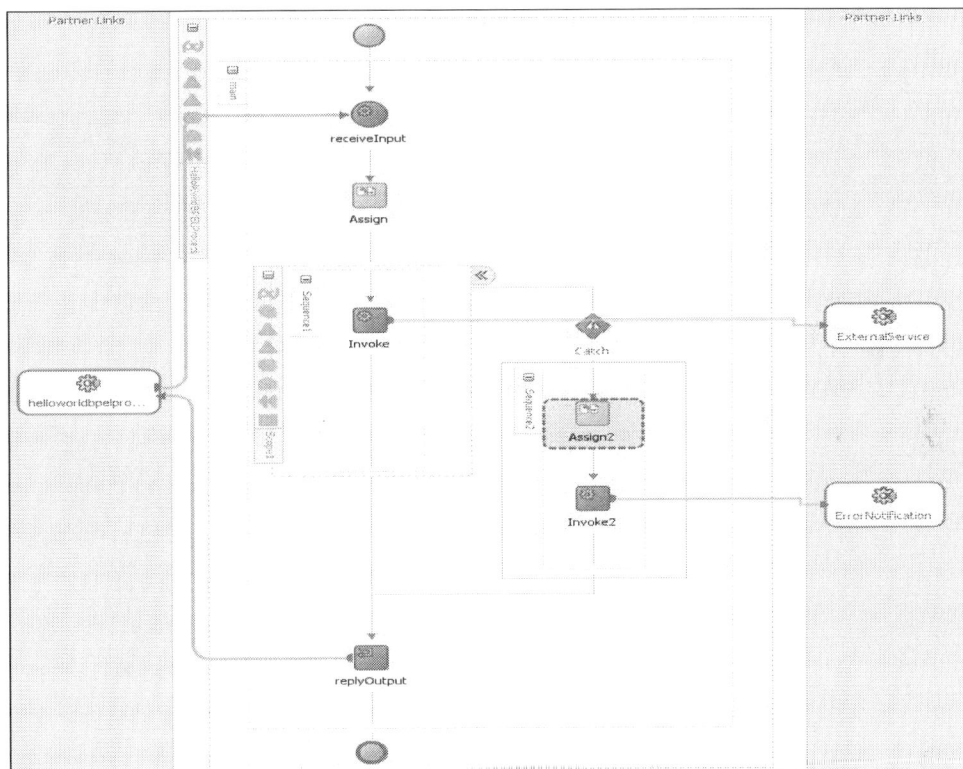

 Notes: The Oracle Mediator component can handle both the business faults and systems faults. In AIA, the components that are built on mediator components can handle both faults.

# System faults

System faults are errors that occur within the running SOA components such as BPEL and Mediator. The internal errors include process failures, transformation failures, and exceptions in handling variables. Composite fault policy framework can be used to handle the system faults. The system's faults can also be captured within the scope of the execution by using scope and throw activities. Such exceptions should be caught by the catch activity to handle the necessary actions.

# AIA error-handling framework

Oracle AIA frameworks provide predefined data objects, process models, and integration components. Similarly, AIA also provides error-handling API and prebuilt processes to handle the error notification and logging.

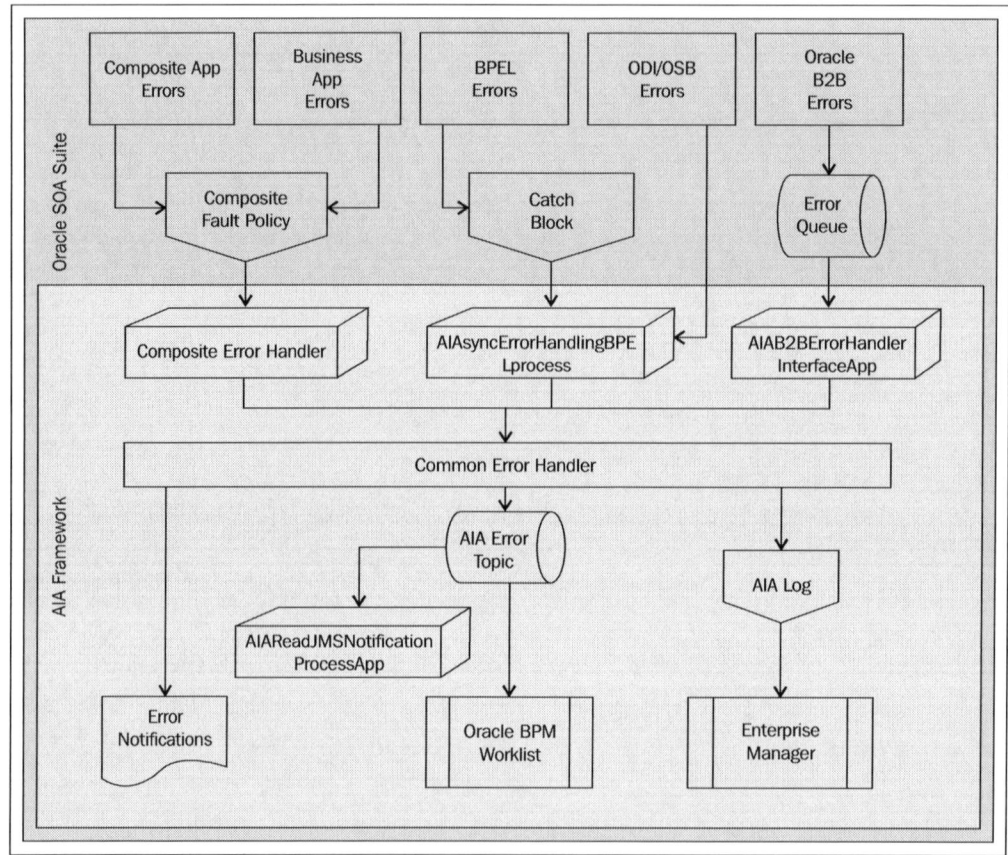

The preceding diagram shows the structure of the AIA framework components, and extended components of the Oracle SOA suite. AIA error-handling framework extends error-handling mechanisms of Oracle SOA suite components such as Mediator, BPEL, and B2B. In addition, the out of box AIA comes up with prebuilt error handler processes for easy implementation. Referring the preceding diagram, all composite application errors and business errors (application connection errors) are handled by the SOA composite fault policy declared in the SOA enterprise manager.

Oracle AIA provides a composite fault handler that can trigger the common error handler component (`oracle.apps.aia.core.eh.InvokeBusinessErrorHandler.process`). Similarly, BPEL, **OSB (Oracle Service Bus)**, and **ODI (Oracle Data Integrator)** related errors will be caught by the catch block component in the process flow. Such catch blocks can send the error notification by invoking the `AIAAsyncErrorHandlingBPELProcess` application. `AIAASyncErrorHandlingBPELProcess` is a skeleton composite application with WSDL and BPEL that can be extended to send the error notification to AIA error topic or AIA logger depending on the implementation needs. Oracle Fusion and AIA handles the B2B errors through error queue mechanism. In a B2B model, the error messages are published in the error message queue to facilitate the business process continuation. Custom error notification applications such as Oracle BPM worklist and Enterprise Manager are common end systems used to view and analyze the error which occurred in the AIA integrations. Oracle AIA provides the framework and process to make use of that in integrations. It is the implementation team's responsibility to identify the approach and implementation models.

The following points are the key features of the Oracle AIA error-handling implementation:

- AIA error handing framework provides a uniform implementation approach for various technologies such as BPEL, Mediator, and B2B
- The framework can accommodate various error categories such as business, systems, and technical faults
- AIA framework approach can be easily adopted by AIA design patterns such as Synchronous Request-Response, Asynchronous Request pattern, and so on
- AIA error notification services can be configured to send notifications to different groups of people such as admin, manager, and CSR based on roles configuration
- Oracle SOA Suite provides integration with Oracle Enterprise Manager Console to trace the AIA faults as well
- Framework provides skeletons, so it can be extended to accommodate different notification contents depending upon needs
- Also it provides the facility to control the flow of errors through error throttling mechanism
- Oracle SOA infrastructure provides mechanisms to log various errors that occur in the server
- AIA fault definition captures B2B-specific errors by routing the errors that occur in the B2B components

# Fault handling in AIA

Fault handling mechanism in AIA approach is almost similar to the approach followed in BPEL and Mediator. However, the AIA approach involves more standardized configuration such as AIA fault policies and binding. In addition, AIA console provides supports to configure the error notification for each process to make the error handling flexible. Implementing the AIA approach of fault handling requires two fundamental steps. They are as follows:

1. Configuring AIA fault policy files.
2. Implement fault handling in AIA processes.

# Configuring AIA fault policy files

Oracle AIA provides policy files to facilitate the policies to be applied to the fault handling situations. AIA out of box installation brings two fault configuration files. They are as follows:

1. Fault policy file.
2. Fault policy binding file.

The fault policy binding files are associated with the fault policy files defined for every SOA composite application. The fault policy binding files must be named as `fault-bindings.xml`. Therefore, the name of the scheme file of the fault policy-binding file should be `fault-bindings.xsd`.

There is no naming standard condition for the policy files. However, AIA recommends following naming convention as `<Service Name>FaultPolicy.xml`. AIA recommends that following the fault policy binding file should be defined in order to associate the policies defined in the fault policies file.

Oracle AIA Foundation Pack 11gR1 installation comes up with a default policy and binding files under the Metadata repository. To locate the fault policy and binding files, go to the `$aia_home\AIAMetaData\faultPolicies\V1\` path. The filenames are as follows:

- `fault-bindings.xml`
- `fault-policies.xml`

While developing the service constructor using JDeveloper, if we select the default fault policies, then the service constructor screen should look like the following screenshot (please refer to *Chapter 6* for systematic instruction for creating the AIA service constructor):

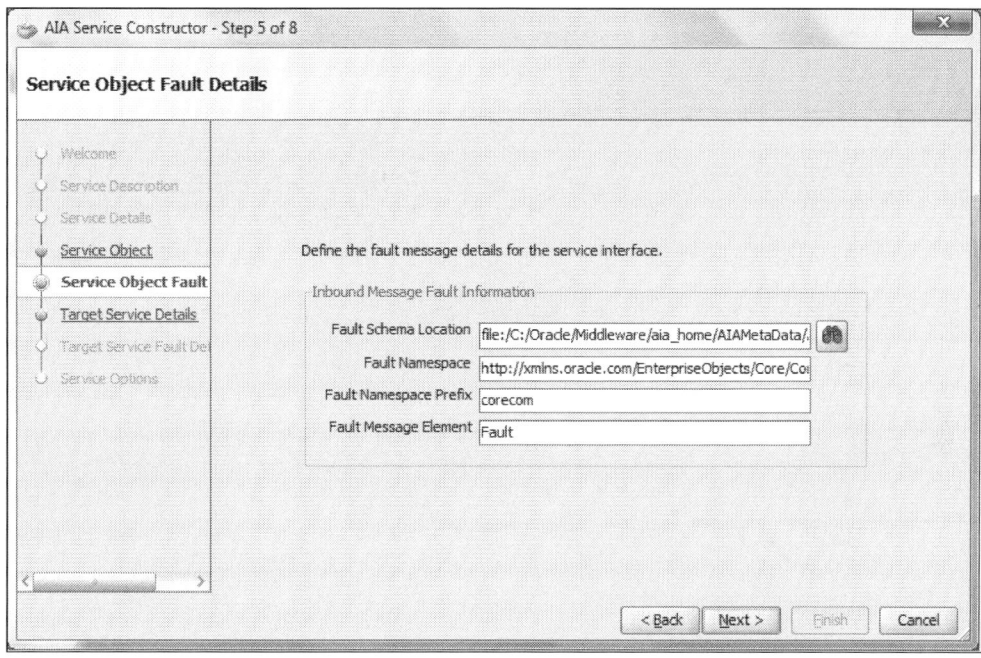

If we choose the default fault policies, then the service constructor composite application should have the following entry in the `composite.xml` file:

```
<property name="oracle.composite.faultPolicyFile">
  oramds:/apps/AIAMetaData/faultPolicies/fault-
  policies.xml</property>
<property name="oracle.composite.faultBindingFile">
  oramds:/apps/AIAMetaData/faultPolicies/fault-
  bindings.xml</property>
```

For the preceding fault policies selection, the composite application should be in design view, which should look like the following:

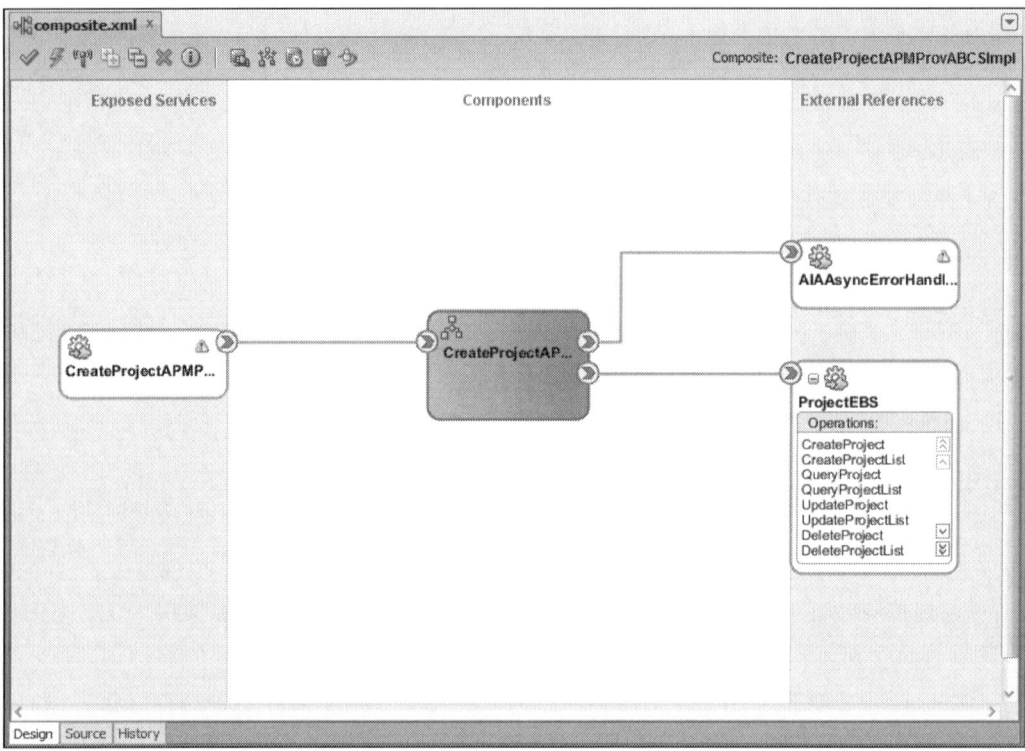

Instead of the default fault policies, if we prefer to include the custom fault policies and binding files, then Oracle recommends to import the AIA default fault policies and binding template files into the same path of the composite.xml file and add the following elements in the composite.xml:

```
<property name="oracle.composite.faultPolicyFile">
  Customfault-policies.xml</property>
<property name="oracle.composite.faultBindingFile">
  Customfault-bindings.xml</property>
```

Once we complete the service constructor along with default fault handling policies, the BPEL process should include all the necessary steps to handle the different catch mechanisms to handle the error situations. The BPEL process may looks like the following screenshot (this BPEL process generator for provider ABCS uses default Project EBM and Project WSDL schema).

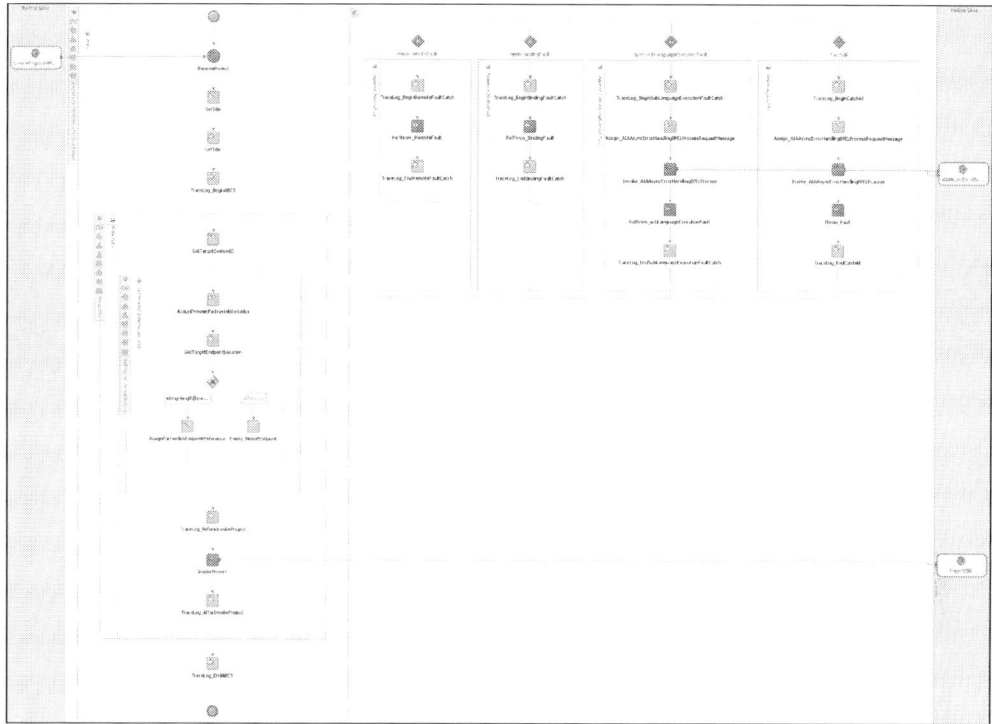

## Customize the association between custom fault polices and bindings

If we prefer to use custom fault policies instead of default fault policies and binding files, then we should associate the custom fault policies with the custom binding configuration manually. The following steps will show the approach to be followed to create the association:

First step, take the copies of the AIA out of box `fault-policies.xml` and `fault-bindings.xml` from the `$aia_home\AIAMetaData\faultPolicies\V1` path and rename the files as per your service constructor requirement. For example, we name them as follows:

- `QueryAgileProjectProviderABCSImplFaultPolicy.xml`
- `fault-bindings.xml` (remember, we should not rename this file)

*Error Handling and Logging*

Open the custom fault policies file in the editor tool (any editor tool that you have installed in your system) and modify the fault policies ID element to the name of the policies file.

```
<?xml version="1.0" encoding="UTF-8"?>

<faultPolicies xmlns="http://schemas.oracle.com/bpel/faultpolicy"
   xmlns:xsi="http://www.w3.org/2001/XMLSchema-instance">

<faultPolicy version="3.0" id="
   QueryAgileProjectProviderABCSImplFaultPolicy"
   xmlns:env="http://schemas.xmlsoap.org/soap/envelope/"
   xmlns:xs="http://www.w3.org/2001/XMLSchema"
   xmlns="http://schemas.oracle.com/bpel/faultpolicy"
   xmlns:xsi="http://www.w3.org/2001/XMLSchema-instance">
```

Now, we must associate the preceding policies defined in the policies file with a level of fault policy binding. In that case, it could either be SOA composite level or any BPEL or Mediator level. Therefore, open the fault bindings file in the editor tool and modify the associate as shown in the following code snippet:

```
<?xml version="1.0" encoding="UTF-8"?>
<faultPolicyBindings version="3.0"
   xmlns="http://schemas.oracle.com/bpel/faultpolicy"
   xmlns:xsi="http://www.w3.org/2001/XMLSchema-instance">

<!-- AIA Domain level Default Policy -->
<composite faultPolicy="
   QueryAgileProjectProviderABCSImplFaultPolicy "/>
</faultPolicyBindings>
```

Oracle AIA recommends configuring the binding association at SOA composite level to compliance with the standard that each composite should be built with a single component. So far, we have learned to customize the fault handling configuration according to our custom requirements. Now we have to handle the same in the BPEL to catch the business errors.

## Enabling error notification

AIA out of box provides value added solutions to handle the integration exception by enabling the error notification. In the SOA design, one of the mature approach is adding error notification service in the stack to provide common notification mechanism. As the AIA framework provides the best practical approach in integration, it also includes the error notification component.

By default, error notification is enabled in AIA. To make sure of this, go to the folder at `$aia_home\aia_instances\aiasoa\AIAMetaData\config` and open `AIAConfigurationProperties.xml` in the XML editor or JDeveloper. In the configuration properties file, the property name `EH.INVOKE.NOTIFY` should be set as `TRUE`.

```xml
<AIAConfiguration xmlns="http://xmlns.oracle.com/aia/core/config/V1"
  version="1.0">
<!-- System-wide configuration -->
<SystemConfiguration>

  <ModuleConfiguration moduleName="ErrorHandler">

    <Property name="EH.INVOKE.NOTIFY">true</Property>

  </ModuleConfiguration >
</SystemConfiguration>
```

As the error notification is enabled by default, the error notification mechanism uses the default configuration provided by the out of box AIA configuration. The default error notification template is available in the `AIAEHNotification.xml` file. The error notification template file includes error and FYI e-mail templates that have a subject and the body of the e-mail content.

However, there are additional configurations required for the customized error notification. The following configuration setup should be followed to make use of custom error notification:

- In order to make sure that the appropriate user receives an error notice from the AIA processes, the first step would be to configure different roles in the WebLogic domain.
- The next step would be to associate the user roles with the e-mail addresses configured in the SOA user-messaging channels.
- The final step would be error-handling configuration in the AIA console. In the AIA console, go to the error notification tab and enter the required details including service name, user role, FYI user role, error type, and handlers.
- All the preceding configuration changes will be stored in the `AIA_ERROR_NOTIFICATION` table.

>  Notes: AIA out of box error notification does not require any entry in the `AIA_ERROR_NOTIFICATION` table. If there is no entry in the `AIA_ERROR_NOTIFICATION` table, then the user and FYI user roles specified in the `AIAConfigurationProperties.xml` file will be used for error notification. By default, the user role is set to `AIAIntegrationAdmin`. Therefore, the default configuration will send the error notification e-mail to the e-mail ID configured for the `AIAIntegrationAdmin` role.

## Disable error notification

As mentioned in the preceding section, AIA error notification is enabled by default. In some of the real-time scenarios, highly efficient error notification may be required which can be achieved using Oracle SOA Suite. In that case, it is reasonable to disable the AIA inbuilt error notification mechanism.

To disable the error notification, go to the folder at `$aia_home\aia_instances\aiasoa\AIAMetaData\config` and open `AIAConfigurationProperties.xml` in the XML editor or JDeveloper. Then, change the value of the `EH.INVOKE.NOTIFY` property as `FALSE`.

```
<AIAConfiguration xmlns="http://xmlns.oracle.com/aia/core/config/V1"
  version="1.0">
<!-- System-wide configuration -->
<SystemConfiguration>

  <ModuleConfiguration moduleName="ErrorHandler">

    <Property name="EH.INVOKE.NOTIFY">False</Property>

  </ModuleConfiguration >
</SystemConfiguration>
```

Once the configuration file `AIAConfigurationProperties.xml` is modified, we should update the configuration by updating the **MDS (Metadata Services)**. To update the MDS, execute the steps given in the *Updating MDS* section of this chapter.

# Updating MDS

Once the preceding configuration is modified, make sure that the modified `AIAConfigurationProperties.xml` file is stored in the `$aia_home\aia_instances\aiasoa\AIAMetaData\config` path. It is mandatory to update the SOA MDS in every time we modify or add new value in the configuration files. While updating the MDS you are required to keep the modified configuration file in this path.

The following steps should be followed to update the MDS in order to ensure that the changes are affecting the system:

1. Go to the folder at `$aia_home\aia_instances\aiasoa\bin` where we can find an environment file named as `aiaenv.sh` or `aiaenv.bat` (if it is Windows).
2. If it is a Windows environment, then go to the command window, go to the path `$aia_home\aia_instances\aiasoa\bin` and execute `aiaenv.bat` file as shown in the following screenshot:

3. If it is an UNIX environment, then go to the path `$aia_home\aia_instances\aiasoa\bin` and execute the `source aiaenv.sh` command.
4. The preceding command execution will set the environment to update MDS.
5. Now we have to make sure that the deployment file has proper configuration before executing the MDS update command.
6. Go to the folder at `$aia_home\aia_instances\aiasoa\config` and open the deployment file named `UpdateMetaDataDP.xml`.

7. Now make sure that the AIAMetaData path is properly configured in the fileset attribute, as follows:

```xml
<?xml version="1.0" standalone="yes"?>
<DeploymentPlan component="Metadata" version="3.0">
  <Configurations>
    <UpdateMetadata wlserver="fp" >
      <fileset dir="${AIA_HOME}/AIAMetaData">
        <include name="xref/AIADEMOORDERS.xref" />
      </fileset>
    </UpdateMetadata>
  </Configurations>
</DeploymentPlan>
```

8. To update the MDS, to go the folder at $aia_home\Infrastructure\Install\config and locate the UpdateMetaData.xml file. Execute the update command by using the ant script, as follows:

    **Command**: ant -f UpdateMetaData.xml

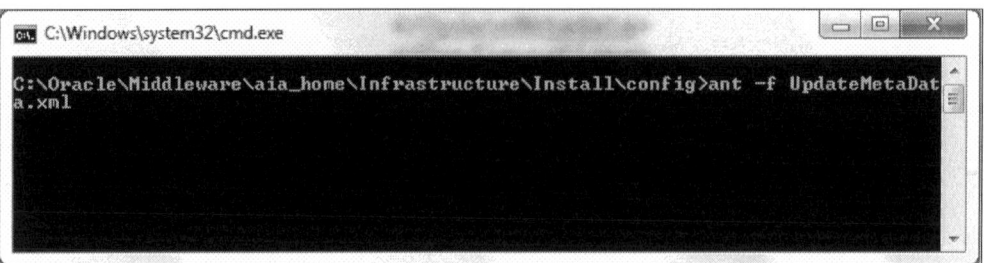

9. At the end of the execution, the MDS update should display a **Build Successful** message, as shown in the following screenshot. If there is any issue, then it will display as **Build failed**. In that case, we should revisit all the preceding sets to make sure everything is configured properly.

10. The MDS update command returned is **Build successful**. It means we have updated the MDS successfully.

# Error logging

In general, error tracing and logging is important and is a good practice that we should follow in software development. Logging and tracing mechanism is helpful to identify issues when the application is serving from a production environment. In the integration environment, when systems interact with each other, it is hard to identify whether the errors are occurring in the system layer or transport channel. So, enabling and disabling of tracing and logging are considered as important system requirements. Oracle AIA supports to enable the tracing and error logging mechanism by configuration. The AIA configuration will be helpful when troubleshooting processing issues.

System tracing helps to keep track of system-general activities. AIA tracing log should be configured to capture the activities by making explicit calls using the trace logging custom XPath and Java API.

The error logging component is used to capture and record all the errors that occur during service or process execution. In AIA, there is no configuration required to enable the BPEL and Mediator to record the errors. The AIA error-handling framework is designed to trigger an error logging event when errors occur in the AIA services. AIA error-handling framework records all errors in a non-disturbing mode.

# Enable trace logging

AIA helps to enable the tracing by configuring in the properties file. AIA out of box provides a configuration file named `AIAConfigurationProperties.xml` located under the `$aia_home\aia_instances\aiasoa\AIAMetaData\config` folder.

>
> Notes: The `AIAConfigurationProperties.XML` file can be located in the `$aia_home\aia_instances\aiasoa\AIAMetaData\config` path only if you have selected the "Complete" installation during the AIA installation. If you selected the AIA "Copy" installation, then you may not find the above path. So you have to take the configuration file from an alternate path: `$aia_home\AIAMetaData\config\`.

AIA supports to enable the trace logging at two different levels. They are as follows:

1. Entire system level.
2. Individual service level.

>
> Note: Please note that logging enabled at service level will override the property enabled at system level.

## Enabling system/service level tracing

AIA supports enabling the tracing at system level. If the tracing is enabled at system level, then that is applicable to all the services that are running at that instance. Let's see how we can enable the tracing at system and service level.

Go to the AIA instance path `$aia_home\aia_instances\aiasoa\AIAMetaData\config` and open the `AIAConfigurationProperties.xml` file in any XML editor tool or JDeveloper.

The `AIAConfigurationProperties.xml` file should look like the following screenshot:

```
AIAConfigurationProperties.xml.tmpl
<?xml version="1.0" encoding="UTF-8"?>
<AIAConfiguration xmlns="http://xmlns.oracle.com/aia/core/config/V1" version="1.0">
    <!-- System-wide configuration -->
    <SystemConfiguration>
        <!-- System configuration properties -->
        <Property name="O2C.EnablePriceListMapping">false</Property>
        <Property name="Routing.ActiveRuleset">DEFAULT</Property>
        <Property name="TRACE.LOG.ENABLED">false</Property>
        <Property name="DIAG.SYSTEM.CONFIG">AIADiagnosticsSystemProperty</Property>
        <ModuleConfiguration moduleName="DiagnosticsModule">
            <Property name="DIAG.MODULE.CONFIG">AIADiagnosticsModuleProperty</Property>
        </ModuleConfiguration>
        <ModuleConfiguration moduleName="ErrorHandler">
            <Property name="COMMON.ERRORHANDLER.IMPL">oracle.apps.aia.core.eh.AIAErrorHandlerImpl</Property>
            <Property name="COMMON.ERRORHANDLER_EXT.IMPL">oracle.apps.aia.core.eh.AIAErrorHandlerExtImpl</Property>
            <Property name="LOGGER.TRACE">oracle.aia.logging.trace</Property>
            <Property name="LOGGER.ERROR">oracle.aia.logging.error</Property>
            <Property name="COMMON.ERRORHANDLER.JAXB.CONTEXT">oracle.apps.aia.eh</Property>
            <Property name="EH.AQ.SUBSCRIPTION">AIA_ERROR_SUBSCRIPTION</Property>
            <Property name="EH.HOSTNAME">$managed.host$</Property>
            <Property name="EH.PORT">$managed.port$</Property>
            <Property name="EH.JNDIURL">$jndiurl$</Property>
            <Property name="EH.USERNAME">$server.username$</Property>
            <Property name="EH.PASSWORD">fp.server.password</Property>
            <Property name="EH.INVOKE.H4F">false</Property>
            <Property name="EH.INVOKE.NOTIFY">true</Property>
            <Property name="EH.AGGR.NOTIFY">false</Property>
            <Property name="FROM.EMAIL.ID">Email:AiaAdmin@server.com</Property>
            <Property name="EH.DEFAULT.ACTOR.ROLE">AIAIntegrationAdmin</Property>
            <Property name="EH.DEFAULT.FYI.ROLE"></Property>
            <Property name="EH.AIADEMO.ERRORHANDLER.IMPL">oracle.apps.aia.demo.AIADemoErrorHandlerExtImpl</Property>
            <Property name="EH.B2B.AIAFAULTENRICH.REQ">true</Property>
            <Property name="EH.B2B.HOSTNAME">$managed.host$</Property>
            <Property name="EH.B2B.PORT">$managed.port$</Property>
            <Property name="EH.AIACOM_OFM_EXT.IMPL">oracle.apps.aia.industry.comms.eh.AIAOrderFalloutErrorHandlerExte
        </ModuleConfiguration>
        <ModuleConfiguration moduleName="CAVS">
```

If you want to set the tracing at system level, then set the TRACE.LOG.ENABLED property as TRUE under <SystemConfiguration>, as shown in the following code snippet:

```
<SystemConfiguration>
   <!-- System configuration properties -->
   <Property name="O2C.EnablePriceListMapping">false</Property>
   <Property name="Routing.ActiveRuleset">DEFAULT</Property>
   <Property name="TRACE.LOG.ENABLED">TRUE</Property>
   <Property name="DIAG.SYSTEM.CONFIG">
      AIADiagnosticsSystemProperty
   </Property>
   <ModuleConfiguration moduleName="DiagnosticsModule">
   <Property name="DIAG.MODULE.CONFIG">
      AIADiagnosticsModuleProperty
   </Property>
</SystemConfiguration>
```

If you want to set the tracing at service level, then set the TRACE.LOG.ENABLED property as TRUE for each service, as shown in the following code snippet:

```
<ServiceConfiguration>
<!-- Service configuration properties -->
..........
<Property name="TRACE.LOG.ENABLED">TRUE</Property>..........
</ServiceConfiguration>
```

*Error Handling and Logging*

Now we should update the MDS by following the instructions provided in the *Updating MDS* section of this chapter.

## Configuring system log level

Once the system is configured and updated by using the preceding approach, we may need to ensure the log level in the server configuration to make sure everything is set according to the environment. Some environments, such as development and test, require detailed tracing, whereas production may not require very detailed logging. We can configure the level of logging depending on the environment by using the Oracle Enterprise Manager console.

The following steps should be executed to validate or modify the logger level in the AIA infrastructure:

1. Open the browser and access the Oracle Enterprise Manager of the AIA domain (http://hostname:port/em). Log in to the enterprise manager and go to the default page.

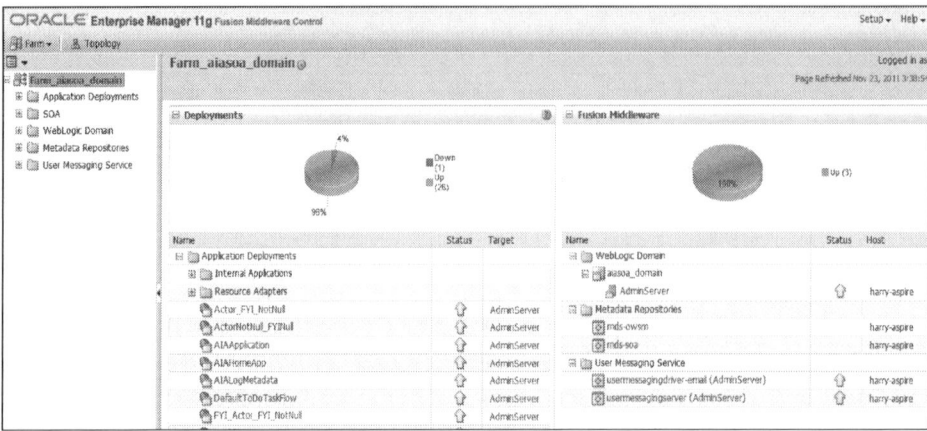

2. Expand the WebLogic domain and navigate the to the SOA domain. Right-click on the domain and select **Logs | Log Configuration**.

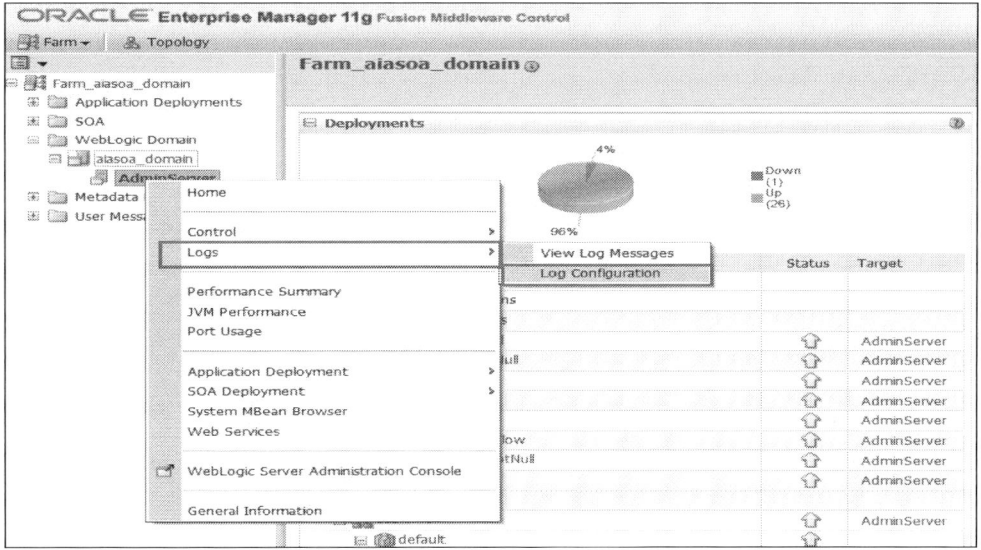

3. Now the page should display the log configuration page of the domain. Select the **Log Levels** tab in the log configuration page (by default it should display the log level page in most of the cases).

4. From the **View** drop down, select **Runtime Loggers** (by default this page may show the Runtime Loggers). Enter **aia** in the **Search** field and execute the search option. The search should locate logger name **Oracle.aia**.

5. Click on the expand icon on the left side of search result (here it is **Oracle.aia**) which should expand all the loggers that belong to AIA.

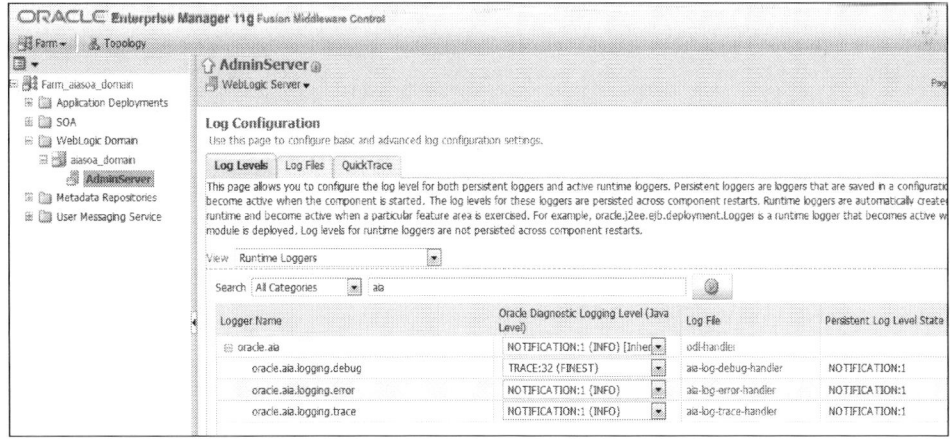

*Error Handling and Logging*

6. Now we can select the level of logging required from the drop down of the Oracle Diagnostic Logging Level. Depending on the need of logging we have many options, as shown in the following screenshot:

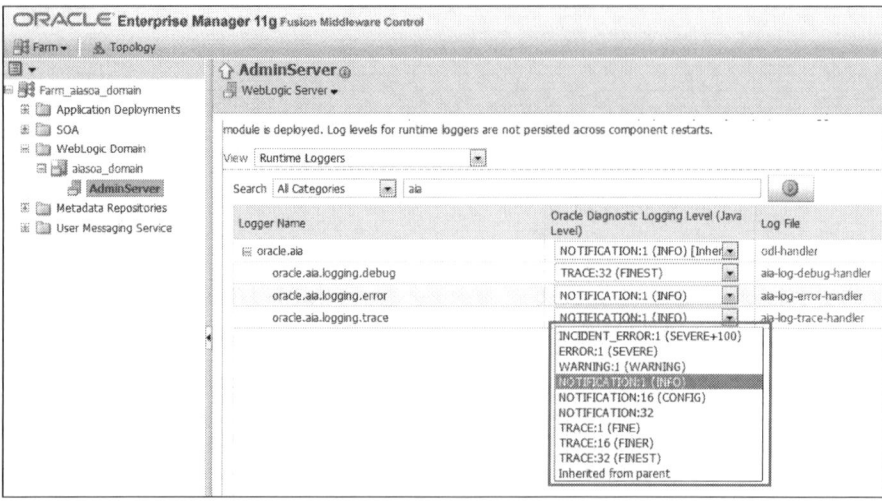

# View logfiles

Oracle AIA error logfiles can be viewed in the Oracle Enterprise Manager. To view the AIA logfiles, go to the Oracle Enterprise Manager console and select the domain in which AIA is configured.

1. Expand the **WebLogic Domain** and navigate to your domain. Right-click on the domain and select **Logs | View Log Messages**.

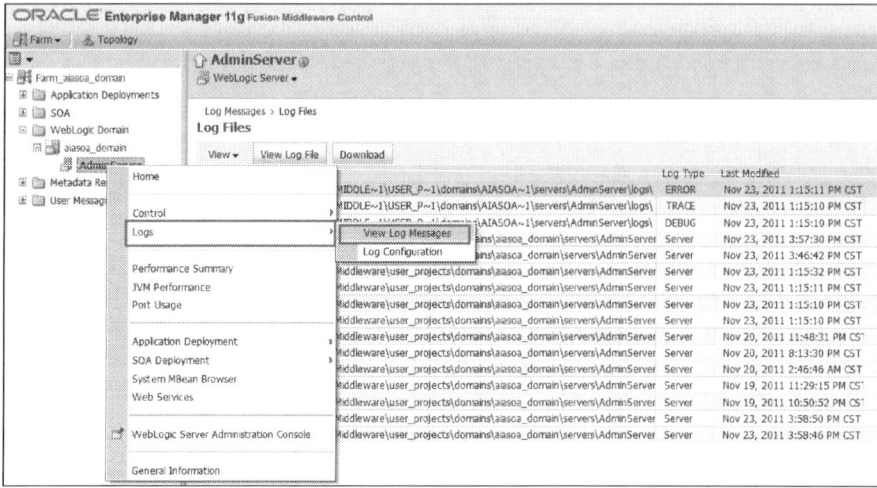

2. Now select the **Target Log Files**... button on the top-right corner of the page. This should display all the logfiles in the page. Now click on the **View Log File** button to view the log errors.

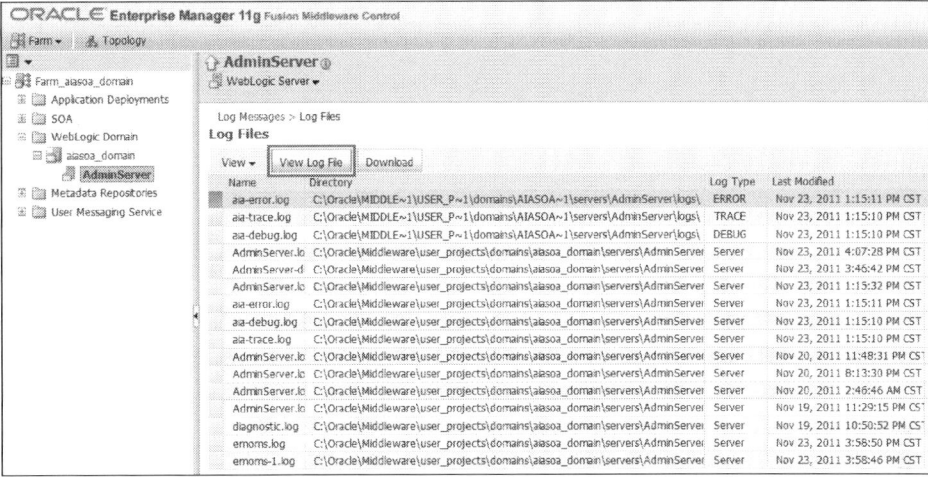

3. Alternatively, we can access the AIA trace-and-error logfile from the following directory:

   ```
   $<domain_home>\servers\<weblogic.domain>\logs\aia-error.log
   $<domain_home>\servers\<weblogic.domain>\logs\aia-trace.log
   ```

# Summary

As we have seen in this chapter, error handling is important and the best practice that makes the integration system stable and self-intelligent. Oracle AIA provides very extensive and mature error handling approach by out of box. It also enables customization of the error-handling by changing the configuration in error logging, error notification, and tracing. In this chapter, we have learned to customize the error-handling, error notification, and logging components provided by AIA. In the next chapter, we are going to explore AIA services-harvesting approach using Oracle Enterprise Repository.

# 11
# Service Management using Oracle Enterprise Repository

In this chapter, we are going to learn about managing the Application Integration Architecture (AIA) services with the help of **Oracle Enterprise Repository (OER)**. From AIA Foundation Pack 11g onwards, Oracle supports the Oracle Enterprise Repository instead of Business Service Repository for AIA service management. As OER has features of centralized web interface and repository, it is naturally efficient for managing various versions of AIA components, EBO, EBS, metadata, and schema models. In order to understand the approach, the following sections are covered in this chapter:

- SOA Governance
- OER as AIA repository
- Configuring OER as AIA repository
- Accessing AIA contents in OER
- Project lifecycle workbench and OER
- Harvesting design-time composites in OER
- Harvesting deployed composites in OER

Before we get into OER, AIA, and configuring AIA with OER, we must understand the fundamental needs and best practices for managing the service infrastructure. Therefore, we must understand all about **SOA Governance** and **service management** during various phases of SOA implementation.

# SOA Governance

**Service Oriented Architecture (SOA)** provides a new dimension for IT strategy and implementation, by breaking the systems into smaller loosely coupled services. This approach helps us to build dynamic systems infrastructure that allows the enterprises to align the business systems to meet the long-term business demands. It is important to reuse the services to build new applications or processes to respond quickly to business needs. As this approach breaks the overall IT systems into smaller services, managing the overall enterprise services becomes challenging. It also increases the dependencies between services and processes. So, more than building service components, it is very important to manage various versions of services, metadata, and schema models to realize better Return of Investment (ROI). In order to resolve this governance issue, the ideal approach would be to build a centralized repository where all the service components, dependencies, and artifacts are stored and maintained efficiently. The central repository also should provide facilities to manage the service lifecycle.

The purpose of the SOA governance model is to manage efficiently all the services, policies, people, processes, and metadata. Efficient SOA governance strategy must include approaches for design and implementation, and maintenance phases. Generally, the SOA governance is divided into **design-time** governance, **implementation-time** governance, and **run-time** governance.

## Design-time governance

During the design-time, governance approach includes identifying, analyzing, and designing service candidates, policies, processes, and information. All metadata and design components should be stored in the central repository for implementation references. The relationship between design components, schema models, and metadata should be captured to make sure that they are referred to during implementation.

## Implementation-time governance

Implementation governance approach helps us to make sure that all captured information in the design-time is validated and approached properly. An effective implementation governance process includes service candidate dependencies validation, policy validation, and logical separation of service components. Once the implementation is completed, the process should promote candidate services that are developed as service components. Once all the services are developed, the implementation should be promoted to next phase of implementation lifecycle.

# Run-time governance

The run-time governance helps to control the run-time aspects of the SOA. The run-time governance includes monitoring the performance of services, security processes, and policy management. The run-time governance approach helps to identify the less utilized or inefficient services and processes, and identify the solution for improvement of these services or processes. Run-time governance also promotes the unused or unwanted services from run-time status to retirement in service lifecycle.

Oracle Enterprise Repository (OER) is a web-based repository product provided by Oracle to manage the service lifecycle efficiently at various stages. The following sections will expose the OER and its role in AIA service management.

# OER as AIA repository

Oracle Enterprise Repository (OER) is a repository solution that provides a solid approach for SOA governance by acting as single source of repository for service asset and dependencies management. OER provides web-based user interface and automated exchange of metadata information between service consumer, provider, and policy channels. Oracle AIA can be implemented to collaborate with OER for managing AIA service components, metadata, and custom schema models. Oracle AIA can deliver all metadata, prebuilt schema models, and service interface descriptions that include EBO, EBM, ESB, WSDL, ABCS, and their relationship through OER. Apart from that, OER can also be used to publish and manage the lifecycle of service composites, especially design-time and run-time components. Building centralized enterprise repository using the Oracle Enterprise Repository product may provide the following benefits:

- Complete service lifecycle management for AIA and SOA services.
- Enterprise-wide visibility for SOA assets and services.
- Minimizes the redundancy of service development.
- Improves service reusability as it has enterprise-wide visibility.
- Provides a graphical representation of dependencies between services.
- Provides complete control on the governance implementation and adoption.

# Configuring OER as AIA repository

In order to make use of OER as enterprise repository for AIA implementation, we must configure the OER to understand the components of AIA and its portfolio. Oracle Enterprise Repository's out-of-the-box installation imports various solution packs including the prebuilt AIA solutions. Solution packs are container mechanisms used to deliver the content as a single bundle. However, we must import AIA solution pack into the OER instance in order to access, operate, and validate AIA portfolio.

The following instructions should be executed to import the AIA solution pack into the OER instance:

1. First, we should import the harvester solution pack known as **OER Harvester Solution pack**. OER's out-of-the-box installation imports the OER harvester pack. In order to validate this, go to the folder at $OER_HOME\repository111\core\tools\solutions where we can find the archive file named as <$version_number>-OER-Harvester-Solution-Pack (if you have installed OER version 11.1.1.5.0 then the archive filename should be 11.1.1.5.0-OER-Harvester-Solution-Pack). In order to import the harvester solution pack, start the OER instance and log in to the web console as administrator. (If you have already imported the harvester solution pack in your OER instance then you can skip the following steps).

2. Once logged in as an OER admin, click on the **Admin** menu from the top menus. This action should load the admin page in the OER, as shown in the following screenshot:

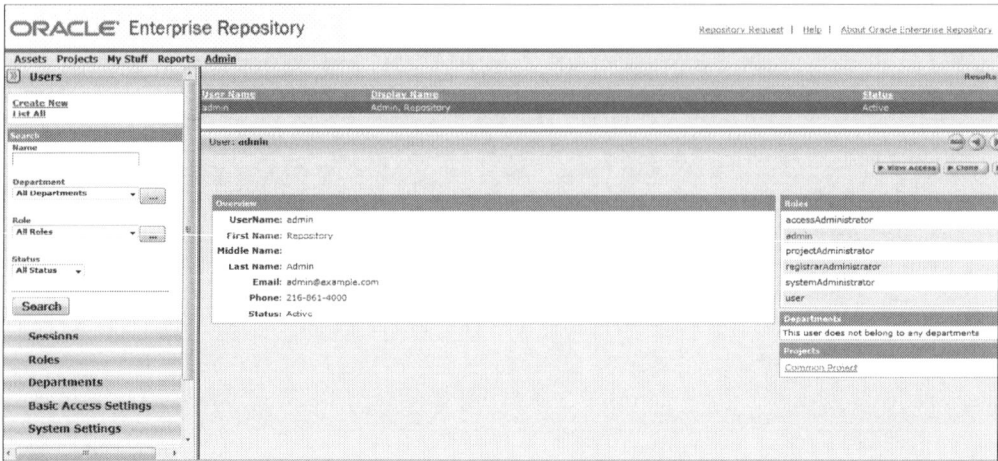

Chapter 11

3. Click on the **Import Export** menu from the side menu and click on the **Import/Export Client** menu item from the side menu as shown in the following screenshot

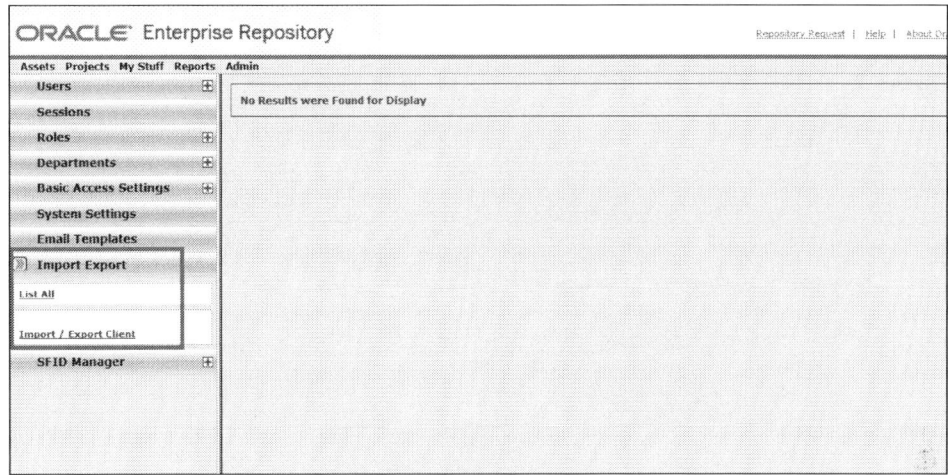

4. It should load the **Web Start** and request permission to run the client application on your PC, shown as follows:

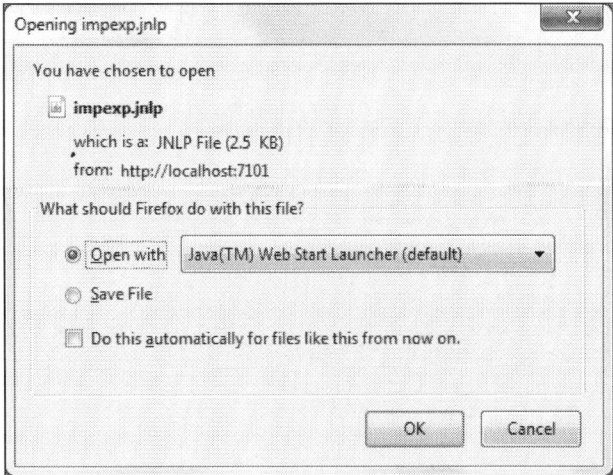

5. The **Web Start** application should load the OER client application. On this screen, click on the **Import** tab. The **Import** page of OER should be displayed as shown in the following screenshot:

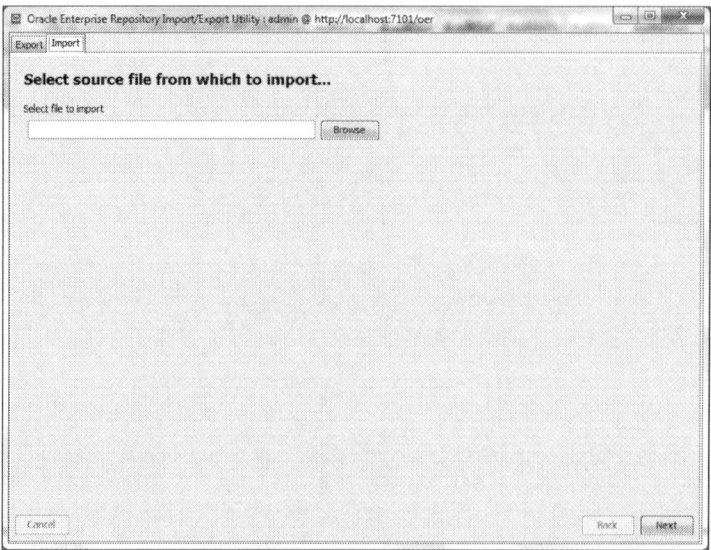

6. Enter the absolute path as **OER-Harvester-Solution-Pack** or click on the **Browse** button to select the solution pack. Then click on the **Next** button. The client application should be ready to import the pack, shown as follows:

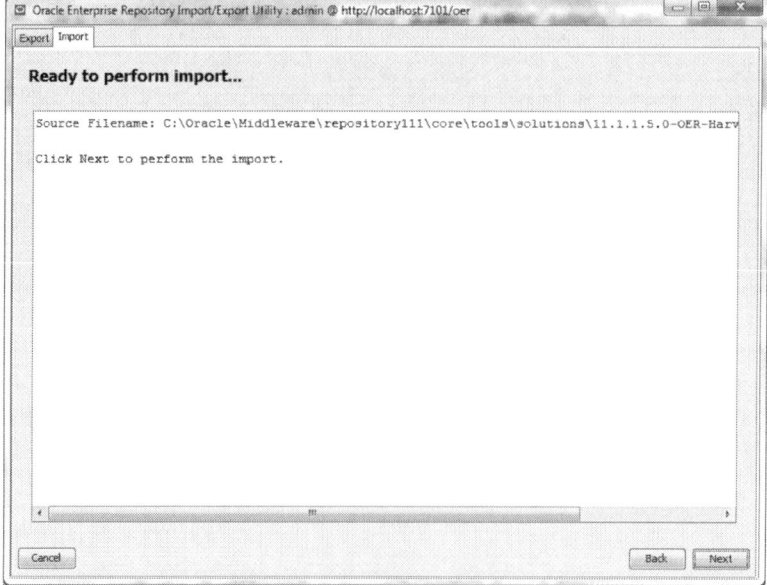

7. Click on the **Next** button to import the harvest solution pack. It should import the solution pack and display the status as completed, as shown in the following screenshot:

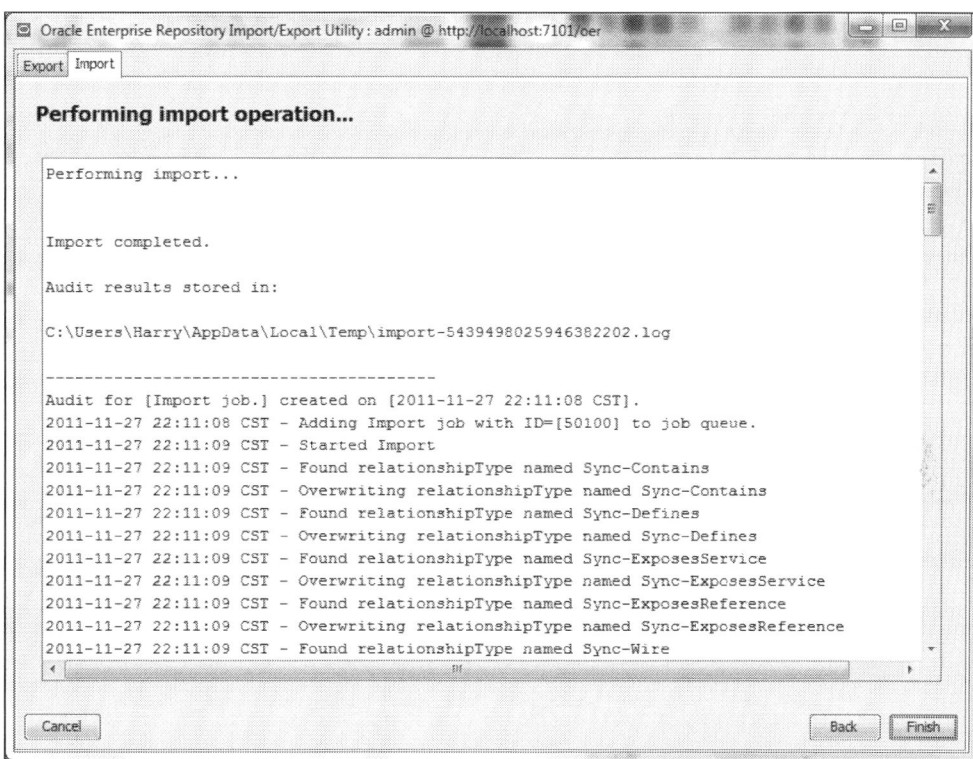

8. Now the OER harvesting solution pack is successfully imported into the OER instance. It is time to import the AIA asset definition file into the OER instance.

9. Go to the folder at `$aia_home\Infrastructure\LifeCycle\solutionpack` and locate the `AIAAssetTypeDef` file.

10. Repeat the previous steps to import the `AIAAssetTypeDef` file into the OER instance. Once the AIA asset definition file is imported successfully, we should import the AIA solution pack.

11. In order to import the AIA solution pack, go to the folder at `$aia_home\Infrastructure\LifeCycle\solutionpack` then locate the following files:

    ◦ `AIA-Types-Solution-Pack`
    ◦ `AIA-Assets-Solution-Pack-part1`
    ◦ `AIA-Assets-Solution-Pack-part2`

12. Repeat the previous import steps for all the three AIA solution packs as per the order given. While importing AIA solution pack, we should not execute any other activities in the OER instance.

> Note that importing a large volume of solution packs into the OER instance requires a lot of memory because the AIA solution pack requires a large volume of memory. If there is any memory issue then just increase the default JVM heap size.

# Accessing AIA contents in OER

Once all the AIA solution packs are imported into the OER instance, we can start exploring the AIA out-of-the-box assets and custom assets using the OER web console. The following steps should be executed to search AIA assets in the OER instance:

1. Log in to the OER instance in which solution packs are imported as an admin user.

2. In the **Search** window, we can narrow down our search for better and accurate results. Enter the string and select the type of AIA content from the drop-down list. You can also select the asset type as EBM, EBO, EBS, ABM, ABO, EBF, or ABCS from the list. For example, in the **Enter Search String** textbox enter **AIA**, from the **Type** drop-down select **AIA:EBM**, and from the **Registration Status** drop-down select **All Assets**, as shown in the following screenshot:

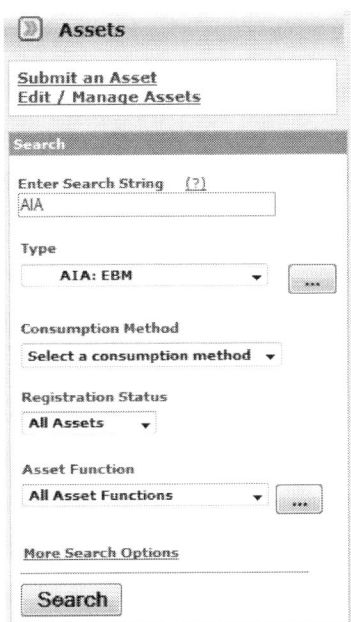

3. Click on the **Search** button to begin the search operation in the OER. The search results should be displayed, as shown in the following screenshot (if you have imported the AIA solution packs successfully):

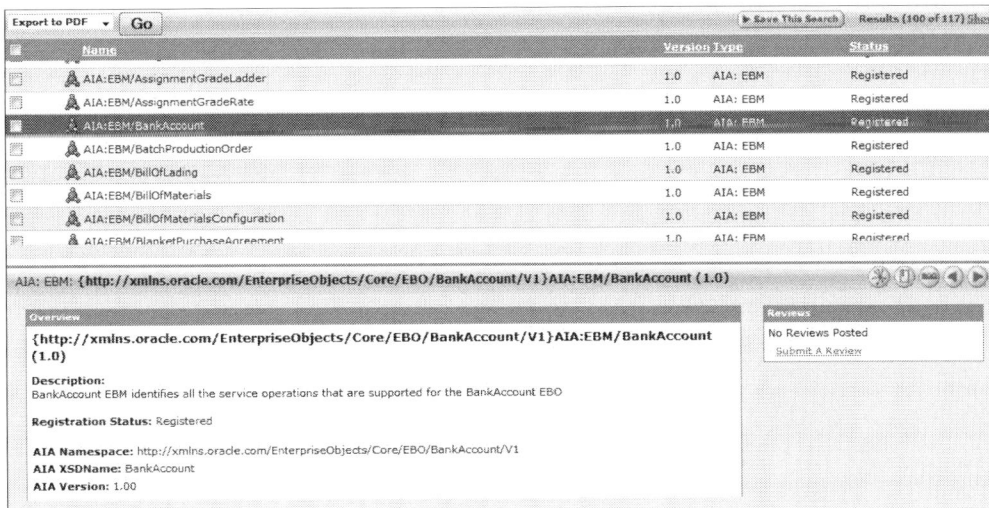

# Project lifecycle workbench and OER

Oracle AIA project is more about a development lifecycle for building service-oriented business processes. In a business process development, the outcome of the analysis phase would lead into service designing, planning, development, deployment, and support, which is similar to a typical SOA implementation. The AIA approach of development is similar to SOA practices.

The following diagram shows the typical lifecycle of AIA process implementation:

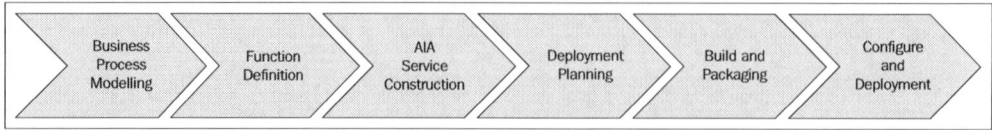

## Business process modeling phase

Process modeling will help you to draw the blueprint of the process implementation for an enterprise. During the business process modeling phase, existing processes are analyzed and categorized as business processes, business activities, and business tasks. At the end of the modeling phase, the outcome should include a set of reusable business activities and tasks that help in reducing the duplication of services. All solution components that are identified should be captured by the project lifecycle workbench.

## Service design and construction phase

In service design and construction phase, the design and development team should extend the existing AIA services, and design new services based on the tasks and activities indentified in the analysis phase. The identified solution components should be referred to during the design and construction phase. At the end of the construction phase, all the physical components should be recorded in the project lifecycle workbench.

## Deployment planning phase

During the deployment planning phase, the installation developer should select the list of components to be deployed and accordingly plan the packing and deployment approach. As service-oriented architecture brings in many service components, a proper deployment plan is required to minimize the impact in the infrastructure.

# Deployment phase

During the deployment phase, the AIA installer helps to deploy the AIA composite applications and other artifacts to the designated environment. It deploys the AIA composite application to the environment as per the deployment plan generated in the planning phase. It also publishes modified and new assets into the SOA repository.

Even though there any many Oracle and AIA tools that can support an AIA project lifecycle management, the primary tools are AIA Project Lifecycle Workbench and Oracle Enterprise Repository.

# AIA Project Lifecycle Workbench

The AIA Project Lifecycle Workbench application can be configured on the AIA workstation. The AIA implementation team members can use the AIA Project Lifecycle Workbench application. It is necessary to import all the AIA assets into the AIA Project Lifecycle Workbench application before you start using the lifecycle management tool.

# Harvesting design-time composites into OER

Once we have completed the AIA composite implementation, we need to preserve the design-time composites into the project lifecycle workspace and the OER. When harvesting the AIA composite application, annotations created after deployment help to identify the components. When we select OER as a repository for AIA harvesting, annotations on the ABCS WSDL file, EBS WSDL file, EBO XSD file, and EBM XSD files are published in the OER.

Oracle recommends harvesting the AIA composites in both the AIA Project Lifecycle Workbench and Oracle Enterprise Repository. If you do not have an OER product, then we may publish it only to Project Lifecycle Workbench.

Oracle recommends harvesting the AIA composite component only after the installation of stage components.

# Set up design-time harvesting using AIA Foundation Pack

Oracle AIA provides support to set up an environment in order to enable design-time harvesting using command-line tools. The following steps should be executed to enable design-time harvesting:

1. Run the AIA environment setup file by executing the `aiaenv.sh` or `aiaenb.bat` from the folder at `$aia_home\<instance_name>\aiasoa\bin`.

2. Prepare the harvesting configuration file `HarvesterSettings.xml`, which has the file directory path of the new `composite.xml`.

3. In order to run in OER, execute the `encrpt.sh` or `encrypt.bat` file from the folder at `$aia_home\Infrastructure\LifeCycle\AIAHarvester\Harvester` to generate a new `harvestersettings.xml` file

# Harvesting deployed composites into OER

At the end of AIA implementation, we would have deployed many AIA composites in the Oracle SOA platform. These composites are either prebuilt or custom-made composites. We should publish the same into the OER environment for harvesting. Publishing run-time composites into OER helps to keep track of the run-time components and service points.

The following steps should be executed to deploy the run-time composite application into OER:

1. Open the `HarvesterSettings.xml` file in an editor or JDeveloper to modify and add the following under specific sections.

2. Update the OER access information under the `<repository>` element as per your OER environment. You may have to configure the URI and access credentials such as username and password to access the OER.

3. Update the `<serverType>`, `<projectName>`, SOA Server access URI, and credentials under the `<remoteQuery>` attributes as per the following sample:

```
<remoteQuery>
  <serverType>SOASuite</serverType>
  <projectName>MyComposite_rev1.0</projectName>
  <uri>http://hostname:port/</uri>
  <credentials>
    <user>xxxxxxxx</user>
```

```
         <password>xxxxxxxxx</password>
     </credentials>
 </remoteQuery>
```

4. Finally execute the `AIAHarvest.sh` or `AIAHarvest.bin` from the command prompt using the following command:

**Example: AIAHarvest.bat -partial true -mode OER -settings HarvesterSetting.xml**

# Summary

In this chapter, we have learned to integrate the Oracle Enterprise Repository in the AIA environment to implement the AIA lifecycle management and harvesting. In order to recap, we have learned to set up the OER environment for importing the AIA solution packs, configuring the AIA repository in the OER environment, then learned about querying AIA service assets from the enterprise repository. Finally, we learned about harvesting the design-time and deployment-time composite applications in the Oracle Enterprise Repository.

In the next chapter, we are going to learn about testing AIA components using the AIA testing framework and a tool called Composite Application Validation Systems (CAVS).

# 12
# Composite Application Validation System

In any software development lifecycle, testing is an important phase in which the development of the system's quality and performance are quantified. Especially in an SOA world, many services are developed to meet various requirements and business tasks. So testing the service functionalities and input, and output message model are the most important to build a successful service solution. However, requirements will differ depending on the style of the testing approach and tools to certify a service.

Oracle AIA provides enormous support to validate various integration services built based on the AIA approach. In order to understand the AIA testing approach, we are going to learn the following topics in this chapter:

- Composite Application Validation System testing framework
- AIA architecture and CAVS
- Test Definition and Simulator Definition
- Using the CAVS user interface
- Enabling the ABCS route through CAVS
- CAVS routing

# Composite Application Validation System testing framework

The **Composite Application Validation System (CAVS)** is a testing framework that provides a structured approach to test AIA integration services. CAVS includes testing initiators to simulate the web service endpoints and invocations. We need to understand how importantCAVS is in the AIA integration service development. In AIA integration implementation, we have to build various levels of service and invoke those services sequentially. The sequence of invocation includes connecting ABCS, EBS, EBF, and participating in application-specific services. The CAVS testing initiator and simulator enables testing each component thoroughly without accounting the dependent services.

In addition to that, during the integration enhancement and development we may end up adding some integration service components to the existing infrastructure. CAVS supports building the testing scripts for the new components alone and that adding those as part of the existing testing subsets. The CAVS has the ability to isolate and test the individual service components by narrowing downthe test scopes.

CAVS provides an inbuilt repository to store the test initiator and simulator definitions created by a CAVS user and other external users. All these test definitions can be created, configured, and run as an individual test execution or batch test execution.

# AIA architecture and CAVS components

Before we go into the CAVS framework and its components, we should know the role of CAVS in the AIA architecture. As we have seen, the CAVS framework helps to validate the various service components built for integration. As there are various types of service interfaces involved in the AIA approach, CAVS should be capable of validating all the service interfaces.

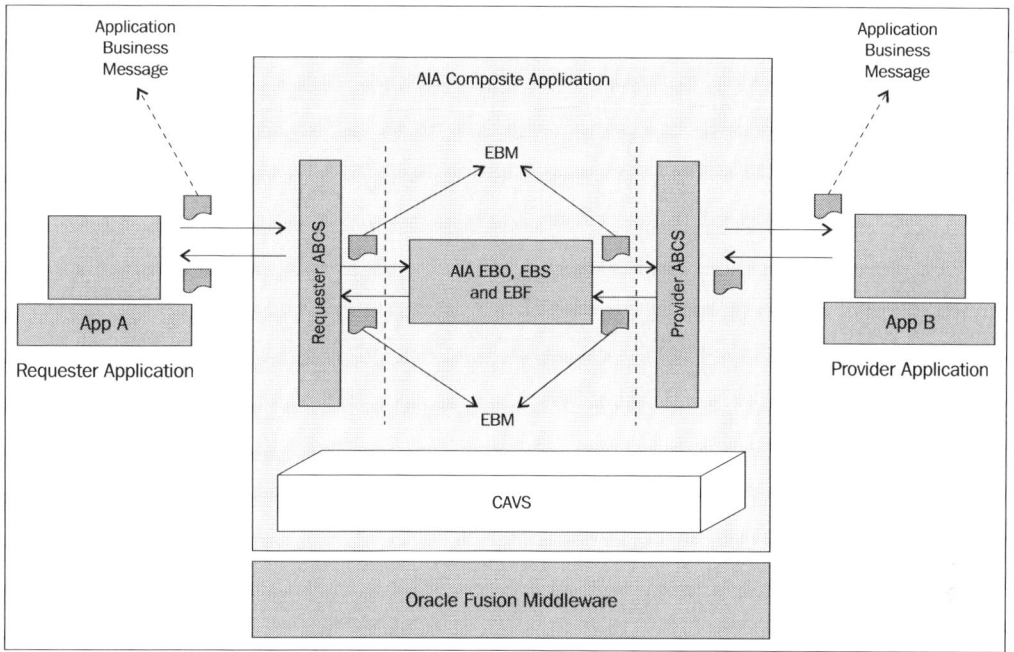

The precedingdiagram represents the overall AIA approach of implementation. In the precedingarchitecture,CAVS plays a foundational role that covers all the services including provider ABCS, EBS, requester ABCS, and so on. Therefore, it is capable of validating the end-to-end integration services. CAVS testing framework supports the following testing scenarios:

- Creating and executing test definition against participating application services
- Creating and executing test definition against test simulators that simulate the integration services
- Combining the actual application services along with simulated services for combined test simulation

In CAVS, two major components help to build and execute the test simulation and test definitions. They are called as **Test Definition** and **Simulator Definition**. Let us understand these key components.

## Test Definition

Fundamentally, the test initiator reads the test data from the repository and feeds it to the target web service to be tested. Test definitions are nothing but configuration and test instructions for the test simulators. The CAVS user can create these test definitions using CAVS user interface and stores it in the CAVS repository. During execution, the test simulator takes the test definition from the repository and acts accordingly. While creating the test definition, the CAVS should configure the target web service endpoint URL, input message model, and metadata. The test initiator is a logical unit that executes the test definition by calling the target endpoint URL according to the test definition. It can also validate the response against the predefined response configured in the test definition.

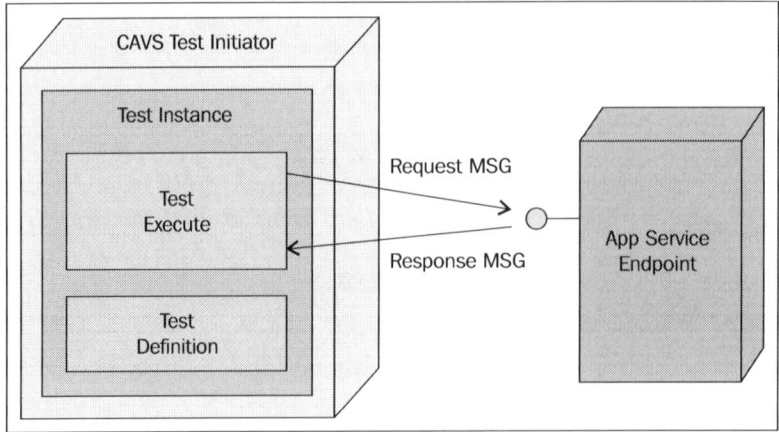

## Simulator Definition

Test initiators are fundamentally for testing the service endpoints according to the configuration defined in the test definition. CAVS simulators are used to simulate the web service endpoints. In real-time development, we may not have the endpoint ready for testing, or the endpoint may be a third party service that cannot be invoked for testing. In such ascenario, we can use the CAVS simulator to define the action of target endpoint service. A CAVS user can create several simulators to validate different sets of messages. During runtime, the CAVS simulator receivesthe request from the test initiator, locates the simulator definition from the CAVS repository and responds according to the definition configured.

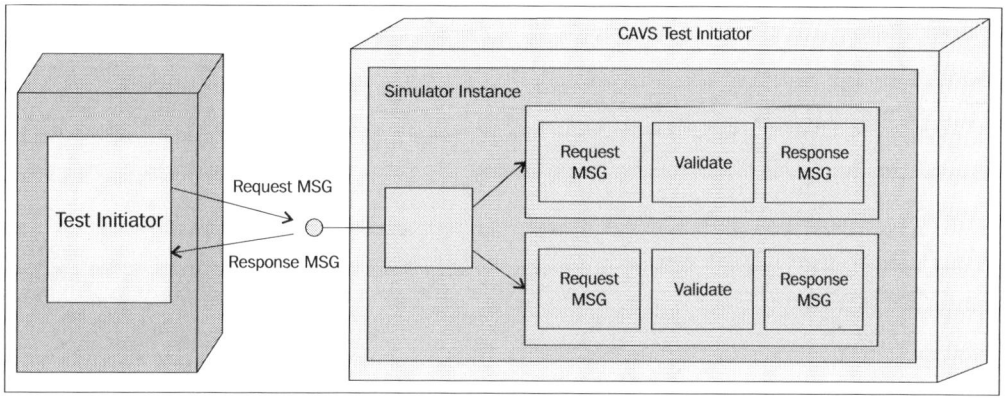

# Design prerequisites for CAVS enabling

As per Oracle AIA recommendations, the following key design requisites should have been followed while designing the AIA services:

- The requester and provider ABCS should be implemented using Oracle BPEL.
- While preparing the test definition and simulator definition, the request and response messages should be an entire SOAP payload. It includes the SOAP header, the SOAP envelope and the SOAP body messages. CAVS does not prepare the entire SOAP message by default.
- If it is a secure AIA service, then CAVS does not support authentication security information while executing the test definition or simulator definition. However, security information passed through the system can be validated by CAVS.
- If any one of the participating applicationsis involved in the CAVS testing flow, then there is a higher chance of the message being modified by the application. Therefore, the end response may be differing in each similar execution.
- The correlation logic between the test initiator and response simulator is purely based on timestamp or the request payload sent from ABCS to CAVS.

# Using CAVS user interface

The CAVS supports all the entire testing-related functionalities such as configuring the test definition, testing data and executing the test definition, reviewing the test result and migrating test. We need to follow a high-level procedure to define and execute the AIA testing using the CAVS user interface. The following is the systematic procedure to be followed:

1. Gather the required information and test message before the kickoff of the configuration.
2. Create test definition for testing the application or AIA service instances.
3. Create test simulator to simulate the service interfaces for service invocation.
4. Define the test groups and routing configuration for executing the testing flows.
5. Execute the test definition and testing simulator using CAVS user interface.
6. Finally, review the test results and execution, and correct the implementation if any.

We will go through the preceding procedure in the following sections.

## Gathering test information

The first step would be, before creating the test definition or simulator, we need to prepare the testing details. In order to prepare for testing configuration, we need the following information:

- We need to know the type of service interface, either synchronous, asynchronous, notify, and so on.
- If we are going to test the application service or any other service interface, then we need the endpoint URL of the service interface.
- When we configure the WSDL URL of the service interface for testing, we need to know the name of the operation where we are going to test and type.
- We should have the request message payload and response message payload that includes SOAP header, SOAP envelopment, and SOAP body as CAVS does not prepare the entire payload while testing the service interface.
- If it is a BPEL-based service interface, then we can gather a sample request message and response message from the BPEL console.

*Chapter 12*

# Create and execute a test definition using CAVS user interface

A test definition is a configuration to be created in the CAVS UI for a single execution of a test simulator instance. A test definition includes the test data and test execution instructions that can be executed alone or in a batch as part of a group definition.

To create the test definition in the CAVS user interface, the following steps should be executed one-by-one:

1. To access the CAVS user interface, we must log in as the admin user in the AIA console by accessing the URL (http://<hostname>:<port>/AIA/) of the AIA instance.

2. To access the CAVS test page, click on the **Go** button in the AIA console home page.

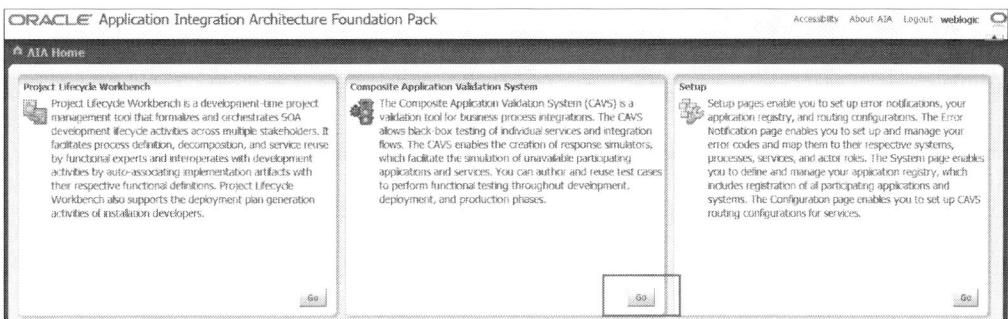

3. Now, we are in the CAVS testing page. To create the test definition, click on the **Create Test** button in the definition tab. It should load the create test page, as shown in the following screenshot:

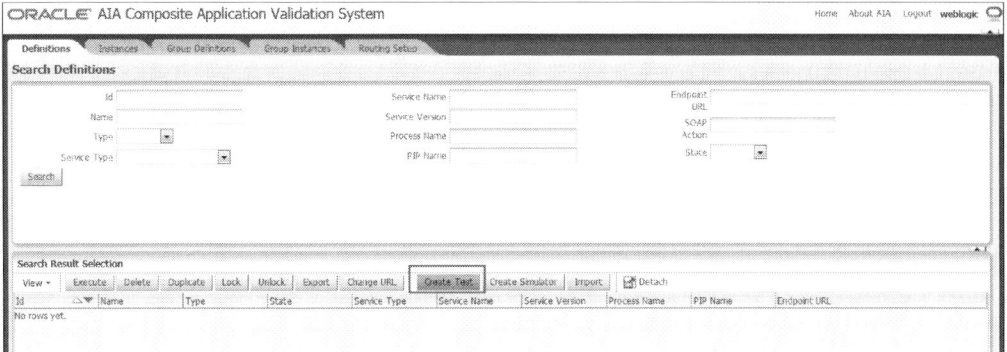

[ 221 ]

## Composite Application Validation System

4. In the create test page, we need to configure all necessary data to create the test definition. Enter the test name, service type, service name, version, and endpoint URL (not WSDL URL). Once the endpoint URL is entered, click on the **Get Operations** button. It should popup a window to select the SOAP action name (operation from the service endpoint).

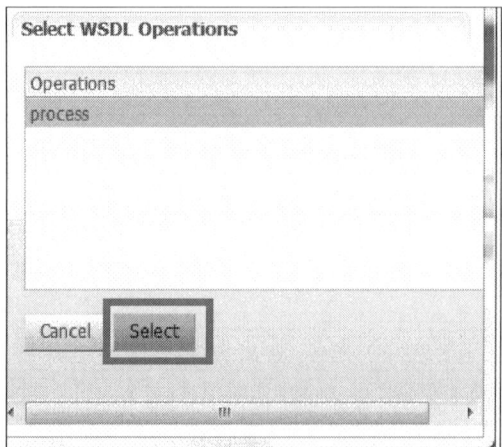

5. Select the name of the operation and click on the **Select** button to load the test page with operations. Once the operation is selected, enter the valid request message in the **Request Message** text area, as shown in the following screenshot:

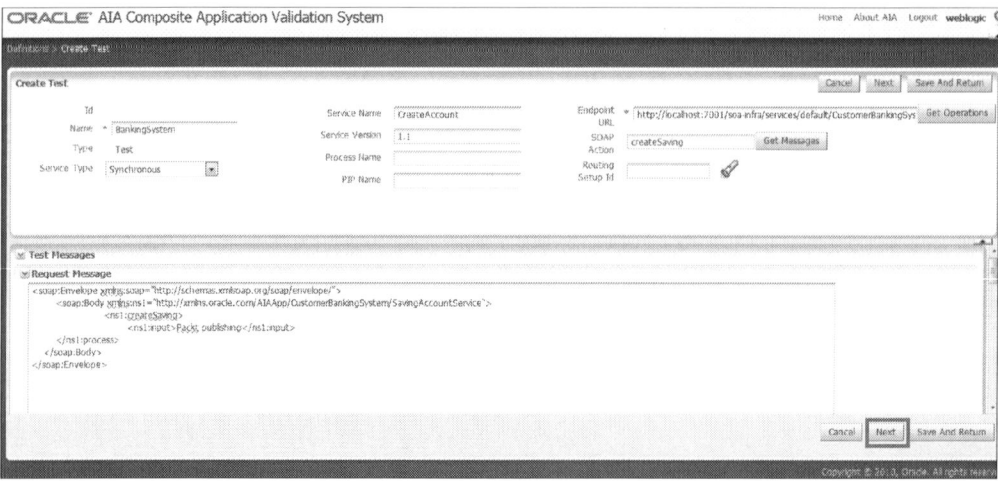

Chapter 12

6. Similarly, enter the expected response message in the **Response Message** text area and click on the **Generate Xpath** button to generate the Xpath values, as follows:

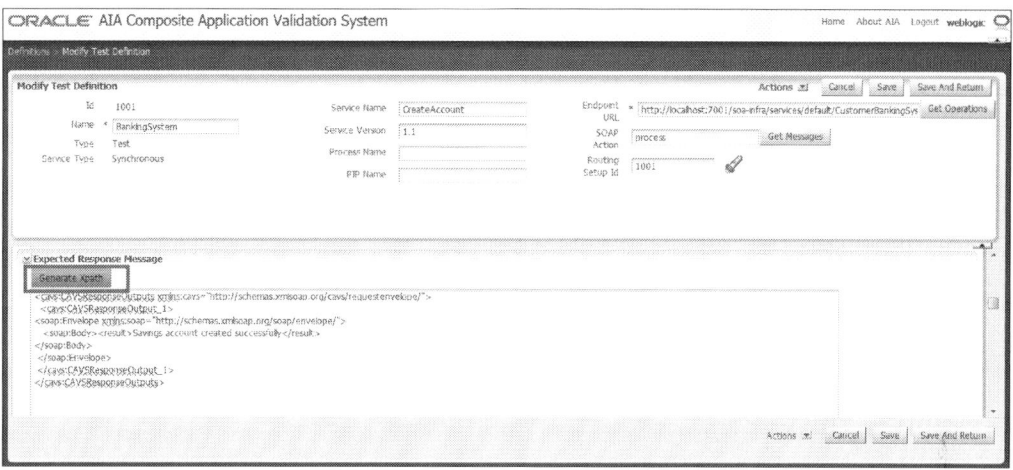

7. Once the Xpath generates the paths, enter the expected node value corresponding to the Xpath declaration, so that while testing the test definition, the CAVS will notify the pass and failed test scenarios.

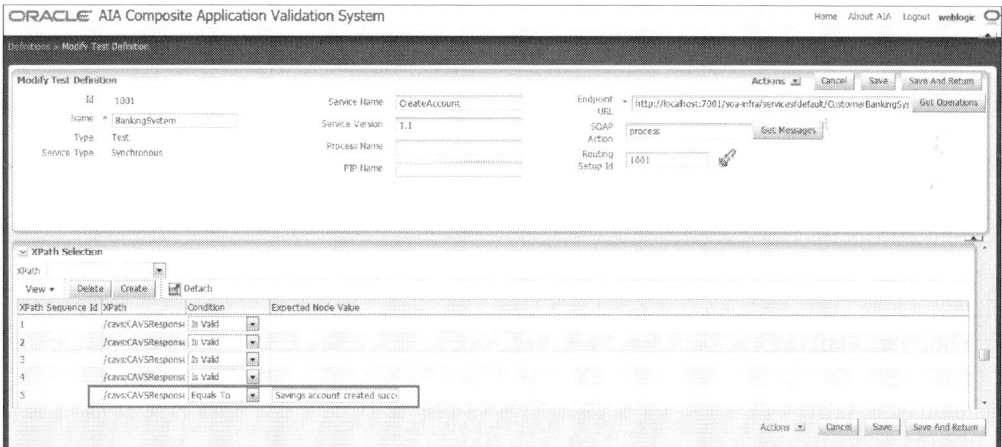

## Composite Application Validation System

8. Before completing, review the configuration and click on the **Save and Return** button to store the test definition in the AIA repository. Once the test definition is stored, it should return to the CAVS home page and display the newly created test definition, as follows:

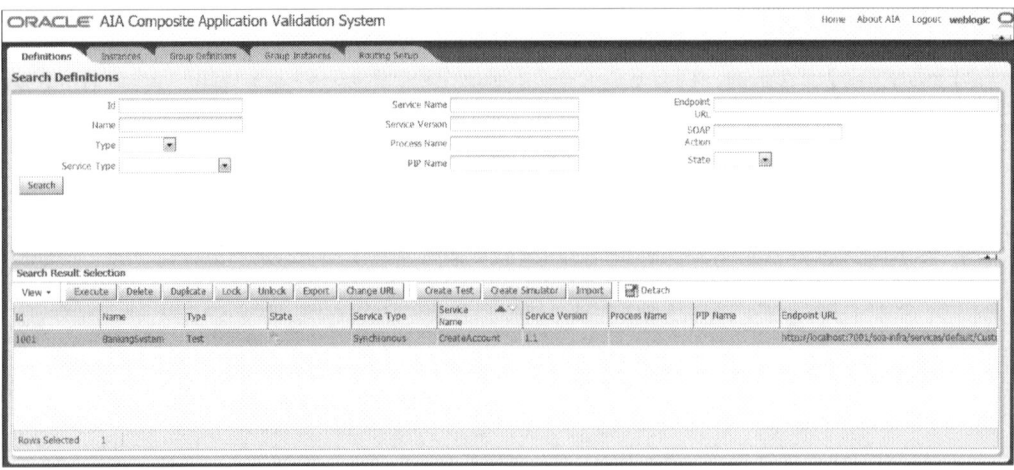

9. Now that we have created the test definition successfully in the CAVS UI, we have to execute the test definition to make sure we have configuredit properly.

10. To execute the test definition, go to the CAVS home page where we can see the newly created test under the **Search Result Selection** section. Select the newly created test from the list of test definitions, and click on the **Execute** button to run the test.

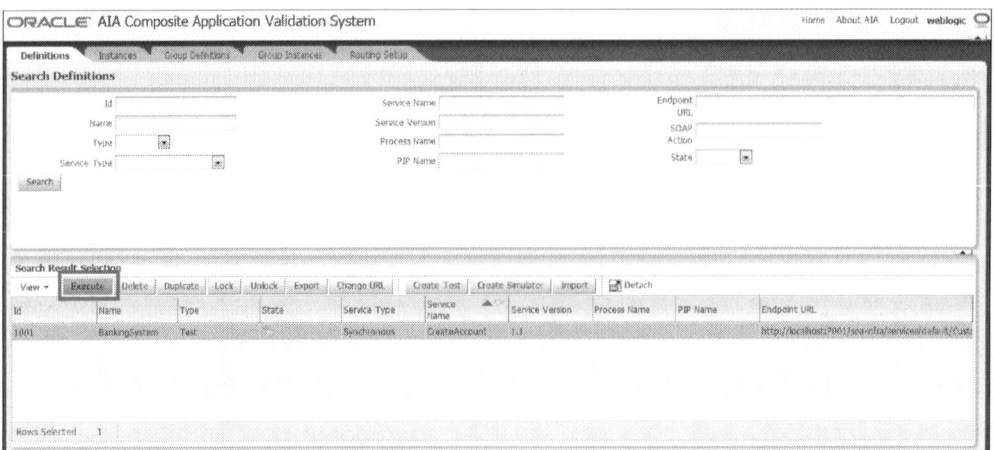

11. Once we have executed the test, the CAVS user interface should show the test results by displaying the request and response received from the service interface, as follows:

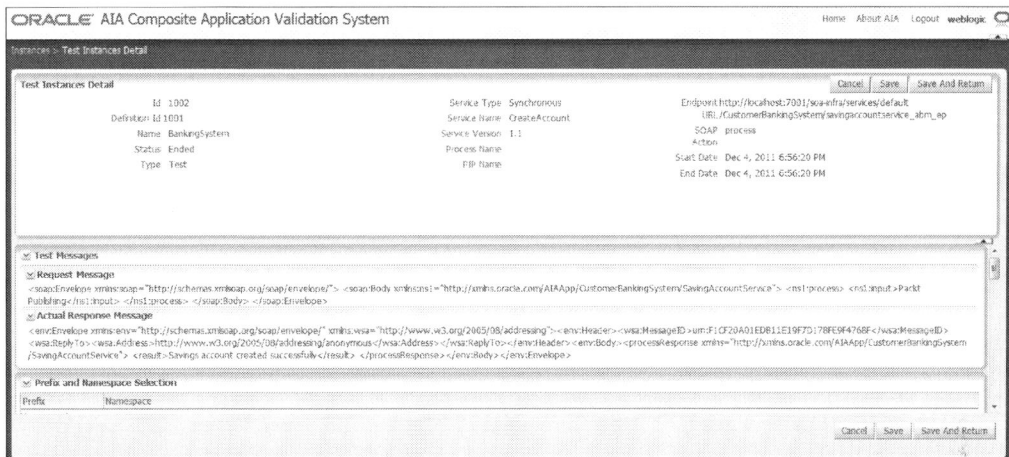

12. If the response message shows the expected response from the service interface, then we have successfully tested the test created using the CAVS user interface.

# Create Simulator Definition using CAVS user interface

As mentioned earlier, simulator definitions are used by the CAVS to simulate the service interface, so that the AIA service and invoking applications can consume the simulated services to validate the service calls. This approach helps to validate the service invocation before invoking the concrete service interfaces.

The following steps will help to create the simulator definition using CAVS user interface:

1. To access the CAVS user interface, we must log in as admin user in the AIA console by accessing the URL (`http://<hostname>:<port>/AIA/`) of the AIA instance.

2. To access the CAVS test page, click on the **Go** button in the AIA console home page.

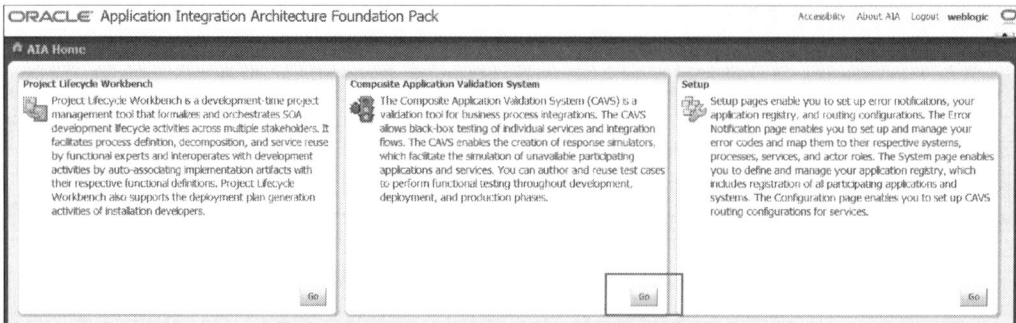

3. Now, we are in the CAVS testing page. To create the simulator definition, click on the **Create Simulator** button in the **Definitions** tab. It should load the simulator page, as shown in the following screenshot:

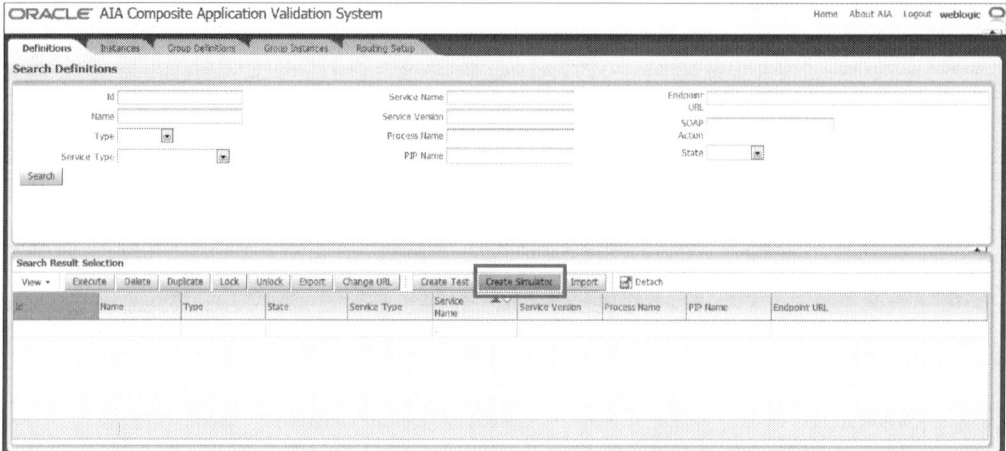

4. Now in the create simulator page, enter all required values which includes the name of the simulator, service type, service name, and service version. Most importantly, we should enter both the expected request message and response message in the respected text area, as shown in the following screenshot:

Chapter 12

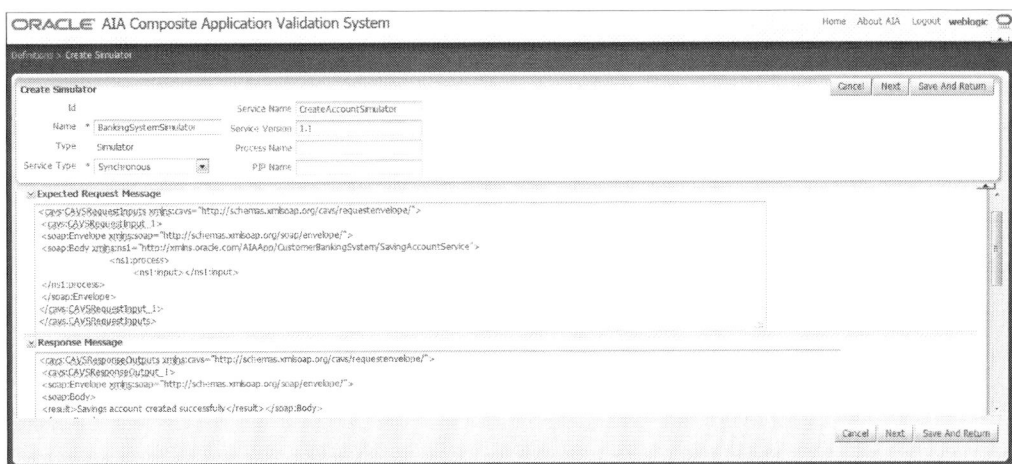

5. Now similar to the test definition, we need to generate the Xpath to validate the request message. Simulators are required to validate the request message before processing the message. Go to the **Expected Request Message** text area and click on the **Generate Xpath** button to generate Xpath values based on the expected request message configured in the text area.

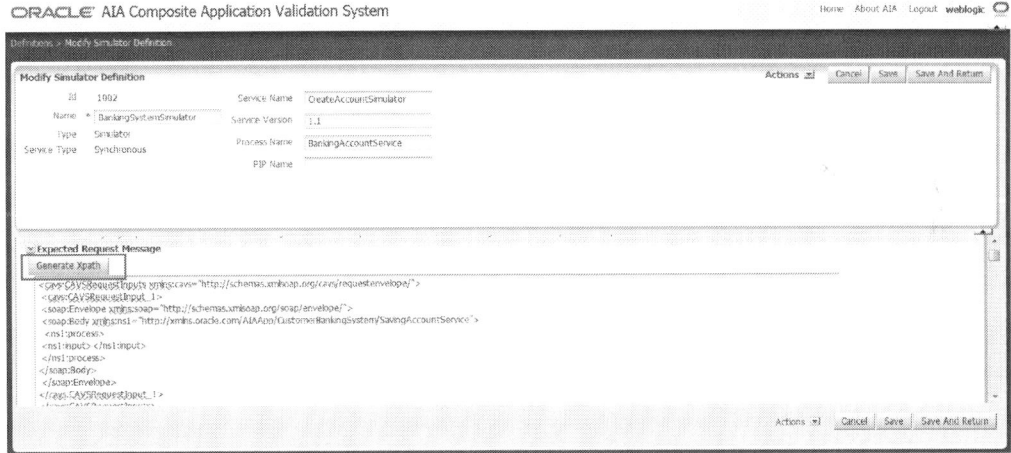

[ 227 ]

6. Once the Xpath is generated, go to the generated Xpath section and check the **Is Node Key** checkbox against the required validation paths, then enter the **Expected Node Value** text field to force the simulator to validate the input message.

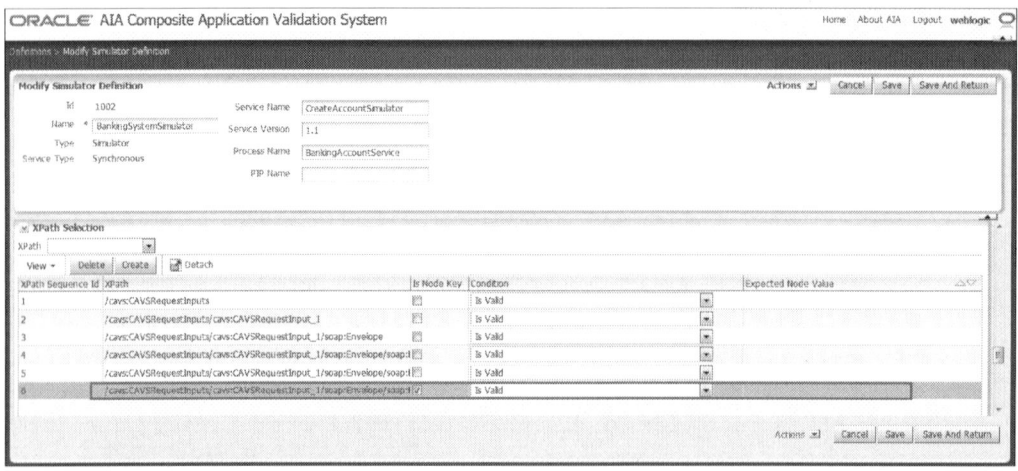

7. After all the required fields are entered in the create simulator page, click on the **Next** button to proceed further. The CAVS user interface will load the **Modify Simulator Definition** page as shown in the following screenshot. In this page, we can generate the XPath, define namespace standards, and instance configuration. Once you have modified the required configuration, click on the **Save and Return** button to complete the configuration, as shown in the following screenshot:

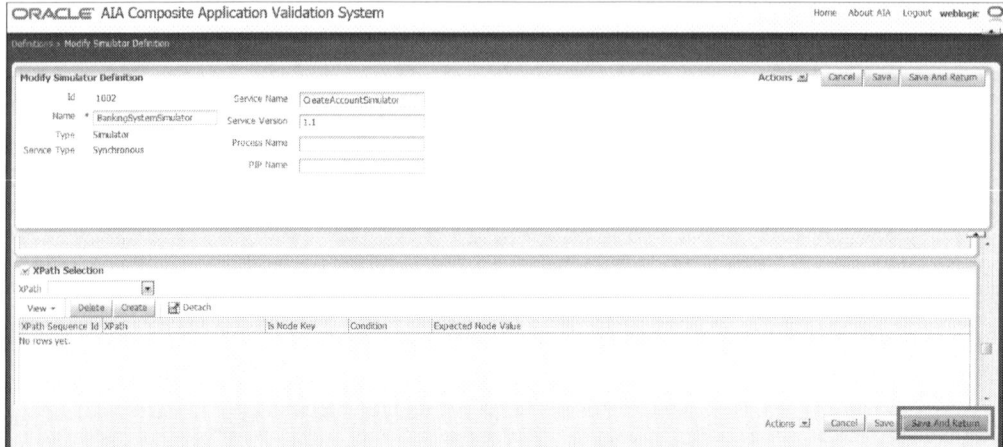

8. Once the configurations are created, the CAVS definition page will display the newly created simulator definition, as shown in the following screenshot:

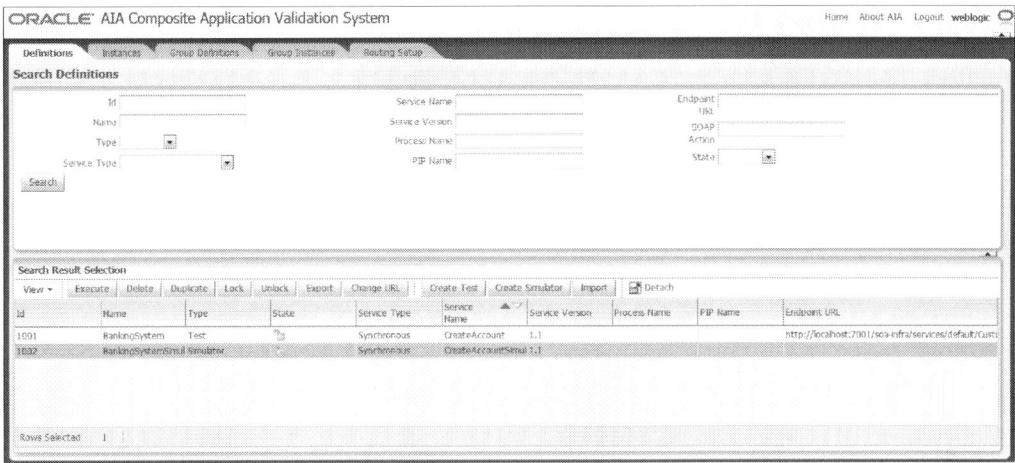

9. Once we complete the simulator part, we need to configure the simulator ID in the ABCS through routing mechanism.

> Note: We cannot execute the CAVS simulator definition directly by clicking on the **Execute** button. CAVS simulator can be executed through associating test definition and web services by configuring the CAVS routing mechanism.

# Enabling ABCS to route through CAVS

It is important to enable the ABCS service components created using JDeveloper in orderto route through the CAVS. That will help the CAVS route the service to the simulator definition created in the CAVS.

There are various approaches followed to enable the CAVS to route through CAVS simulation. The simplest approach would be to enable that in JDeveloper itself. While creating the ABCS service requester/provider, open the `AIAServiceConfigurationProperties.xml` file. Set the value of property name `"Routing.[PartnerLink].RouteToCAVS"` to `TRUE`.

# Composite Application Validation System

The followingimage will show the modified configuration file:

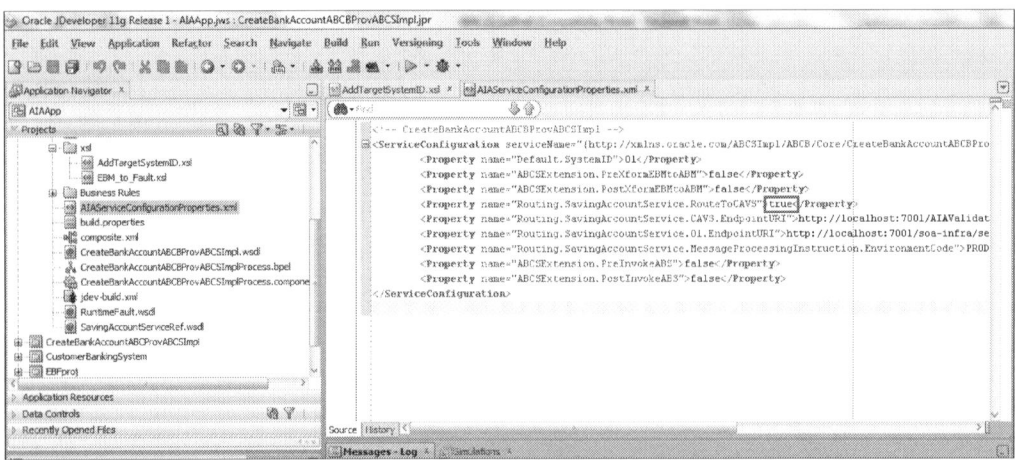

While deploying the ABCS service implementation in the AIA server, the AIA deployment framework will add `AIAServiceConfigrationProperties` to the `AIAConfigurationProperties.xml` file located in the `$AIA_HOME\aia_instances\<name of the instance>\AIAMetaData\config`folder.

Once the ABCS service provider/requester is deployed in the server go to the AIA configuration tab in the AIA console and update the ABCS service deployed to include the simulator ID created earlier.

>  Notes:When we mention a simulator ID which does exist, it will create the stuck threads in the server and it might bring down the CAVS (which can be fixed by restarting the server). So we should be cautious while performing this activity.

## CAVS routing

AIA CAVS provides a routing set up mechanism to achieve the following scenarios:

- If you want to test the provider services (ABCS) without invoking the actual service, then we can create the CAVS simulator and route the actual invocation from provider service to simulator.
- The requester application and service can call the CAVS simulator instead of calling the actual provider services.

How does the CAVS routing mechanism work? CAVS provides routing setup using the setup ID that is used to route the service calls to the CAVS simulators. CAVS routing set ups are stored as `RouteToCAVS` properties in the `AIAConfigurationProperties.xml`. That means while creating the ABCS services using the service components creator we should enable the ABCS to invoke the simulator service instead of the actual services.

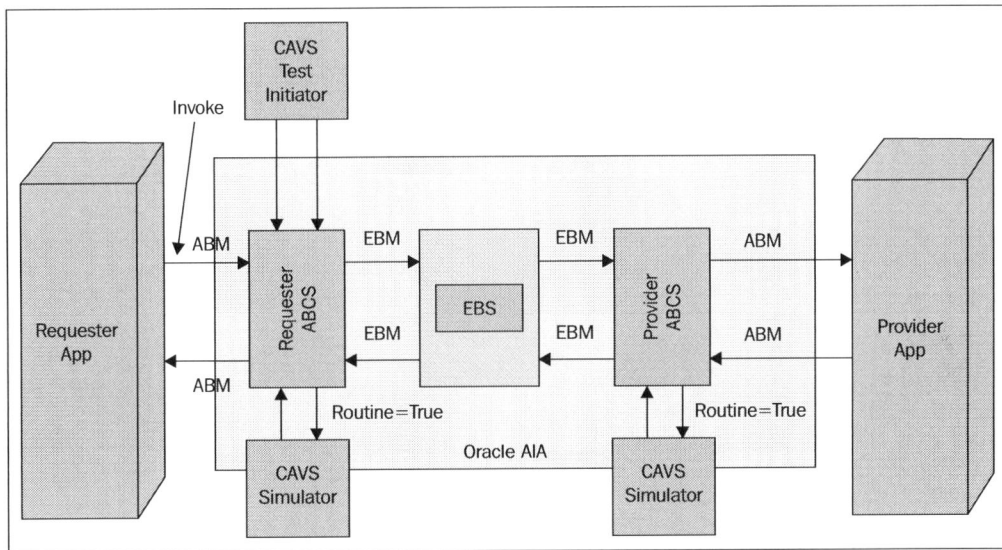

The preceding diagram represents the various CAVS simulator scenarios. If the requester ABCS or provider ABCS are configured routing to CAVS as true, then the actual invocation to the service provider will be routed to the simulator service. This approach will cover the scenario such as to test the requester ABCS service without invoking the actual AIA service, or to test the provider ABCS service without invoking provider application service or combining the simulation of both requester ABCS and provider ABCS. The CAVS routing setup determines the configuration that is required and automatically applies it before executing the test.

There are two approaches available to create and configure the CAVS routing mechanism. They are as follows:

1. Creating CAVS routing set up IDs using CAVS user interface
2. Creating CAVS routing configuration without creating routing setup IDs

For this chapter, we will go through the approach of creating CAVS routing configuration without creating the routing setup IDs.

# Create routing setup ID in CAVS user interface

To create the CAVS routing set up ID, go to the CAVS definition page and click on the **Routing Setup** tab. It should load the routing setup page. In that page, enter the Description field and click on the **Add** button in the simulator ID column to add the simulator with ABCS service.

Once all the configurations are completed, click on the **Save and Return** button to save the routing configuration changed, as shown in the following screenshot:

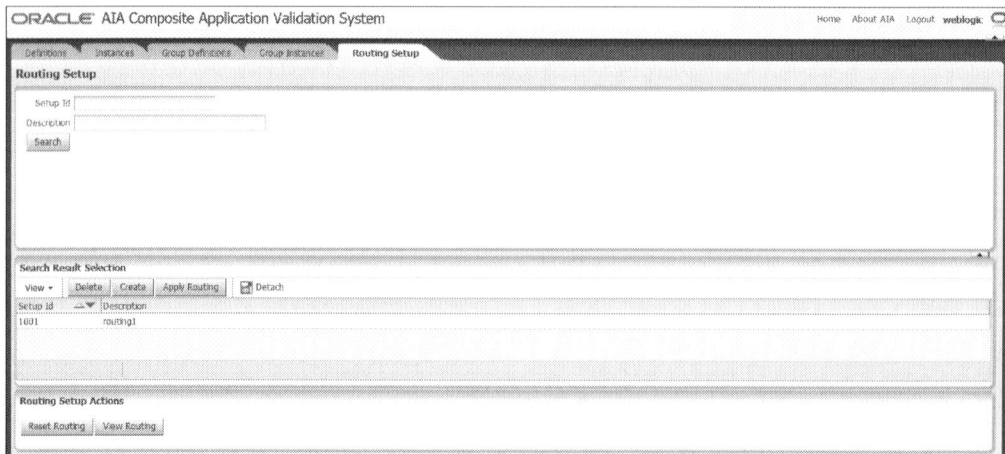

Now all the configurations are completed to execute the test definition that will trigger the test simulator and capture all testing results.

> Note: There are various mechanisms and configurations provided by the CAVS component in the AIA architecture. For other configuration mechanisms and details, you must read the AIA infrastructure guidelines provided by Oracle.

# Summary

In this last chapter, we learned the AIA testing framework and the Composite Application Validation System. The AIA CAVS provides two major definition approaches to test the service components and requester components. In this chapter, we learned about CAVS testing framework's test definition and simulator definition approaches that help to build the test scripts for the services. Furthermore, we learned about creating test definitions using the CAVS user interface and the execution approach. Finally, we touched on the ABCS configuration and routing approach. All the precedingsections of this chapter help us understand the fundamentals of the AIA Composite Application Validation System.

# Case Study

In the previous chapters, we learned about Oracle Application Integration Architecture Foundation Pack framework, its components, and development approaches. Now, you should have a good understanding of Oracle AIA framework and its components. You might have developed some sample EBS and ABCS using the Oracle JDeveloper. However, it is always better to have knowledge about how to apply this Oracle AIA integration approach to real world use cases. This case study will be helpful in leveraging your confidence for applying Oracle AIA integration approach.

As we know, Oracle AIA Foundation Pack is based on Oracle SOA Suite's tools and technologies. The AIA framework will help you to build integrations based on Service Oriented Architecture (SOA) approach and principles. Predominantly, Oracle AIA foundation pack has been adopted to integrate with other Oracle applications or to integrate an Oracle application with other systems such as legacy systems or web portals in order to leverage the SOA approach. In this chapter, we are going to understand how Oracle AIA foundation pack has been used to integrate Oracle JD Edwards application with a web portal.

## Sales and distribution

One of the top global pharmaceutical, biologic, and vaccine healthcare companies in North America made a decision to expand their vaccine's supply channel aggressively in northern regions. The business team identified various key sales channels that included effective e-commerce channels and quicker distribution and delivery channels. Therefore, the business and the IT department decided to expand the existing e-commerce portal to include the languages of target regions and effective shipment facilities. Oracle JD Edwards Sales Order Management module used to process the sales orders received through the e-commerce channels.

Case Study

In addition, the business team also engaged with a major shipment service provider to maintain the warehouse at various locations so that the shipper can quickly deliver the products to the customers. There were various integration requirements that were identified including customer, product, and pricing data synchronization between JD Edwards and the e-commerce portal, order flow synchronization, shipping partner systems integration, and so on. One of the important integrations is the one between JD Edwards and shipment partner systems, so that the orders and shipment notice can be delivered to the shipper seamlessly. For this case study, we will focus on the approach followed to integrate JD Edwards with a third party shipment provider. Due to confidentiality, this case study will only analyze the approach and components used for this integration.

# Business / data flow

Before we jump to the technical side, we need to understand the business process flow of the sales order and shipment. The following diagram will show the business flow along with its data flow:

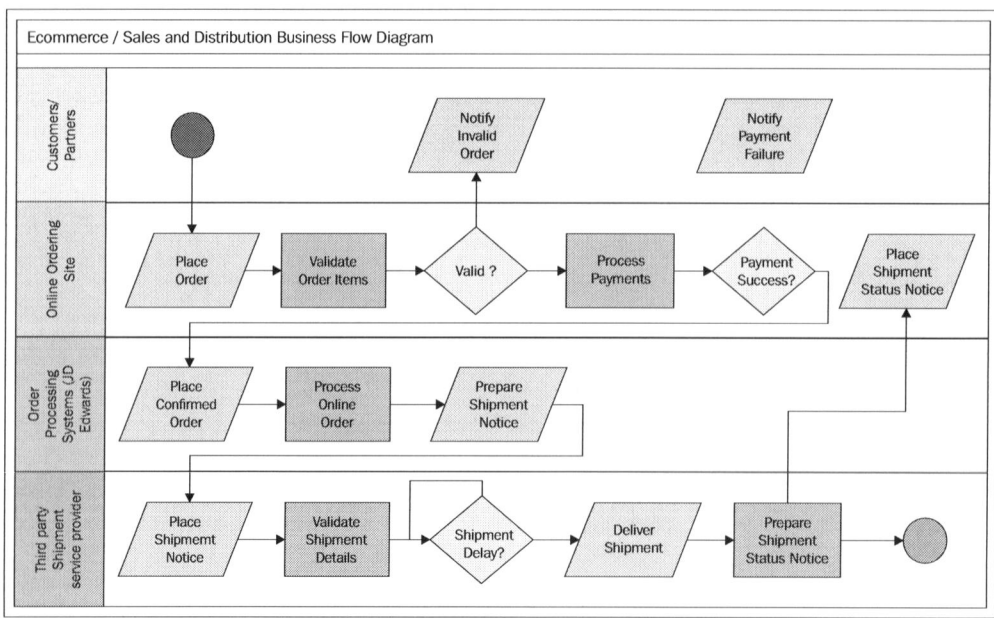

Customers and partners will have access to the online e-commerce website, where they can place the orders and make payments. Some customers may have credit eligibility. Once the customer places the order and makes a successful payment, the orders data is transferred to JD Edwards through an integration channel. All online orders will be processed in JD Edwards by the order management team, who can also contact the customer to correct the order details if there is any inadequate data. Once the order is processed in the JD Edwards application, a shipment notice will be generated, which should be transferred to the third party shipment service provider through another integration channel. After the delivery, order status update notice should be generated by the shipment provider, which will also be updated in the online e-commerce site.

# Integration flow

In order to meet the business flow, there are various integrations required between the business systems and partners. Oracle SOA Suite and AIA Foundation pack was identified as a framework for integrating the systems in mature SOA approach. The Oracle AIA foundation pack provides a proven approach of adopting SOA integration and the availability of EBO and EBM canonical message schema helps to build the integration solution quickly. The integration between the e-commerce portal and JD Edwards also flows through Oracle Fusion middleware. However, we are going to focus on the integration between JD Edwards and the shipment provider for this case study.

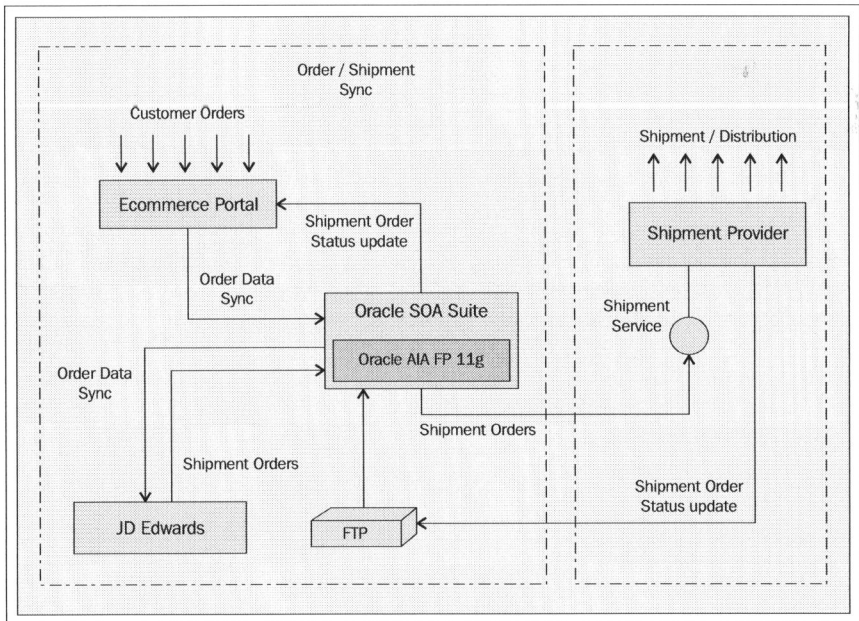

*Case Study*

As shown in the preceding diagram, the order data synchronization between the e-commerce portal and JD Edwards goes through Oracle SOA infrastructure. Once the online order is processed in the JD Edwards application, the processed order generates a shipment order, which has been delivered to the shipment provider through the service interface provided by the shipment service provider. Once the vaccines are delivered to the customer, the shipment provider generates a list of order status in a file format that can be delivered back through FTP. Oracle SOA infrastructure picks up those files through the FTP adapter, processes each order status, and updates it in the e-commerce portal. As our focus is on the shipment order flow between JD Edwards to shipment provider, the following sections will detail out the approach followed to identify the EBO, EBM, and EBS development.

## AIA Integration Reference Architecture

As mentioned earlier, Oracle AIA played a middleware role to integrate the internal and external systems. The following diagram will show the shipment order integration through Oracle AIA approach:

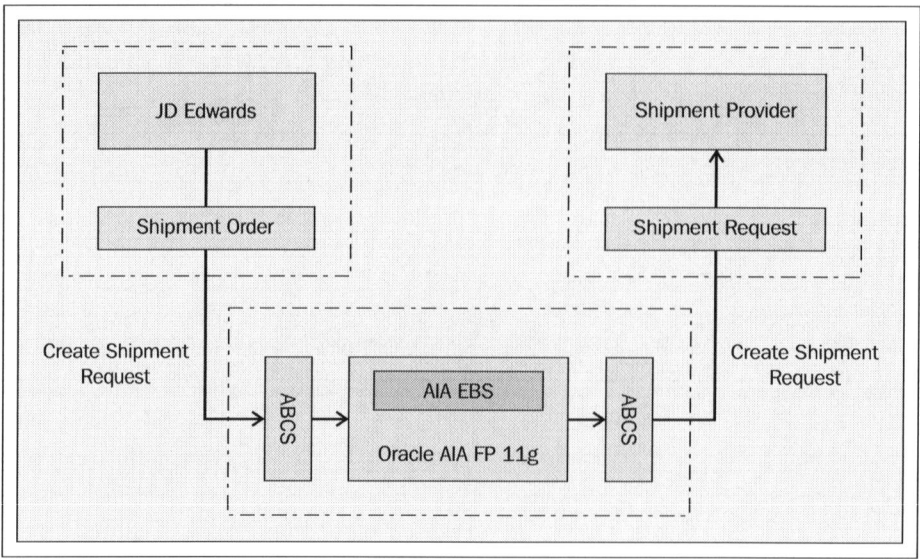

In the shipment order integration, JD Edwards will generate the shipment request message. Oracle AIA will then transform the message into a shipment request format as expected by the shipment provider. The transformed shipment request will be sent to the shipment provider through the shipment request interface. In order to meet the approach, we need to carry out the following steps:

1. Identify the EBO first and then the EBM.
2. Identify the EBS Service Operations from EBS WSDL.
3. Define ABCS process for applications interfaces.
4. Validate the integration interfaces using CAVS.

# Identifying EBO followed by EBM

The development team decided to implement the EBO format provided by Oracle AIA to meet the message structure between the JD Edwards and the shipment provider. Oracle AIA foundation pack's out-of-box installation comes with various predefined business objects as EBO and EBMs. For shipment, the development team decided to use the `ShipmentRequestEBO` and `ShipmentRequestEBM` that come as parts of AIA Metadata. However, `ShipmentRequestEBO` and `ShipmentRequestEBM` do include various data elements to meet a wide range of integration needs. Therefore, it has been decided to customize the `ShipmentRequestEBO` and `ShipmentRequestEBM` to meet the specific requirement. Oracle AIA foundation pack's EBO and EBM schema covers wide range of requirements. In most of the use case scenarios, it is required to customize the EBO and EBM schema model to meet the requirements. In addition, it is not a good approach to contain the entire used elements as parts of the message schema. The customized EBO and EBM are separated from the original EBO and EBM for better handling during development and upgrades.

The EBM message model, which is used for creating a shipment request and response from the `ShipmentRequestEBM.xsd`, is shown as follows:

```
<!-- Create ShipmentRequest Response Service -->
<xsd:complexType name="CreateShipmentRequestResponseEBMType">
<xsd:complexContent>
<xsd:extension base="corecom:EBMType">
<xsd:sequence>
<xsd:element name="DataArea"
  type="CreateShipmentRequestResponseDataAreaType"/>
</xsd:sequence>
</xsd:extension>
</xsd:complexContent>
/xsd:complexType>
```

```xml
<xsd:element name="CreateShipmentRequestResponseEBM"
  type="CreateShipmentRequestResponseEBMType"/>
<xsd:complexType name="CreateShipmentRequestResponseDataAreaType">
<xsd:sequence>
<xsd:element ref="corecom:CreateResponse"/>
<xsd:element ref="CreateShipmentRequestResponse"/>
</xsd:sequence>
/xsd:complexType>
<xsd:complexType name="CreateShipmentRequestResponseType">
<xsd:complexContent>
<xsd:extension base="ShipmentRequestEBMType"/>
</xsd:complexContent>
</xsd:complexType>
<xsd:element name="CreateShipmentRequestResponse"
  type="CreateShipmentRequestResponseType"/>
```

# Identifying EBS Service Operations from EBS WSDL

Once the EBO and EBM are identified, it is obvious that we should use the EBS that accommodates the identified EBM in the service operation. In this use case, we should use `ShipmentRequestEBS` to meet the requirement. Therefore, it has been decided to use the `ShipmentRequestEBS` as the EBS operation; however, Oracle AIA `ShipmentRequestEBS` includes many request and response operations including create, update, query, cancel, , and so on. As it is required to receive a confirmation message from the shipment provider for every shipment request, they decided to use the request and response type operations for this requirement.

The request operation used for this requirement from the `ShipmentRequestEBSV1.WSDL` is shown, as follows:

```xml
<operation name="CreateShipmentRequestResponse">
<documentation>
<svcdoc:Operation>
<svcdoc:Description>This callback operation will be used to
  provide the CreateShipmentRequest Response.</svcdoc:Description>
    <svcdoc:MEP>ASYNC_REQ_RESPONSE</svcdoc:MEP>
<svcdoc:DisplayName>CreateShipmentRequestResponse
  </svcdoc:DisplayName>
<svcdoc:LifecycleStatus>Active</svcdoc:LifecycleStatus>
  <svcdoc:Scope>Public</svcdoc:Scope>
<svcdoc:InitiatorService>ShipmentRequestEBSV1
  </svcdoc:InitiatorService>
```

```
            <svcdoc:InitiatorInterface>CreateShipmentRequestResponseEBM
                </svcdoc:InitiatorInterface>
            <svcdoc:InitiatorOperation>CreateShipmentRequestRequest
                </svcdoc:InitiatorOperation>
        </svcdoc:Operation>
    </documentation>
    <input message="ebs:CreateShipmentRequestRespMsg"/>
</operation>
```

# Defining ABCS process for application interfaces

As of now, we have identified the AIA integration message model and the operations to be used to communicate the message between application systems. In order to meet the end-to-end integration, the enterprise objects have to be converted to application-specific formats. Therefore, we have to identify the transformation approach to meet the application-specific message structure. As service provider's shipment service interface requires an application-specific message format (ABM) for request messages, a separate provider Application Business Connector Service (ABCS) is required to handle the transformation from `ShipmentRequestEBM` to shipment-provider ABM format.

On the other hand, interfacing with JD Edwards can be achieved through various methods. Oracle provides Oracle Applications that are specific to the adapters in order to connect to an application system that includes JD Edwards. However, the solution team decided to use the JD Edwards' temporary DB repository where shipment orders will be placed as records for processing. Oracle SOA Suite DB adapter will be used to consume the records from the JD Edwards, which will be passed to the AIA interface to submit shipment request to the shipment provider. It is required to build an ABCS interface to handle transformation to map the records generated by the JD Edwards to `ShipmentRequestEBM`. Therefore, this approach meets the AIA integration framework and reference model.

As we have seen in the *Chapter 5, Application Business Connector Services*, AIA service constructor in JDeveloper helps to build the provider and requester ABCS. The JDeveloper builds the ABCS component by mapping the Application Specific Message (ABM) and Enterprise Message Model (EBM). Therefore, the development team builds the `ShipmenRequesterABCS` and `ShipmentProviderABCS` using JDeveloper AIA Service Constructor Wizards.

The following diagram will show the overall components of the shipment integration architecture:

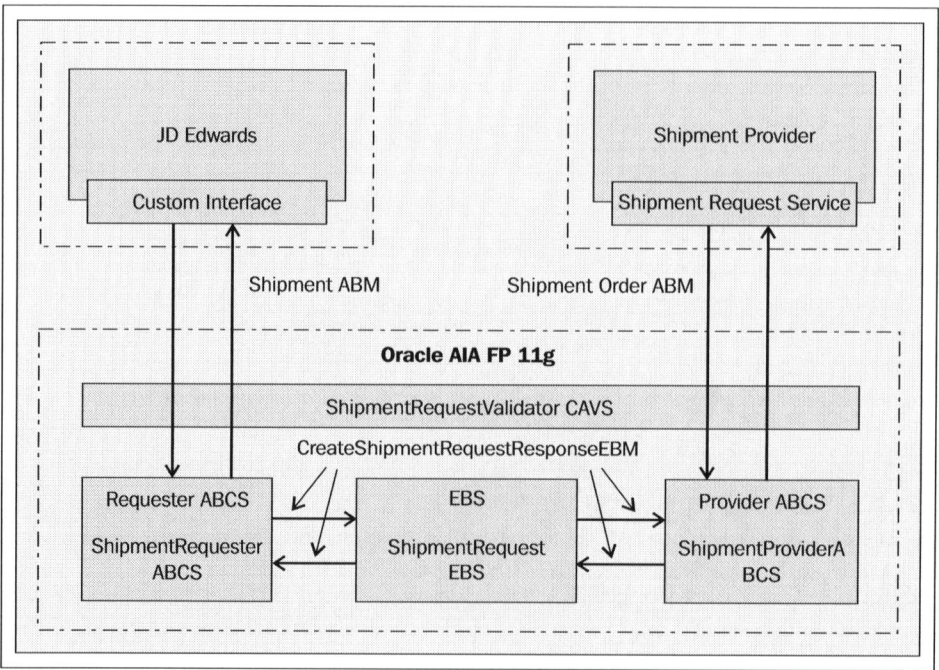

# Validating the integration interfaces using CAVS

As we have seen in *Chapter 12, Composite Application Validation System*, CAVS provides framework to build the test definitions to validate the services built on the AIA framework and provides simulator components to simulate the external services for complete end-to-end testing. During the design phase, the implementation team decided to use the CAVS feature to qualify various services component of the AIA approach to save time and efforts.

As it was decided to use the CAVS during unit testing and integration testing phases, the design includes enabling the ABCS routing through CAVS by configuring it in `AIAServiceConfigurationProperties.xml`. Therefore, the CAVS test definition created in the CAVS user interface will be executed to validate the integration performance before taking it into the production environment. In addition, CAVS is used to unit test both the provider ABCS and the requester ABCS for this integration process.

# Key benefits of using AIA

As we have seen in various chapters of this book, the Oracle AIA foundation pack provides various components to build integrations between applications. As expected, the following benefits are realized by using the AIA FP for this integration use case.

- AIA foundation pack provides prebuilt Enterprise Service Objects and Services for shipment related integration that made this implementation achievable and more quickly than expected. Even if the EBO/EBM for the domain requirement is not available or suitable for the AIA integration, the default template can be used to speeding up custom development.
- AIA has an inbuilt consumer component (provider ABCS) to establish connection with the shipper interface seamlessly.
- Prebuilt AIA error handling framework helps to implement the error handling as a part of the integration process.
- AIA proven architecture methodology helps to adopt service-oriented integration without spending efforts on identifying the methodologies or architecture concepts.
- CAVS support helps to build the test definitions and third party service simulation (in this use case, it is the shipper service) quicker and easier, and reduce the environment configuration overheads.

# Summary

At the end of this implementation, the entire integration was achieved in much lesser time due to the prebuilt EBM and EBS components. In addition, the AIA approach helped to build the integration based on mature SOA approach without any deviation in identifying the service granularity, message model, and interaction complexities. Similar to the shipment integration, other integration requirements such as maintaining products, customers, and pricing data integrity between JD Edwards and the e-commerce website has been implemented through the AIA approach. The data integrity process has been built as separate provider ABCS for each data model such as products, customers, and pricing, which has been consumed by the automated requester ABCS to import into the e-commerce site.

Overall, the entire project was implemented in a much quicker and easier way by using the Oracle AIA Foundation Pack 11g.

# Index

## Symbols

(Advanced Message Queue Protocol)
  about 11
<definitions> element 71
<message> element 72
<portType> element
  about 73
  one-way operation pattern 73
  two-way or request/response operation pattern 73
<types> element 72

## A

ABCS
  about 24, 99, 100
  design principles 105
  developing 106
  developing manually, Oracle JDeveloper used 120-123
  extending, custom code used 124
  in AIA 100
  in AIA architecture 100
  provider ABCS 100
  requester ABCS 100
  securing 152
  VETORO 101
ABCS Architecture
  about 101
  diagram 102
  enrich 103
  key definitions 104
  operate 103
  route 103
  Route 101
  transform 103
  validate 102
ABCS development
  about 106
  AIA Service Constructor, used 106
  Oracle JDeveloper used 120-123
ABCS development, with AIA Service Constructor
  ABCS service solution, creating 107-113
  about 106
  Additional Target Systems screen 117
  manual configurations 119
  Options and Generation 107
  Service Description 106
  Service Description screen 108
  Service Details screen 110
  Service Interface 106
  Service Object Fault screen 113, 116
  Service Object screen 111
  Service Option screen 117
  Target Service 107
  Target Service Fault screen 116
  Target Service screen 113
  WSDL text field, selecting 114
ABCS process
  defining, for application interfaces 241
ABCS security implementation 153
ABCS versioning 164
ABCS WSDL file 211
ABM Schema
  designing 105
access control level security 144
ActivityDateTime, EBMTracking elements 61

Adapters 15
Additional Target Systems screen 117
Agile PLM 16
AIA
  error logging 193
AIAAsyncErrorHandlingBPELProcess application 183
AIA contents
  accessing, in OER 208, 209
AIA EBMs
  exploring 50
AIA error handling framework
  about 182
  diagram 182
  features 183
AIA fault policy files
  association, configuring 187, 188
  configuring 184-186
AIA Foundation Pack. See Orcale AIA Foundation Pack
AIA Integration Reference Architecture 238
AIA message processing patterns
  about 166
  asynchronous delayed response pattern 170-172
  asynchronous fire-and-forget pattern 168, 169, 170
  competing consumers pattern 175
  guaranteed delivery pattern 172, 173
  other patterns 174
  service routing pattern 174
  synchronous request-response pattern 166-168
AIA Process Reference Model 27
AIA Project Lifecycle Workbench 211
AIA Security
  about 143, 145
  security implementations levels 143
AIA Service Constructor
  about 106
  used, for ABCS development 106
AIA Service Constructor wizard 118
AIA services
  predefined policies, applying 148-152
  securing 147, 148
AIA versioning
  ABCS versioning 164
  about 157, 158
  major versioning 159
  minor versioning 158
  schema (EBO/EBM) versioning 159-162
  services (EBS) versioning 162, 163
Apache Qpid 11
Application Business Connector Services. See ABCS
Application Business Message (ABM) 48, 99
Application Layer 24
Application, Sender sub elements 59
Application Servers 15
asset centralization pattern
  about 175
  data model centralization 175
  service contract centralization 176
asset extensibility patterns
  about 176
  EBF and transformation, extending 177
  EBO/EBM, extending 176
  EBS and ABCS, extending 177
asynchronous delayed response pattern
  about 170-172
  diagrammatic representation 170
asynchronous fire and forget pattern
  about 84, 168-170
  diagrammatic representation 168
asynchronous one-way pattern EBS
  developing 96
asynchronous request and delayed response pattern 85-87
asynchronous request delayed response pattern EBS
  developing 96

# B

B2B integration 9
B2BProfile elements
  about 62
  ReceiverTradingPartner 62
  SendingTradingPartner 62
BankAccountEBS.wsdl definition 68
bottom-up approach 88
BPEL 15
Business Activity Monitors 15
business components

about 38
characteristics 38
diagrammatic representation 38
business / data flow 236
business data types 45
business entity EBS implementation 88
business faults 180
Business Message 47
business object 22
Business Process Execution Language (BPEL) 126
business process integration 8
Business Process Management (BPM) 15
business process modeling phase, Oracle AIA project life-cycle 210
Business Rules Engine 15
BusinessScope elements
  about 60
  BusinessScopeTypeCode 61
  Custom 61
  EnterpriseServiceName 61
  EnterpriseServiceOperationName 61
  ID 61
  InstanceID 61
BusinessScopeTypeCode, BusinessScope elements 61
Business Service Repository (BSR) 25
business to business integration 9
business use case, for EBF 138-140

# C

CallingServiceName, Sender sub elements 59
Canonical Layer 48
canonical versioning patterns 156
Canonical XML 15
CAVS 25, 57
characteristics, EBF 126
characteristics, EBS 70
coarse-grained web services 23
common business objects 35
common components
  about 40
  ComponentIndentificationType 40
  OperationType 40
  ShipmentType 40
Common EBO
  about 35
  diagrammatic representation 36
  example 36
  extending 36, 37
  ItemLotBalance EBO 36
competing consumers pattern 175
complex data types 44
Complex Event Processer 15
ComponentIndentificationType 40
Composite Application Validation System. See CAVS
construction phase, AIA Project Life Cycle 106
ContactEmail, Sender sub elements 59
ContactName, Sender sub elements 59
ContactPhoneNumber, Sender sub elements 59
context-oriented EBMs 48
CORBA 11
core data types 45
Core EBO
  about 34, 35
  groups 35
Core EBO components 35
Core EBO Groups
  about 35
  Common EBO Group 35
  Custom EBO 41
  EBOs Components Group 38
Core EBO package 50
CreateBankAccount 68
CreateBankAccountEBM 68
CreateBankAccountEBO 68
CreateBankAccountResponse 68
Create SalesOrderEBM 22
CreationDateTime element 55
current-datetime() function 55
Custom, BusinessScope elements 61
custom code
  used, for extending ABCS 124
Custom EBO 41
Custom element 62
Custom, Sender sub elements 59

## D

DataArea element 62, 63
data integration 8
data model centralization 175
data types 45
DateTimeType data type 55
DefinitionID attribute 57
DeleteBankAccount 69
Delete SalesOrderEBM 22
deployed composite
  harvesting, into OER 212
deployment phase 211
deployment planning phase 210
Description, Sender sub elements 59
design patterns 165
design pattern solutions, Oracle AIA
  about 165
  AIA message processing patterns 166
  asset centralization pattern 175
  asset extensibility patterns 176
design principles, ABCS
  ABM Schema, designing 105
  about 105
design-time composites
  harvesting, into OER 211
design-time governance 202
design-time harvesting
  setting up, AIA Foundation Pack used 212
diagrammatic relationship, EBS-EBM-EBO 78

## E

EBF
  about 24, 125
  architecture 126, 127
  building 128
  business use case 138-140
  characteristics 126
  overview 125
EBF and transformation
  extending 177
EBF architecture 126, 127
EBF, building
  as, BPEL Service 131-137
  EBF candidate, identifying 128, 129

  service contract, creating 129-131
  service contract, identifying 128
EBF candidate
  identifying 128, 129
EBM characteristics 49
EBM global attributes
  about 53
  languageCode 53
  versionID 53
EBM Header 53
EBM Header child components
  about 57
  B2BProfile element 62
  BusinessScope 60
  custom element 62
  EBMTracking elements 61
  FaultNotification element 62
  MessageBatch element 62
  MessageProcessingInstruction 57
  Sender element 58
  Target element 60
EBM header components
  about 55
  CreationDateTime 55
  EBMID 55
  EBMName 55
  EBOName 55
  RequestEBMID 56
  VerbCode 56
EBMID element 55
EBMName element 55
EBM Request - Response Message use case 64, 65
EBMs
  about 22, 48
  characteristics 49
  overview 48
  physical structure 50
  structure 51, 52
EBM schema model 90
EBM structure
  about 51
  DataArea 51-63
  EBM header 53
  global attributes 53
  header 51
EBMTracking elements

ActivityDateTime 61
ExecutionUnitID 61
ExecutionUnitName 61
ImplementationCode 61
SequenceNumber 61
**EBM use cases**
  EBM Request - Response Message 64, 65
**EBM XSD files 211**
**EBO/EBM**
  extending 176
**EBO group as directories**
  about 33
  Core EBOs 34
  Industry EBOs 34
  Infrastructure components 34
**EBOName element 55**
**EBOs**
  about 22, 31, 32
  exploring 33, 34
  extending 42, 43
  identifying 239
  overview 31, 32
  structure 40, 41
**EBOs Components Group**
  business components 38
  common components 40
  reference components 39
**EBO XSD file 211**
**EBS**
  about 23, 67
  characteristics 70
  developing, Oracle Mediator used 91-4
  overview 67, 68
  roles 69
  structure 71
  types 75
**EBS and ABCS**
  extending 177
**EBS architecture**
  about 79
  entity services EBS 80
  MEP 82
  message pattern, identifying 87
  process services EBS 81
**EBS design principles 88, 89**
**EBS implementation**
  about 90
  asynchronous one-way pattern EBS, developing 96
  EBS, developing using Oracle Mediator 91, 92-94
  JDeveloper, used 90
  synchronous request and response pattern, developing 94
  synchronous request delayed response pattern EBS, developing 96
  WSDL, constructing for process service EBS 90
**EBS library**
  about 74
  exploring 74
**EBS message exchange patterns**
  about 82
  asynchronous fire and forgot pattern 84
  asynchronous request and delayed response pattern 85, 86
  identifying 87
  synchronous request-response pattern 83
**EBS routing principles 89, 90**
**EBS Service Operations**
  identifying, from EBS WSDL 240
**EBS structure**
  <definitions> element 71
  <message> element 72
  <portType> element 73
  <types> element 72
  about 71
**EBS types**
  entity type EBS 75
  process type EBS 75, 77
**EBS WSDL file 211**
**enrich, ABCS Architecture 103**
**Enterprise Application Integration (EAI) 100**
**Enterprise Business Flow.** *See* **EBF**
**Enterprise Business Message (EBM) 100**
**Enterprise Business Messages.** *See* **EBMs**
**Enterprise Business Objects.** *See* **EBOs**
**Enterprise Business Services.** *See* **EBS**
**Enterprise Object Library (EOL) 34**
**Enterprise Service Bus (ESB) 15**
**EnterpriseServiceName, BusinessScope elements 61**

EnterpriseServiceOperationName, BusinessScope elements 61
entity services EBS
  architecture 80
entity type EBS 75
EnvironmentCode attribute 57
error log files
  viewing 198, 199
error logging, AIA
  about 193
  error log files, viewing 198, 199
  system log level, configuring 196-198
  system/service level tracing, enabling 194-196
  trace logging, enabling 194
error notification
  disabling 190
  enabling 188, 189
ESBHeader, Sender sub elements 59
ExecutionUnitID, EBMTracking elements 61
ExecutionUnitName, EBMTracking elements 61
eXtensible Access Control Markup Language. *See* XACML

## F

FaultHandlers 180
fault handling, AIA
  about 184
  AIA fault policy files, configuring 184, 185, 186
  association, customizing between custom fault polices and bindings 187, 188
  error notification, disabling 190
  error notification, enabling 188, 189
  MDS, updating 191-193
fault handling, BPEL
  about 180
  business faults 180
  system faults 181
FaultName 180
FaultNotification element 62
FaultVariable 180
fine-grained web services 23

functional integration 8
fundamentals, for implementing and designing EBS 88, 89

## G

guaranteed delivery pattern
  about 172, 173
  diagrammatic representation 172

## H

Human Workflow 29

## I

IBM WebSphere MQ 11
ID, BusinessScope elements 61
ID, Sender sub elements 59
ImplementationCode, EBMTracking elements 61
implementation-time governance 202
Industry EBOs
  about 34, 44
  diagrammatic representation 44
infrastructure components
  about 34, 44
  business data types 45
  complex data types 44
  core date types 45
  data types 45
  simple data types 44
InstanceID attribute 57
InstanceID, BusinessScope elements 61
integration architectures
  about 9
  Message oriented middleware (MOM) 11
  one-to-one integration 9
  point-to-point integration 9
  Remote Procedure Call (RPC) 10
  Service Oriented Architecture (SOA) 13
  shared data repository 10
  web service integration 12
integration flow
  about 237
  AIA Integration Reference Architecture 238
  EBO, identifying 239

EBS Service Operations, identifying from
    EBS WSDL 240
**integration interfaces**
    validating, CAVS used 242
**integration types**
    about 8
    business process integration 8
    business to business integration 9
    data integration 8
    functional integration 8
    presentation (UI) integration 8
**IPAddress, Sender sub elements 59**

# J

Java Messaging Service (JMS) 11
Java RMI 11
JDeveloper IDE 29
JDeveloper WSDL Editor 90

# K

key definitions, ABCS Architecture 104

# L

languageCode attribute 53

# M

**MDS**
    updating 191-193
**MessageBatch element 62**
**message level security 144**
**Message oriented middleware (MOM)**
    about 11
    architecture 11
**MessageProcessingInstruction element**
    about 57
    attributes 57
    DefinitionID attribute 57
    EnvironmentCode attribute 57
    InstanceID attribute 57
**Message Queue (MQ) 11**
**Messaging Services 15**

# O

**OAGIS 32**

ObjectCrossReference, Sender sub elements 59
**ODI(Oracle Data Integrator) 183**
**OER**
    about 25, 201, 203
    AIA contents, accessing 208, 209
    as, AIA repository 203
    benefits 203
    configuring, as AIA repository 204-207
    deployed composite, harvesting 212
    design-time composites, harvesting 211
    design-time harvesting, setting up using
        AIA Foundation Pack 212
**OER Harvester Solution pack 204**
**one-to-one integration 9**
**one-way operation pattern 73**
**operate, ABCS Architecture 103**
**OperationType 40**
**optimized enterprise service-oriented solution**
    implementing 15
**Options and Generation 107**
**Oracle AIA**
    ABCS 100
    ABCS process, defining for application
        interfaces 241
    ABCS, securing 152, 153
    about 16, 67
    benefits 243
    business / data flow 236
    error handling framework 182
    error log files, viewing 198, 199
    fault handling mechanism 184
    integration flow 237
    integration interfaces, validating using
        CAVS 242
    Oracle AIA Foundation Pack 16
    Oracle AIA Process Integration Pack 16
    overview 7
    project life-cycle 210
    sales and distribution 235, 236
    security, implementing 146
    versioning 155
**Oracle AIA EBO components 31**
**Oracle AIA Foundation Pack**
    about 17, 18
    components 21

features 20
Oracle AIA Foundation Pack 11g 34
Oracle AIA Foundation Pack 11g R1 165
Oracle AIA Foundation Pack components
   Application Business Connector Services (ABCS) 24
   Composite Application Validation System (CAVS) 25
   Enterprise Business Flow (EBF) 24
   Enterprise Business Messages (EBM) 22
   Enterprise Business Objects (EBO) 22
   Enterprise Business Services (EBS) 23
   Oracle Enterprise Repository (OER) 25
Oracle AIA FP
   design pattern solutions 165
Oracle AIA FP 11g 62
Oracle AIA Process Integration Packs (PIPs) 16, 17
Oracle AIA product 14
Oracle AIA reference architecture
   about 26, 27
   AIA Process Reference Model 27
Oracle AIA reference architecture model 26
Oracle Application Integration Architecture. See Oracle AIA
Oracle B2B 29
Oracle BPEL
   fault handling mechanism 180
Oracle BPEL Process Manager 29
Oracle BPM worklist 183
Oracle Business Activity Monitor 29
Oracle Business Rules 29
Oracle Complex Event Processing 29
Oracle E-Business Suite 16
Oracle Enterprise Manager 29
Oracle Enterprise Repository. See OER
Oracle Fusion Middleware
   about 28
   diagrammatic representation 19
Oracle Fusion platform 145
Oracle JDeveloper
   used, for ABCS development 120
Oracle Mediator
   about 29, 79
   used, for developing EBS 91-94
Oracle Mediator component 181
Oracle Metadata Repository 29

Oracle Service Bus 29, 183
Oracle SOA Suite 11g
   about 29
   components 29
Oracle SOA Suite 11g components
   Human Workflow 29
   JDeveloper IDE 29
   Oracle B2B 29
   Oracle BPEL Process Manager 29
   Oracle Business Activity Monitor 29
   Oracle Business Rules 29
   Oracle Complex Event Processing 29
   Oracle Enterprise Manager 29
   Oracle Mediator 29
   Oracle Metadata Repository 29
   Oracle Service Bus 29
   Oracle Technical/Application Adapters 29
   Oracle Web Service Manager 29
Oracle Technical/Application Adapters 29
Oracle Web Service Manager. See OWSM 29
OSB (Oracle Service Bus) 29, 183
OWSM 29, 143, 145

# P

parameters, Service Details screen
   application name 110
   application short name 110
   industry 110
   product code 110
   Service Operation 111
   Service Type 111
   Service version 111
   system code 110
parameters, Service Object screen
   Input Message 112
   Message Exchange Pattern 112
   Namespace 112
   Object Name 112
   Output Message 112
   Prefix 112
   Schema (XSD) 112
   Version 112
PeopleSoft 16
PO EBO
   customizing 42, 43

point-to-point integration 9
Portal 16
presentation (UI) integration 8
primary header components 55
process services EBS
 about 81
 architecture 81
process type EBS 77
project life-cycle, Oracle AIA
 AIA Project Lifecycle Workbench application 211
 business process modeling phase 210
 deployment phase 211
 deployment planning phase 210
 service design and construction phase 210
provider ABCS 100

## Q

QueryBankAccount 69

## R

Rabbit MQ 11
ReceiverTradingPartner child element 62
reference components
 about 39
 advantages 39
Remote Procedure Call (RPC) 10
Repository and Security 15
RequestEBMID element 56
request routing model 174
Return of Investment (ROI) 202
roles, EBS 69
route, ABCS Architecture 103
run-time governance 203

## S

SalesOrder EBO 22
SalesOrderFormat 32
SAP 16
schema (EBO/EBM) versioning 159-162
secondary header components 55
security implementation levels
 about 143
 access control level security 144
 message level security 144
 transport level security 144
security models 145
security, Oracle AIA
 about 145, 146
 AIA services, securing 147, 148
 implementing 146, 147
 predefined policies, applying to AIA Services 148-152
Sender element
 about 58
 Application, sub elements 59
 CallingServiceName, sub elements 59
 ContactEmail, sub elements 59
 ContactName, sub elements 59
 ContactPhoneNumber, sub elements 59
 Custom, sub elements 59
 Description, sub elements 59
 ESBHeader, sub elements 59
 header elements 59
 ID, sub elements 59
 IPAddress, sub elements 59
 ObjectCrossReference, sub elements 59
 SenderMessageID, sub elements 59
 sub elements 59
 TransactionCode, sub elements 59
SenderMessageID, Sender sub elements 59
SendingTradingPartner child element 62
SequenceNumber, EBMTracking elements 61
service contract
 creating 129-131
 identifying, for EBF 128
service contract centralization 176
Service Description screen 106-108
service design and construction phase 210
Service Details screen
 about 110
 parameters 110
Service Details screen, parameters
 application name 110
 application short name 110
 industry 110
 product code 110
 Service Operation 111
 Service Type 111
 Service version 111
 system code 110

service granularities 23
Service Interface 106
Service Object Fault screen 113
Service Object screen
  about 111
  parameters 112
Service Object screen, parameters
  Input Message 112
  Message Exchange Pattern 112
  Namespace 112
  Object Name 112
  Output Message 112
  Prefix 112
  Schema (XSD) 112
  Version 112
Service Oriented Architecture. *See* SOA
Service Registry 15
service routing pattern 174
services (EBS) versioning 162, 163
services version management
  about 156, 157
  diagrammatic representation 157
shared data repository 10
ShipmentType 40
Siebel CRM 16
simple data types 44
SOA
  about 13, 15, 100, 179, 202
  diagrammatic representation 14
SOA design pattern
  canonical versioning patterns 156
SOA Governance
  about 202
  design-time governance 202
  implementation-time governance 202
  purpose 202
  run-time governance 203
structure, EBM 51
structure, EBOs 40, 41
synchronous request and response pattern EBS
  developing 94, 95
synchronous request-response pattern
  about 83, 166-168
  block diagram 166

system faults 181
system log level
  configuring 196-198
system/service level tracing
  enabling 194-196

## T

Target element 60
targetNamespace attributes 71
Target Service 107
Target Service Fault screen 116
Target Service screen 113
TCP/IP protocol 11
TIBCO EMS 11
top-down approach 88
trace logging
  enabling 194
TransactionCode, Sender sub elements 59
transform, ABCS Architecture 103
two-way or request/response operation pattern 73
typical structural relationship, EBS-EBM-EBO 76

## U

UN/CEFACT Core Component Technical Specification 32
UN/CEFACT XML Naming and Design Rules 32
UpdateBankAccount 69

## V

validate, ABCS Architecture 102
VerbCode element 56
versionID attribute 53
versioning 155
version management
  about 155
  importance 155
VETO 101
VETORO 101
VETRO 101

## W

Web Service Definition Language (WSDL) 68
web service integration
  about 12
  REST (Representational State Transfer) 13
  SOAP 13
  WADL (Web Application Description Language) 13
  WSDL (Web Service Description Language) 13
  XML 12
  XML schema 12
web services-based service architecture 13
Web Start application 206
WSDL
  constructing, for process service EBS 90
WSDL portTypes 91

## X

XACML 148
xmlns:corecomEBO attribute 162
XML Schema Definition (XSD) 32
XPath function 55

## Thank you for buying
## Oracle Application Integration Architecture (AIA) Foundation Pack 11gR1: Essentials

# About Packt Publishing

Packt, pronounced 'packed', published its first book "Mastering phpMyAdmin for Effective MySQL Management" in April 2004 and subsequently continued to specialize in publishing highly focused books on specific technologies and solutions.

Our books and publications share the experiences of your fellow IT professionals in adapting and customizing today's systems, applications, and frameworks. Our solution based books give you the knowledge and power to customize the software and technologies you're using to get the job done. Packt books are more specific and less general than the IT books you have seen in the past. Our unique business model allows us to bring you more focused information, giving you more of what you need to know, and less of what you don't.

Packt is a modern, yet unique publishing company, which focuses on producing quality, cutting-edge books for communities of developers, administrators, and newbies alike. For more information, please visit our website: www.packtpub.com.

# About Packt Enterprise

In 2010, Packt launched two new brands, Packt Enterprise and Packt Open Source, in order to continue its focus on specialization. This book is part of the Packt Enterprise brand, home to books published on enterprise software – software created by major vendors, including (but not limited to) IBM, Microsoft and Oracle, often for use in other corporations. Its titles will offer information relevant to a range of users of this software, including administrators, developers, architects, and end users.

# Writing for Packt

We welcome all inquiries from people who are interested in authoring. Book proposals should be sent to author@packtpub.com. If your book idea is still at an early stage and you would like to discuss it first before writing a formal book proposal, contact us; one of our commissioning editors will get in touch with you.

We're not just looking for published authors; if you have strong technical skills but no writing experience, our experienced editors can help you develop a writing career, or simply get some additional reward for your expertise.

## Oracle Service Bus 11g Development Cookbook

ISBN: 978-1-84968-444-6      Paperback: 522 pages

Over 80 practical recipes to develop service and message-oriented solutions on the Oracle Service Bus

1. Develop service and message-oriented solutions on the Oracle Service Bus following best practices

2. Extend your practical knowledge of building solutions on the Oracle Service Bus

3. Packed with hands-on cookbook recipes, with the complete and finished solution as an OSB and SOA Suite project, made available electronically for download

## Oracle JDeveloper 11gR2 Cookbook

ISBN: 978-1-84968-476-7      Paperback: 406 pages

Over 85 simple but incredibly effective recipes for using Oracle JDeveloper 11gR2 to build ADF applications

1. Encounter a myriad of ADF tasks to help you enhance the practical application of JDeveloper 11gR2

2. Get to grips with deploying, debugging, testing, profiling and optimizing Fusion Web ADF Applications with JDeveloper 11gR2

3. A high level development cookbook with immediately applicable recipes for extending your practical knowledge of building ADF applications

Please check **www.PacktPub.com** for information on our titles

## Oracle Essbase 11 Development Cookbook

ISBN: 978-1-84968-326-5　　　Paperback: 400 pages

Over 90 advanced development recipes to build and take your Oracle Essbase Applications further

1. This book and e-book will provide you with the tools needed to successfully build and deploy your Essbase application.
2. Includes the major components that need to be considered when designing an Essbase application.
3. This book can be used to build calculations, design process automation, add security, integrate data, and report off an Essbase cube

## Oracle Database 11gR2 Performance Tuning Cookbook

ISBN: 978-1-84968-260-2　　　Paperback: 542 pages

Over 80 recipes to help beginners achieve better performance from Oracle Database applications

1. Learn the right techniques to achieve best performance from the Oracle Database
2. Avoid common myths and pitfalls that slow down the database
3. Diagnose problems when they arise and employ tricks to prevent them
4. Explore various aspects that affect performance, from application design to system tuning

Please check **www.PacktPub.com** for information on our titles

Made in the USA
Lexington, KY
16 April 2012